PSYCHOLOGY 101
Frontiers of Psychology

Fall 2007

Edited by

James B. Maas

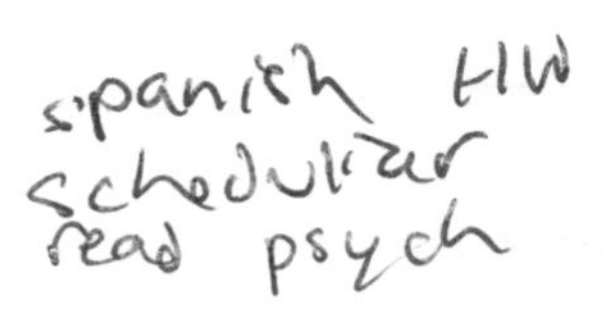

Cover photo *Mars Rover*, courtesy of Daniel J. Maas, Maas Digital, LLC.

Back cover painting, *The Maze*, by William Kurelek, The Isaacs Gallery, Toronto

This manuscript is the property of ____
____
____
____
Telephone ____

Printed in the United States of America

10 9 8 7 6 5 4 3 2 1

ISBN 0-536-40223-X

2007500087

CS/MJ

Please visit our web site at *www.pearsoncustom.com*

PEARSON CUSTOM PUBLISHING
501 Boylston Street, Suite 900, Boston, MA 02116
A Pearson Education Company

Contents

COURSE DESCRIPTION AND GOALS

Purpose

Psychology 101 will provide you with a broad, general introduction to the scientific discipline that attempts to understand human and animal behavior. The course will cover Psychology's basic subject matter, its approaches to gathering and evaluating evidence about the correlates and causes of behavior, and also the means by which psychological knowledge is (or can be) applied to improve the quality of individual and communal life.

Psychology 101 is the typical gateway to more advanced courses in the Department of Psychology, which develop in greater breadth and depth topics covered in the lectures and readings in this basic course. I, and any of the course staff, will be happy to describe these advanced offerings to you, as well as the psychology major and possible career opportunities. Throughout the term we will discuss the relevance of psychology background to careers in law, medicine, social work, psychiatry, education, business, and child care. I'd like you to consider taking advanced courses in the field and hope that your Psychology 101 venture will stimulate you to do so.

Objectives

1. *Knowledge of Psychology.* This is the primary goal we attempt to evaluate directly by examinations. It includes (a) awareness of major psychological approaches to the study of the behavior of organisms; (b) awareness of the major problems of psychology (c) knowledge of its origins and important contributors; (d) knowledge of research findings, concepts, and basic terminology; (e) understanding of its methodology and its limitations.

2. *Development of Scientific Values and Skills.* Some of these goals are testable; others will evolve more slowly, perhaps not completely during the semester. Included are (a) stimulation of intellectual curiosity about human and animal behavior; (b) appreciation of the scientific method; (c) recognition of the operation of individual bias in experimentation, observation, and reporting of what has been observed and/or measured; and (d) a critical attitude toward all generalizations, and an ability to evaluate them on the basis of the evidence upon which they claim to be based.

3. *Personal Development.* Only you can be the judge of whether this goal has been attained, and the evidence might not be manifest for some time. Ideally, contact with psychological knowledge should: (a) increase your understanding and tolerance of your own behavior and that of others, especially a greater acceptance of what is labeled "deviant," "abnormal," "pathological," "crazy," or "different"; (b) provide a better understanding of the forces acting upon you to limit or prevent your freedom of choice or action--those in your past (guilt, traumatic memories, obligations, bad contracts, unrewarded experiences, punishment, low self-esteem, shyness, and others); those in the present (social pressures to conform, comply, obey, perform, to do what others reward you for, and personal pressures to be recognized, approved of, accepted and loved); and those in the future (your unrealistic expectations, aspirations, concern for liabilities and responsibilities, security and death, among others); (c) stimulate your curiosity to explain why people (and you) behave as they (and you) do; (d) help you develop an

intelligent skepticism about accepting unwarranted truths, "psychology in everyday life" conclusions made in the mass media, as well as those made by "authorities."

My Orientation, Expectations and Aspirations for Psychology 101

The central theme of Psychology 101 is to explore human behavior from a biological, cognitive and social viewpoint. My orientation will be one of humanistic behaviorism. I assume all behavior is caused and those causes can be illuminated through empirical research. Thus we shall emphasize the research methodology that allows psychologists to establish functional relationships between behavioral observations and antecedent stimulus events. The new look in behaviorism which I endorse is "cognitively-flavored," which means treating mental events such as attitudes, expectations and knowledge as acceptable data for systematic investigation. But research must be guided not solely by the intellectual quest to dispel ignorance; humanism introduces a value-laden concern for understanding the whole person and does so with an abiding interest in creating conditions that enable each of us to realize his or her fullest potential. Humanistic behaviorism is only one of several fundamental theoretical/philosophical approaches to explaining behavior. You will be exposed to other points of view, such as psychoanalytic theory, and it is your task to decide which approach is most meaningful to guide your understanding of the human condition. At times I will undoubtedly present personal, opinionated points of view (against bigotry and blind conformity, for sexual equality). I will try to indicate when my teaching is reflecting such biases—if you're not sure, ask. Whenever you encounter a statement in the lectures or readings that you feel is not valid or inappropriate for your gender, race, social class, religion, political background, etc., please indicate to me in writing why it is wrong or limited. I will then discuss the issue with you and modify my future lectures/readings to take valid criticisms into account.

I would like Psychology 101 to become one of the highlights of your educational experience at Cornell, in terms of how it improves your understanding of behavior, and how it helps you reach your goals and aspirations for a rewarding and meaningful life. That's a big order, especially given the encumbrance of a large enrollment and the rather impersonal auditorium setting. You and I and the 101/103 staff must try together to create a unique educational atmosphere where we each contribute essential elements. This means you must not think of yourself as a passive-academic wastebasket into which words are dumped, to be memorized and recycled for examinations. You have to be willing to invest your time and effort in reading each assignment on time, in actively listening and responding to the lecture material, and in seriously thinking about the issues raised. What you will gain from this course will be directly proportional to the intellectual and emotional effort you put into your educational experience. I will not "profess" anything; rather, I will follow the Latin meaning of "educate," that is, to guide and to lead you to your understanding. I will serve as a resource, willing to invest considerable time, energy and enthusiasm into organizing a rigorous and exciting introduction to psychology. The teaching assistants and tutors will also provide a great deal of personal attention and time--if you want or need it. Comments and constructive criticism of the course are always sought.

GENERAL INFORMATION

Lectures

The function of the lectures will be to explore in depth significant psychological concepts and controversial issues at the forefront of research on human behavior. Most of the lectures will introduce new material or go well beyond what is presented in the reading assignments. The lectures are not meant to review text materials, although in a few instances appropriate time will be spent discussing and amplifying what is in the textbook.

The lectures constitute a significant portion of the course. Therefore, it is essential that you take complete notes. To assist you in that endeavor, you might wish to take advantage of the lecture outlines in this manual. The lectures may diverge from the outlines as time and interests dictate, but in general I'll stick closely to what is indicated. Do not rely on notes taken by students in previous semesters; course material undergoes revision each year and new findings replace old "facts." Make sure you bring your "i-clicker" to every class.

Since this course is meant to help you prepare for life in the real world, I expect you to treat coming to class like holding an important job. You are expected to arrive on time and attend every lecture. Our attendance policy rewards responsible behavior. Your Psych 101 tutor will be assigned to your seating area, will take attendance at the start of each lecture, and will sit with you throughout the course. Should you have any questions regarding any course material, just arrange a consultation with your tutor, or visit the Psych 101 Tutor Office, G-94A Uris Hall at times posted at *www.psych101.net.*

The lectures are presented in Bailey Hall. In our large class it is essential that absolute quiet be maintained to minimize distraction to your fellow students. You should plan to come early, relax, and clear your head to think PSYCHOLOGY. All seats are assigned for the semester at the second lecture. The auditorium doors will close at 10:10AM. and nobody will be admitted after that time. If for any reason you must leave a lecture early, sit in the designated area in the balcony on the far right facing the stage balcony (CCC 104–124). Nobody will be permitted to leave the main floor once the lecture has started. If you permit me to begin on time at 10:10 AM, I promise not to keep you past the sacred hour of 11 AM. To do otherwise will disturb the rest of us. (How's that for using peer pressure and group psychology?)

If you have an official university excuse (medical or athletic) for missing a lecture, show that to your own tutor so you don't get marked absent! I do not handle those requests—only your tutor in your seating area has the official records. If you miss two (2) lectures or less (regardless of reason such as weddings, funerals, job interviews) you will receive 3 points additional credit on your final grade calculation.

The lectures are designed to motivate you to want to learn more about psychology, to stimulate your curiosity, to inform you about what is known (and what is not yet known) about behavior, and to make you think about important issues. I will make full use of demonstrations, expert guest lecturers, and media-based educational materials to involve you directly in the excitement of the psychological enterprise. Most of the slides and films were prepared specifically for Psychology 101, although they are frequently used by other universities and occasionally on national television. I firmly believe that academic material should be presented in a stimulating (and sometimes even entertaining) manner, if doing so will aid learning and increase satisfaction with the educational process. I do not subscribe to the theory that lectures have to be dull to be truly sophisticated and intellectually worthwhile. However, if you are (or are not) amused, and still fail to see the academic point behind what is being said, shown, or demonstrated, please ask me immediately to clarify/justify what has been presented.

If you miss a lecture and would like to review the content, audiotapes of Dr. Maas presenting the lectures will be available for your review in the Uris Library Media Center approximately 6 hours after each lecture. These tapes are for review purposes only, and may not be taken from the library listening facility. Due to duplication restrictions, the visuals which are integral to each lecture are not available at any time other than the "live" lecture, so do not rely solely on the audiotapes if you expect to perform well in the course. (Pre-medical students taking Psych 101 at CWMC-Q in Doha, Qatar will be provided access to course materials through the TA in residence).

If you feel that I have made a statement in lecture that contradicts what you know to be true, or that disturbs you in any way, please call it to my attention immediately so we can discuss what were (and were not) my intentions. I deeply appreciate your caring and concerns.

Readings

The required readings are listed on the syllabus contained in this manual. We will be using **Psychology (Myers in Modules—8th edition)** by David Myers. It is the most interesting, relevant and widely used introductory textbook in the field. It will take considerable effort to absorb all the material, but you will be intellectually rewarded for investing your time and attention. The writing style is engaging. While not as encyclopedic as some texts, what is presented is absolutely essential—the core of introductory psychology. Therefore I expect you to know all the material covered in the book. The syllabus assignments do not follow the order of text modules in the book. Don't be concerned about this; Myers' organization of text modules is quite arbitrary. I prefer to assign reading material in an order that parallels the lecture topics.

The assignments are designed to provide a solid background of principles, theories, concepts and research findings across the broad spectrum of psychology. Before you read any textbook assignment, read the overview and preview sections in the **Study Guide to Accompany Myers in Modules 8th Edition.** After you finish any module make sure you complete all the "stepping through the section" and progress tests. If you miss any questions, re-read the relevant part of the text. You'll be amazed at how much the study guide helps you perform well on examinations. For the other reading assignments, which are mostly journal articles or reports of experiments, you should be able to identify the main hypotheses, the key concepts and scientific/conceptual theory, the research design used, the results of the investigation, and the significance or value of the findings.

Some assignments involve using **PsychSim,** a series of interactive graphic computer simulations. You can access the program from: http://bcs.worthpublishers.com/myers8e/content/psychsim/index.htm

If you desire additional stimulation, depth and challenge you might wish to consult the list of suggested readings in this manual. For more specialized references, see me or one of the course tutors or teaching assistants.

PSYCHOLOGY 101 ACADEMIC RESOURCE WEBSITE

As an integral part of your support materials for this course, you will be given access to a highly developed website on the Internet. There is an enormous amount of information that you will be able to conveniently access by pressing "link buttons" on the screen. We encourage you to become familiar with the website and to use its many functions often. *You should check the website for announcements at least once each week.*

We recognize that not all of you own a personal computer. For these individuals, accessing the website will be less convenient than for others. Nevertheless, the information that is available at the site is important to your success in the class, and you should make every effort to integrate website access into your study habits. To help you do this, we are providing you with a list of the many computer labs on campus:

- Martha Van Rensselaer Computer Lab (CIT): 14 Windows PC's, 24 Macs
- Sibley Computer Lab (CIT): 13 Windows PC's, 16 Macs
- Noyes Center (CIT): 8 Windows PC's, 18 Macs
- Robert Purcell Union (CIT): 12 Windows PC's, 20 Macs
- Upson Computer Lab (CIT): 61 PCs
- Uris Library (CIT): 48 PCs
- Riley-Robb (CIT): 20 Windows PC's, 25 Macs
- ILR Computer Lab (ILR): 20 Windows PC's, 10 Macs
- Warren Hall Computer Lab (A&LS): 24 Windows PC's, 25 Macs
- Mann Library Computer Lab (Mann Lib): 20 Windows PC's, 20 Macs

How to connect to the Psychology 101 Academic Course Web

1. Launch your web browser application. Preferred browsers include Internet Explorer, Mozilla Firefox and Netscape. If you use another browser it must be forms and tables capable to view this web site properly.

2. In Internet Explorer:. Click in the navigation text bar at the top of the browser window to enter the web address. Other browsers: Click in the navigation text bar or look for the open location or URL option.

3. Enter the following web address (URL): www.psych101.net and hit "Return." You will then be in the Psychology 101 Course Website.

4. Save this location in your bookmark file for future connections.

Psychology 103 Seminars

If you are interested in exploring a psychological topic in depth and discussing it with others in a small group, you might wish to take Psychology 103 concurrently with 101. Psychology 103 is an optional 1-credit seminar. You may sign up for a specific seminar on a first-come basis. Seminar times and locations are posted on the Psych 101 website *(www.psych101.net)*. You can sign up for a 103 seminar anytime after the second lecture (but before the add course deadline) by going to the Department of Psychology, Room 211 Uris Hall. 103 Seminars begin the third week of the semester. The 1-credit course involves weekly discussions, some reading assignments, and a 10-page term paper. CWMC-Q students will have opportunity for discussions with their TA as part of the regular Psych 101 course.

Tutoring and Special Help

If you need assistance in grasping the lecture or reading material, or are dissatisfied with your performance on course examinations, there is help available. You should consult the Psychology 101 tutors, whose office hours in G-94 Uris Hall are posted there and on the website. You may elect to get your questions answered by using the tutor e-mail address (psych101@cornell.edu), or through the Psychology 101 website section: "Questions and Chat." Students enrolled in Psychology 103 should consult their teaching assistant for 101 and 103 assistance. For CWMC-Q students, there is an on-site Psych 101 TA in Doha.

Contact Hours

I would like to get to know as many of you as possible. In addition to wandering around Bailey Hall before each lecture, I will from time to time hold open discussions. These optional meetings will provide both of us with an opportunity to explore issues of mutual interest. Of course I also hold office hours (see **"My Office Hours"** at the end of this document.) For CWMC-Q students, I will have special contact hours several times during the semester via live satellite transmission.

Course Examination and Grading Policy

There has been considerable debate and research on the assets and liabilities of various examination procedures in large introductory-level lecture courses. It seems that objective (multiple-choice) examinations represent the least objectionable alternative if one considers content validity, objective grading standards, and immediate knowledge of results. Therefore, all exams will consist of objective items that focus on theories, concepts, and results of empirical research. Approximately 50% of each exam will be based on lecture material (including slides and videos), and 50% will cover the assigned readings. After several years of experience, I have decided not to arrange for outside note-taking services. Research has clearly demonstrated the efficacy of active note-taking in terms of learning and performance. Furthermore, note-taking services do not provide for adequate coverage of the extensive audiovisual materials used to teach this course. You may find that some note-taking services offer notes from previous semesters of Psych 101; however, each year new information is added to the course and old information is often revised, so utilizing old notes is NOT recommended. Thus, to perform well in 101 you should attend all the lectures, take good notes, and do all the reading on time. Previous exams can be used for practice and can be found on the Psychology 101 website.

There will be two in-class prelims and a comprehensive final examination. You must take all three examinations to pass the course. **There are no regularly scheduled make-up examinations.** If you are on a University trip, or hospitalized, you should immediately inform my assistant, Cindy Durbin (255-6266). A letter from a University official (teacher, coach, advisor) or physician is mandatory before we will make any arrangements for you to take a makeup exam.

Occasionally multiple-choice examinations contain an item considered ambiguous or misleading by at least some students. In a course of this size, it is virtually impossible to re-grade all the examinations or make item-specific adjustments for particular students. To counter for this we will ask three extra questions on each prelim and five extra questions on the final exam. That is, the prelims will have 50 questions, but will be scored on the basis of 47 items, and the final will have 100 questions, but will be scored on the basis of 95 items. In other words, you can get three questions wrong on each prelim and five questions wrong on the final and still have a perfect score (A+) in the course—go for it! Don't bother arguing about any "ambiguous" questions unless you have a minimum of four such items on a prelim or six on the final—it won't make any difference in your grade!

The examinations are weighted according to the following:

Prelim 1 = 30% of the final grade; Prelim 2 = 30% of the final grade; Final Examination = 40% of the final grade. All grades are calculated on a numerical basis (with no rounding up for any calculation or conversion) and converted to a letter grade scale at the end of the semester (where 97.5 to 100 = A+; 92.5 to 97.4 = A; 90 to 92.4 = A–, and so forth).

You will be graded strictly on the percent of the material an examination indicates you have mastered. This means that your grade on an examination (and, hence, the course) is not affected in any way by anyone else's performance. **Grades are computed strictly on a mathematical basis. To be fair to all, there is absolutely no individual deviation from this policy. There are no "extra credit" papers at the end of the semester to raise grades, so try to work hard from the beginning and you will do just fine.**

You will have access to the correct scoring key for each exam on the Psychology 101 website shortly after each test is administered. Within 72 hours of any exam we will have your grades available (listed, with your permission, by student ID) on the Psychology 101 website. To get to the secure grading section use the following codes:

Name: psych101

ID: gobigred

The grading computer does not make errors. On any exam we, like the LSAT and MCAT, cannot assume responsibility for your carelessness; if you skip or incorrectly record answers, or fail to completely erase unintended responses on an answer sheet, we will not remedy the error after the fact. Therefore, please check your work before you leave the exam room. Any discrepancies between posted grades and your own calculation must be resolved by contacting the course administrator, Cindy Durbin, in person in 211B Uris Hall or by e-mail: (cld1@cornell.edu) within 1 week after prelim grades are posted or within 24 hrs. after the final exam grades are posted. After those deadlines no revisions are possible.

You must take the prelim exams on the date indicated, regardless of how many other prelims you have scheduled for that date or that week. Only if you have three final exams scheduled within 24 hours are you eligible for a make-up final examination. The 101 make-up final examination is usually held in the first scheduled period for make-up examinations after the regularly scheduled final.

S/U Option

The S/U grading option is available in Psychology 101. You should complete the appropriate forms required by your college. University deadlines for adding or dropping the option are strictly maintained. A grade of C- or higher is required for "S" standing in Psychology 101.

Records

All questions regarding official enrollment status, the computation of 101 exam and final grades, and Psychology 103 seminar registration will be handled by the course Administrator, Cindy Durbin. She can be contacted easily via e-mail ***(cld1@cornell.edu)*** or in person in 211B Uris Hall.

Research Participation

Although not formally required, participation in the psychological research of honors students, graduate students and faculty is encouraged. This experience is designed to provide insight into the nature of scientific investigation in psychology. All experimenters must observe the rulings of the American Psychological Association's Ethics Committee and the guidelines instituted by the Cornell University Committee on Human Subjects. After participating in the research each subject will be given an explanation of the purpose of the experiment and its theoretical basis.

One (1) point of additional credit is given for actual participation in the *SUSAN* research program before November 30th, on a limited first come first served basis. To sign up, go to *http://susan.psych.cornell.edu/* Address any questions about SUSAN to Sarah Cargill at sec57@cornell.edu

My Office Hours (211C Uris Hall)

Please feel free to talk to me about the course or any other matter where you feel I could be of assistance. If I cannot be of help, I'll try to refer you to someone who can. In a class of this size it is probably best that you first see the course teaching assistants and tutors if you are having difficulty understanding basic course materials; they are employed specifically to spend time helping you; if they don't satisfy your needs be sure to see me, and I'll be more than happy to work with you. I am most willing to talk to you about psychology as a major or career, or discuss with you anything that is on your mind.

I have regularly scheduled office hours and have found it best for all if I maintain a schedule of appointments. That way you won't have to spend unnecessary time waiting. Appointments can be made by calling my assistant, Cindy Durbin, at 255-6266, or by seeing her in 211B Uris Hall.

I try to answer all my e-mail within 48 hours. My address is: *jbm1@cornell.edu*

Welcome to Psych 101!

Jim Maas

Psychology 101 Course Syllabus
Fall 2007

Note: Readings are due on date indicated. **P=** *Psychology in Modules 8th ed* (Myers Text);
SR= *Supplementary Readings* (Maas/in this book); **SG=** *Study Guide* (Straub);
PSM= *PsychSim Modules* (Ludwig); **PS=** *Power Sleep*

August-September

Monday		Wednesday		Friday
		Please read "Course Description and Goals" and "General Information" in this manual before you come to the first lecture!	***Complete all exercises in Straub (Study Guide) as you read each assignment in the Myers text (P).**	**August** 24 Overview Lecture SR Test of Psych Know. SR Kohn P Introduction P Modules 1-3 *
27 Mind Control and Critical Thinking P Modules 55-56* SR Milgram PSM Not My Type PSM Everybody's Doing It		29 Mind Control and Critical Thinking P Module 57-58* PSM Social Dec.Making SR Zimbardo et al.		31 Mind Control and Critical Thinking PS Maas xiii-44 SR Anderson & Zimbardo
September 3 Mind Control P Module 44* PS 45-100		5 Dream Interpretation; Sigmund Freud P Module 18* PS 101-132		7 Sleep Research PSM EEG & Sleep PS 133-162
10 Psychophysiology of Sleep and Dreaming PS Maas 163-204 **(Psych 103 begins)**		12 Psychophysiology of Sleep and Dreaming SR- Kotler		14 Disorders of Sleep SR Milgram and Sabini SR Weil
17 Current Research on Sleep **Scientific Methodology** SR Kleiber & Devereux SR Horn PSM Helplessly Hoping		19 Scientific Methodology "ESP: Is it real?" P Module 31-32*		21 Naturalistic Observation P Module 33* PSM Get Smart

October

Monday		Wednesday		Friday
September 24 Naturalistic Observation SR Aronson PSM Descriptive Statistics PSM What's Wrong with this Study?		26 Systematic Assessment SR Rosenthal P Module 37, 45-46 PSM Correlation		28 Systematic Assessment P Module 4 - 5*
October 1 Experimental Research PSM Neural Messages PSM Hemispheric Specialization PSM Brain & Behavior	SG Review all assigned modules for Prelim I	**3** **PRELIM I** **IN CLASS 10:10am**		5 Guest Lecture David Dunning "Psych and Law" P Modules 6-7* PSM Dating and Mating
8 **FALL RECESS**	**FALL RECESS**	10 Hypnosis P Modules 19-20* SR Harary SR Kandel & Kandel PSM Your Mind on Drugs		12 Perceptual Organization P Modules 12-13* PSM Colorful World
15 Nature-Nurture and Perception P Modules 14-15* PSM The Auditory System		17 Factors Influencing Perception P Modules 16-17*		19 Subliminal Perception PSM Visual Illusions SR Hidden Messages SR Bower
22 Learning: Classical Conditioning P Modules 21 thru 23* PSM Classical Conditioning		24 Learning: Instrumental Conditioning P Modules 24 thru 26* SR Treffert PSM Operant Conditioning PSM Short Term Memory		26 Operant Conditioning: Behavior Modification P Modules 27 thru 29* PSM Iconic Memory PSM Forgetting

November - December

Monday		Wednesday		Friday
29 Learning (continued) P Module 30* PSM My Head is Spinning		31 TV & Society P Modules 34-35* SR Catalfo SR Rutter PSM Hunger and Fat Rat	SG Review all assigned modules for Prelim II	**November 2** The Psychology of Advertising P Modules 36 * SR Britt
5 **PRELIM 2** **IN CLASS 10:10**		7 Conflict/Defense Mech. Guest Lecture: Dave Myers "Happiness" P Modules 8-9* PSM Cognitive Development		9 Clinical Psychology P Modules 10-11*
12 Clinical Psychology (Film: The Maze) P Modules 38-40* PSM Catching Liars		14 Neuroses P Modules 41-43*		16 Neuroses P Modules 47-48* SR Goode
19 Neuroses P Modules 49-50 * PSM Losing Touch with Reality PSM Mystery Client		21 Optional Statler Discussion	**Thanksgiving**	23 **Vacation**
26 Psychoses P Module 51* SR Szasz SR Rosenhan PSM Mystery Therapist		28 Psychoses P Modules 52-53* SR Trotter (Love)	SG Review all assigned modules for final exam.	30 Parenting P Module 54* SR Meyerhoff & White SR Pittman

PSYCHOLOGICAL MEDIA

Psychology 101 lectures are heavily supplemented by audio visual aids designed to promote understanding of important theories and concepts. The use of films, slides, tapes, and demonstrations brings "real world" phenomena and laboratory experiments into Bailey Hall. The materials should enhance your learning experience. The entertainment value of well-produced media is often high, but in no way should this distract you from the academic message involved. If you are in doubt as to why something was shown, please ask me. Examinations contain questions on the media materials. Feel free to suggest additional media for the course.

The Milgram Studies on Obedience to Authority
The Zimbardo Experiments on Aggression
Candid Camera Observations on Conformity & Obedience
The Zimbardo Prison Experiment
Jonestown
Shyness
Flowers are Red—Harry Chapin on conformity
Sleep and Dreaming in Humans
Sleep Disorders—*60 Minutes*
Keep Us Awake — narcolepsy
When Nights Are Longest—insomnia
Sleep Alert—Chronic Sleep Deprivation
Pretty Teacher/Handsome Teacher—naturalistic observation
Children of the Fields—secondary records
Imprinting and Sign Stimuli—field research
Two Ball Games—secondary records
Unknown Genius—the savant syndrome
Bravo Gloria
Space Doctor—public opinion surveys
Monkey on the Head—interviewing
New Frontiers of the Mind—neurosurgery
Meditation and the Mind—altered states of consciousness
Deeper into Hypnosis
Visual Perception—the illusions
Factors Influencing Perception; American Time Capsule
Listen, Hear
Motion Perception 2-D and 3-D
Perception of the Upright
The Visual Cliff
Living in a Reversed World
Little Francis—classical conditioning
Shaping Public Opinion—operant conditioning
Plato-IV—computer-assisted instruction
Infantile Autism
A Monkey Named Hellion
Rescue at Sea
Teaching Sign Language to Chimpanzees
Television's Greatest Commercials
The Invisible Wall
The Maze—The Story of William Kurelek
Van Gogh Self-Portraits
Until I Get Caught
Powers of Ten

SUPPLEMENTARY SUGGESTED READINGS

These readings are recommended for advanced freshmen and upperclassmen who wish to look deeper into the topics covered by this course. The seminar leaders are most anxious to discuss these and other readings with students, during posted office hours.

History and Systems

Boring, *History of Experimental Psychology*
Heidbreder, *Seven Psychologies*
Hunt, *The Story of Psychology*
Woodworth, *Contemporary Schools of Psychology*

Experimental Methodology

Downie & Heath, *Basic Statistical Methods*
Ford, *The Sleep Prescription*
Foulkes, *The Psychology of Sleep*
Scott & Wertheimer, *Introduction to Psychological Research*
Stevens, *Hand book of Experimental Psychology*
Townsend, *Introduction to Experimental Method*

Neuropsychology, Physiology, Comparative Psychology

Cheney & Seyfarth, *How Monkeys See the World*
Gazzaniga, *Mind Matters*
Isaacson, *Basic Readings in Neuropsychology*
Kandel, Schwartz, & Jessell, *Essentials of Neural Science and Behavior*
Marr, *Vision*
Pinker, *The Language Instinct*
Thompson, *Foundations of Physiological Psychology*
Waters, *Principles of Comparative Psychology*

Perception

Gibson, J., *The Perception of the Visual World*
Gibson, J., *The Senses as Perceptual Systems*
Sekular, *Perception*

Learning and Cognition

Gibson, E., *Principles of Perceptual Learning and Development*
Hilgard, *Theories of Learning*
Medin & Ross, *Cognitive Psychology*
Skinner, *Science and Human Behavior*

Personality, Abnormal and Social Psychology

Brown, *Social Psychology*
Cameron, *The Psychology of Behavior Disorders*
Gay, *Freud*
Hall & Lindzey, *Theories of Personality*
Krech, Crutchfield, & Ballachey, *Individual in Society*
Sampson, *Social Psychology: A Book of Readings*

RESEARCH PARTICIPATION

Although not formally required, participation in the psychological research of honor students, graduate students and faculty is encouraged. This experience is designed to provide insight into the nature of scientific investigation in psychology. All experimenters must observe the rulings of the American Psychological Association's Ethics Committee and the guidelines instituted by the Cornell University Committee on Human Subjects. After participating in the research each subject will be given an explanation of the purpose of the experiment and its theoretical basis.

One (1) point of additional credit on your final course grade is given for one hour of actual participation in the SUSAN research program before November 30, on a limited first come first served basis. To sign up, go to http://susan.psych.cornell.edu/
Address any questions about SUSAN to Sarah Cargill at sec57@cornell.edu

THE "COMMON SENSE" TEST OF PSYCHOLOGICAL KNOWLEDGE

(Note: Please complete this "test" before the second lecture. Mark "T" if you believe the item is True; mark "F" if you believe the item is False. Do not look up the answers – just respond on the basis of your "common sense.")

Response

_____ 1. If a casual acquaintance tells the average college student to deliver a 400-volt electric shock to another person, there is a greater-than-50% chance that he will do it.

_____ 2. Everybody dreams every night.

_____ 3. Dreams take place within a few seconds, although they take much longer to narrate later.

_____ 4. Children from single-child families are usually brighter than children from multiple-child families.

_____ 5. Children who are above average in IQ are below average physically.

_____ 6. "Ability to learn" can be chemically transferred from one animal to another.

_____ 7. A stimulating environment can actually increase the size of your brain.

_____ 8. It is psychologically possible to control sexual behavior or aggression with the flip of an electrical switch.

_____ 9. Subliminal perception can make you do things without knowing why.

_____ 10. If a person born blind were to have his sight restored as an adult, almost immediately he would perceive the world as does a normal adult.

_____ 11. When the moon is on the horizon, we see it as "bigger" than the zenith moon, because we think it is closer at the horizon than when at the zenith.

_____ 12. Hunger can affect our perception of objects.

_____ 13. Lessons learned just before going to sleep are remembered better than those learned in the morning.

_____ 14. When working for several hours, it is better to take a few long rests than several short ones.

_____ 15. Hypnosis can be used for blocking pain in dentistry and will inhibit bleeding after extractions.

_____ 16. Facial expression is an accurate cue as to the emotion a person is experiencing.

_____ 17. A baby can die from lack of love, even though his physiological needs are satisfied.

_____ 18. Anger is the first emotion shown by an infant.

_____ 19. A person with a "multiple personality" is a schizophrenic.

_____ 20. There is a clear distinction between the normal person and the psychotic.

_____ 21. Psychoanalysis has been proven to be more effective than "no treatment" in curing neuroses.

_____ 22. One effective way to cure a child who is afraid of animals is to have him eat candy bars while looking at the animals from a distance.

_____ 23. To change people's behavior toward members of ethnic minority groups, we must first change their attitudes.

_____ 24. Memory can be likened to a storage chest in the brain into which we deposit material and from which we can withdraw it later if needed. Occasionally, something gets lost from the "chest" and then we say we have forgotten.

_____ 25. The basis of the baby's love for his mother is the fact that his mother fills his physiological needs for food, etc.

_____ 26. The more highly motivated you are, the better you will do at solving a complex problem.

_____ 27. The best way to ensure that a desired behavior will persist after training is completed is to reward the behavior every single time it occurs throughout training (rather than intermittently).

_____ 28. Blind people have unusually sensitive organs of touch.

_____ 29. Biologists study the body; psychologists study the mind.

_____ 30. Unlike man, the lower animals are motivated only by their bodily needs—hunger, thirst, sex, etc.

_____ 31. Psychiatrists are defined as medical people who use psychoanalysis.

_____ 32. Children memorize much more easily than adults.

_____ 33. "The study of the mind" is the best brief definition of psychology today.

_____ 34. Genius is closely akin to insanity.

_____ 35. The unstructured interview is the most valid method for assessing someone's personality.

_____ 36. Under hypnosis, people can perform feats of physical strength which they could never do otherwise.

_____ 37. The more you memorize by rote (for example, poems) the better you will become at memorizing.

_____ 38. Children's IQ scores have very little relationship with how well they do in school.

LECTURE OUTLINES

On the following pages you will find the lecture outlines for Psychology 101. You might find it useful to take an outline with you to Bailey Hall, especially if you feel the need for organizational structure or are having difficulty identifying essential material.

The course is divided into several primary units:

1. THE NATURE OF PSYCHOLOGICAL INQUIRY

   Psychology in Action: The Psychology of Mind Control:
   Undue Influences on Critical Thinking and Behavior

2. RESEARCH METHODOLOGY

   The Scientific Study of Sleep and Dreaming—A Multidimensional Approach
   Naturalistic Observation
   Systematic Assessment; Case Histories, Tests, Surveys, and Interviews
   Experimental Paradigms

3. NEUROPSYCHOLOGY

   Cortical Localization of Brain Functions; Psychosurgery
   Altered States of Consciousness: Meditation and Hypnosis

4. PERCEPTION AND LEARNING

   Perception: Organization of the Visual World
   The Nature-Nurture Controversy
   Factors Influencing Perception; Subliminal Perception
   Learning: Classical Conditioning
   Instrumental and Operant Conditioning
   Behavior Modification

5. MOTIVATION, SOCIAL AND APPLIED PSYCHOLOGY

   Television and Society
   Advertising and Motivational Research
   Applied Psychology: Sex Roles

6. CLINICAL PSYCHOLOGY AND PSYCHIATRY

   Paintings as a Mirror of the Mind
   Conflict and Frustration
   Defense Mechanisms
   Clinical Symptoms, Diagnoses, and Causes
   Social Psychiatry: Alcoholism
   Psychotherapy

THE NATURE OF PSYCHOLOGICAL INQUIRY

Questions of Concern to Psychologists

(Note: The first lecture raises some important issues and questions of concern to psychologists. These are a selection of topics to be studied in depth during the semester. There is no need to take notes during this first "overview" lecture.)

General Overview of Psychological Questions

Mind Control and Social Psychology
The Nature of Dreams and Experimental Studies on Sleep
Personality Assessment
The Nature of Intelligence
The Brain and Behavior
Factors Influencing Perception
Learning and Memory
Motivation and Consumer Behavior
Abnormal and Clinical Psychology

Are you Under the Influence?

Resisting the subtle forces
of mind control
in everyday life

(3 Lectures)

I. Social and situational influences on critical thinking and behavior

A. Blind obedience to authority

B. Group pressure:
Groupthink;
Diffusion of responsibility; bystander inaction
Diffusion of guilt

C. Stereotyped roles (management isolation):
Failure to listen,
Failure to ask,
Unwillingness to be questioned

D. Ideologies:
Appealing to overarching principles to justify unethical actions

E. Sleep Deprivation

II. Successful leaders think critically, and develop critical thinking skills in others.

Successful leaders:
A. Recognize undue influences on critical thinking

B. Care deeply for others and what they think

C. Encourage critical thinking

Establishing goals
Coaching for success
Focusing reprimands

D. Encourage creativity

RESEARCH STRATEGIES USED TO INVESTIGATE SLEEP AND DREAMS

A. Hypothesized causes for dreaming

B. The "psychic" theory of dream causation: anecdotal evidence

C. The psychoanalytic theory of dreaming: (Sigmund Freud)
The clinical case history

1. The deterministic viewpoint
2. The tripartite personality: id, ego, superego
3. Dream work; day residue; manifest content & latent content
4. The importance of dream interpretation: cathectic and anti-cathectic energy
5. Criticisms of Freudian dream interpretation
6. The Neo-Freudian theories

D. Physiological and psychological research on sleep and dreams; the experimental method

1. Human physiology during sleep and dreaming: Kleitman, Aserensky and Dement
    a. Electroocular activity (EOG & REM)
    b. Electroencephalographic activity (EEG) — see next page
    c. The sleep-dream cycle (SWS and EEG stages)
    d. Electromyographic activity (EMG)
    e. Middle ear muscle activity (MEMA)
    f. Penile erections and vaginal engorgement

EEG Activity

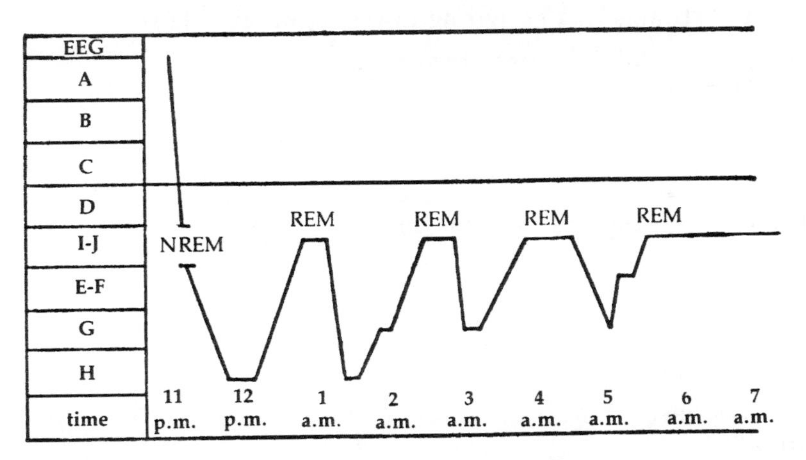

Distribution of EEG Activity in a Typical Night of Sleep.
The letters identify the same EEG and eye-movement patterns as in the preceding outline.

ASCENDING STAGE 1 SLEEP

An EEG with characteristics also observed in wakefulness
Intermittent rapid eye movements
Autonomic nervous system arousal
(heart rate, blood pressure, respiration, body temperature, sexual response)
A high rate of spontaneous firing by individual neurons in the cerebral cortex of the brain (causing less sensitivity to outside stimuli)
A relatively high rate of gross body movement between dream episodes
This regularly recurring stage one sleep becomes increasingly predominant in later hours of sleep and would seem likely to be capable of sustaining relatively intense mental activity.

OTHER PHASES OF EEG SLEEP (particularly stages 3 and 4)

Less organismic arousal than found in ascending stage 1 sleep
Bodily mobility relatively low
The brain is sensitive to external stimulation, as demonstrated by evoked responses, and is capable of reliably discriminating between meaningful and meaningless patterns of stimulation.
Relatively complex motor habits may be performed on appropriate cues.
Integrated voluntary behavior patterns, such as walking and talking, may be initiated.
Meaningful mental activity may occur.

2. Experiments on variables affecting dream content

3. Disorders of sleep — things that go wrong in the night (and day)
   a. Sleep walking; sleep talking; night terror
   b. Narcolepsy; film: *Keep Us Awake*
   c. Insomnia
      (1) Transient
      (2) Chronic
         a) Delayed sleep phase syndrome; chronotherapy
         b) Sleep apnea
         c) Sleep hygiene

4. Applied Psychology and sleep
   a. Infant and adult sleep
   b. REM deprivation
   c. Substances that interfere with sleep
   d. Jet lag — the pilot and the passengers
   e. Sleep learning
   f. Optimal sleep

The Sleep Deprivation Crisis

- Most people are moderately to severely sleep deprived. 71% do not meet the suggested sleep requirement
- High school & college students are walking zombies.
- 75% of people experience sleep problems each week.

The Sleep Deprivation Crisis at Work

- For the majority of the population, sleepiness diminishes:

  Concentration at work

  The amount of work accomplished

  The quality of work

Sleep deprivation costs $66 billion annually

"Sleep debt bigger than our fiscal debt"

Sleep is a Necessity, Not a Luxury

Sleep determines our waking success:

Mood, alertness, energy, thinking performance, productivity, safety, general health & longevity

In sum, sleep deprivation...
makes you clumsy, stupid, unhealthy and shortens your life.

Recent Research on Sleep

- The sleeping brain is highly active:
  1) Regulates immune, hormone & endocrine functions essential for general health

Univ. Chicago– Eve VanCauter

Young Ss restricted to 4 hrs./ night for 6 nights developed "senior citizen" profiles...

>cortisol, > blood sugar levels, < leptin molecules

Leads to: Hypertension (heart attacks & strokes), Type II diabetes, Obesity

Recent Research on Sleep

- The sleeping brain is highly active:
  1) Regulates immune, hormone & endocrine functions essential for general health

Penn State: Alexandros Vgontzas

Ss restricted to 6 hrs./ night for 1 week...

>Cytokines (immune system molecules);
if no invader --> inflammation of arteries

> C-reactive protein

< Leptin levels and > Ghrelin levels

Leads to: Hypertension, Osteoporosis, Type II diabetes, Obesity

Recent Research on Sleep

Less than 4 hrs sleep	73% more likely to be obese than 7-9 hr sleepers
5 hrs sleep	50% more likely...
6 hrs sleep	23% more likely...

S. Heymsfield, J Gangwisch, Columbia Univ.

Recent Research on Sleep

- The sleeping brain is highly active:
  1) Regulates immune, hormone & endocrine functions essential for general health

Dr. Jan Born-- Univ. of Luebeck, Germany found that people who sleep only 6 hours:

Have lowered their resistance to viral infection by 50%

Produce half the flu fighting antibodies after flu shot

Recent Research on Sleep

- The sleeping brain is highly active:
  1) Regulates immune, hormone & endocrine functions essential for general health

Within the last 3 decades:

Males (25-45yrs.) have reduced deep sleep from 20% of total sleep time to 5% , producing less growth hormone...

Causes obesity, loss of abdominal muscle mass, and reduced capacity to exercise -->

Heart disease, Type II diabetes

Recent Research on Sleep

- The sleeping brain is highly active:
  1) Regulates immune, hormone & endocrine functions essential for general health

Blind women have 50% less breast cancer than sighted women.

Night workers have 35% > risk of colorectal cancer.

Recent Research on Sleep

The sleeping brain is highly active:

2) Replenishes brain neurotransmitters that stimulate and organize neural networks into long term physical storage...

essential for memory, learning, performance, problem-solving and creativity

Do we sleep enough for this to occur?

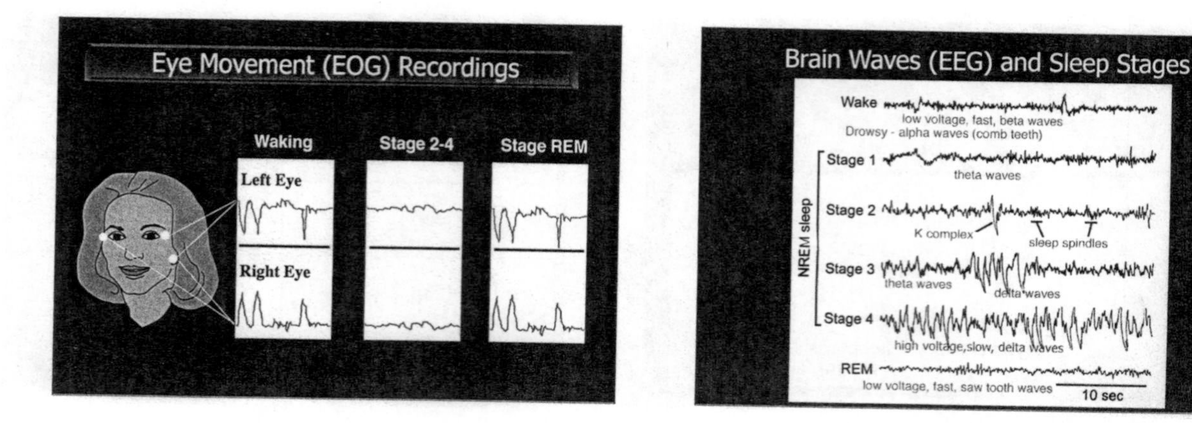

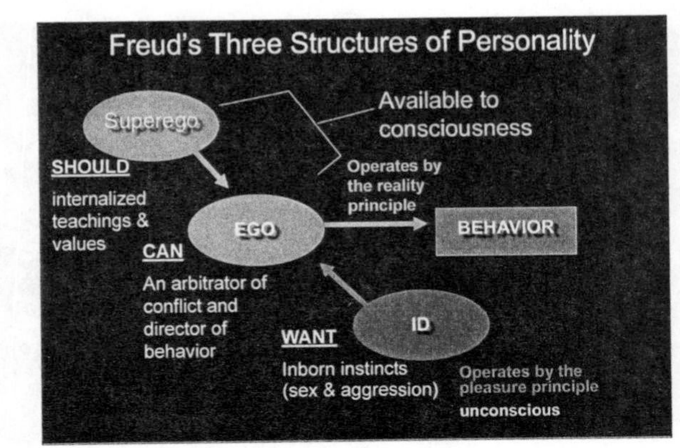

Why is it important to interpret dreams?

- Through dream interpretation unconscious complexes are uncovered/explained and the need for repression is reduced
- Anti-cathectic energy is returned to pool and can be used as cathectic energy

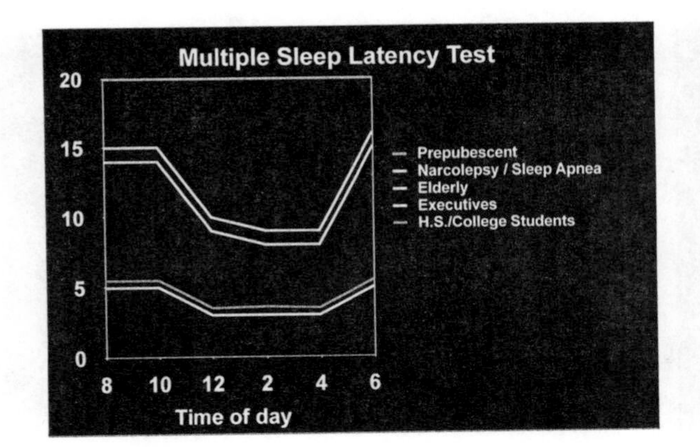

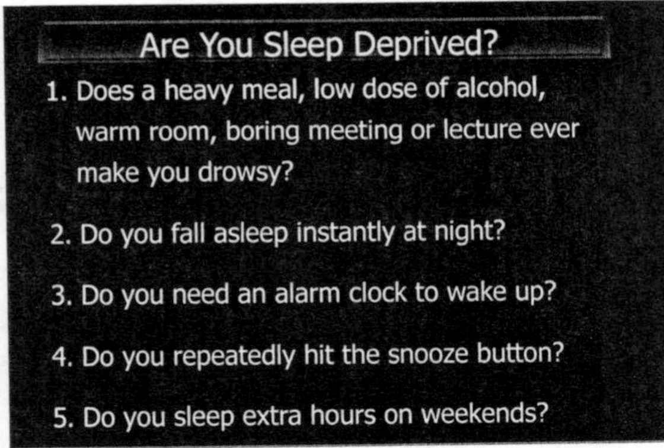

Consequences of Sleep Deprivation

- Poor driving performance:
  - Automatic behavior: "microsleeps"
  - Interaction of alcohol & sleep deprivation 19 hrs. awake worse than .08 BAC
  - Drowsy driver accidents - 37% fall asleep; 1,500 fatalities/yr (5 Boeing-747s)

How do we know the driver fell asleep?

Consequences of Sleep Deprivation

Drowsiness is Red Alert
Driving drowsy is the same as driving drunk

No loud radio, air conditioning, coffee, or food will prevent falling asleep at the wheel

The Drive Cam

Consequences of Shortened Sleep

- Increased heart disease, diabetes, obesity
- Drowsiness/microsleeps/unintended sleep seizures
- Increased irritability, anxiety, depression, weight
- Decreased socialization skills & sense of humor
- Decreased motor skills
- Decreased cognitive performance:
  - Reduced ability to process, concentrate & remember
  - Reduced ability to communicate
  - Reduced ability for complex/multi tasking & creativity
  - Poor decision skills and increased risk-taking
- In sum: Reduced health and performance

Student Sleep Deprivation Crisis

- Students distracted by academics, social life, alcohol and drugs, jobs, cell phones, TV, computer games, internet, IM.
- Hormone changes causing delayed sleep.
- Yo-Yo sleep wake schedules
- Answer: Later school start times
- Results: Academics, athletics, stimulant and drug use, behavioral problems, injuries (Edina, MN)

Fragmented Sleep

Caused by:

- Caffeine (after 2 p.m.)
  - Hint to stay awake -- 2 oz./hr.
  - 2nd largest commodity traded
- Chocolate (after 2 p.m.)
- Nicotine
- Liquor (within 3 hour of bedtime)

Golden Rules for Peak Performance

4) Make up for lost sleep

Sleep loss doesn't dissipate over time

The Sleep Debt Bank Account
"Carrying the Load"

Restorative Nap

- The biphasic sleep pattern
  The modern day siesta

The "Power Nap"

- Duration of naps
- Good for stress reduction/heart
- A stop-gap measure- not for senior citizens if nocturnal insomnia is present

Strategies for POWER SLEEP

1. Setting the bedroom stage
2. Limit TV; Turn clocks
3. A hot bath and easy stretching
4. "Worry Time"
5. Relaxation exercises; Mental imagery; Meditation
6. Reading as a bedtime ritual
7. Pleasurable sexual relations
8. If you toss & turn...
9. Melatonin; Tylenol PM; Sleeping Pills

RESEARCH METHODOLOGY—RESEARCH DESIGNS

A. Naturalistic observation

1. The philosophy and the methodological approaches
2. Advantages and disadvantages of the research strategy
3. "Two Ball Games" — an exercise in naturalistic observation

B. Systematic assessment

1. The philosophy and methodological approaches
2. Test requirements
   a. Reliability
   b. Validity
      (1) Predictive (follow-up)
         a) The correlation coefficient
      (2) Content
      (3) Face
      (4) Personal (MFPT)
   c. Standardization
3. Types of assessment devices
   a. Self-report tests
      (1) Diagnosing normal traits
         ex.: vocational guidance tests
      (2) Hartschorne and May Character Test
      (3) Diagnosing abnormal behavior
         ex.: Minnesota Multiphasic Personality Inventory (MMPI)
   b. Testing for intelligence; film: *The Unknown Genius*
   c. Projective tests
      (1) Philosophy
      (2) Examples of projective techniques
         a) Rorschach Ink Blot Test
         b) Thematic Apperception Test (TAT) — Murray
         c) Rosenzweig Picture-Frustration Study
         d) Play activity
         e) Paintings as projective devices
      (3) Strengths and weaknesses of systematic assessment tests

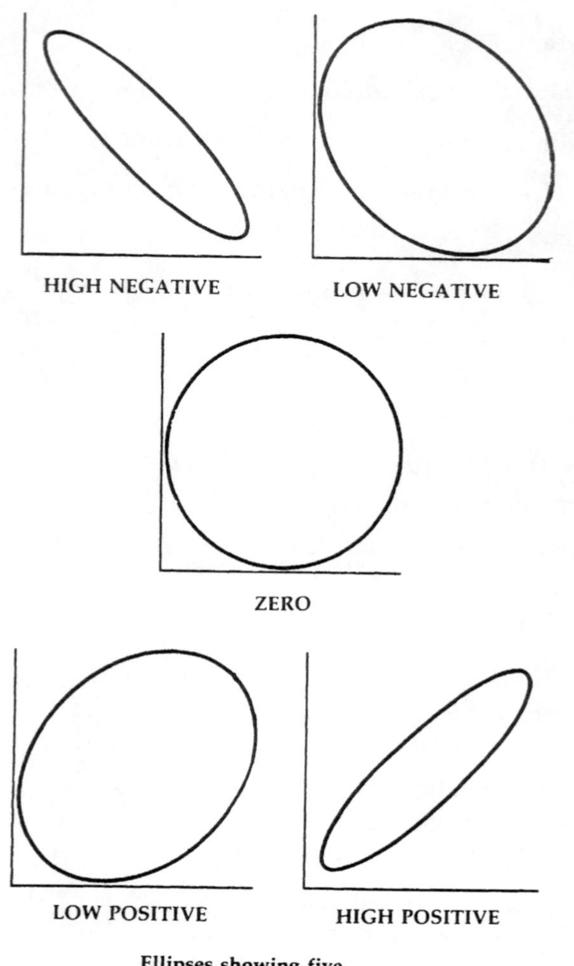

Ellipses showing five different patterns of correlation

CORRELATION

d. Public opinion surveys

e. Ratings from observations of behavior

(1) Naturalistic situations

(2) Interviews — how to make a good impression

(3) Structured situations

The Office of Strategic Services (OSS)

Corporate assessment tests (airline crews)

Medical school admissions tests

(4) Rating errors (for all assessment devices)

Leniency

Central Tendency

Halo

Contrast

C. Experimental psychology

1. Philosophy and design

a. The classical experimental paradigms (designs)

The purpose of experimental and control groups

independent and dependent variables

b. Controls

Placebo—autosuggestion effects

the Hawthorne effect

the John Henry effect

Experimenter expectancy and self-fulfilling prophecies

D. Which strategy to choose

1. Similarities and contrasts among the designs

a. Precision of measurement

b. Generality and applicability

c. Appropriateness of method

d. Representativeness of sample

e. Appropriateness of conclusions

NEUROPSYCHOLOGY AND BRAIN CONTROL

Cortical Localization and the Psychosurgeons
Two Lectures

A. Introduction to the controversy; is there cortical localization? (film): *Overview of Structures*

B. The first observation: phrenology—its friends and enemies

   1. Gall and Spurzheim (1800): inherited neurological structures

   2. Flourens: Law of Mass Action
      Law of Equipotentiality

C. The autopsy

   1. Broca: speech centers (1870s)

   2. Hughlings-Jackson: psychomotor disturbances

D. The neurosurgeons: exploration of the cerebral cortex

   1. Bartholow: the surgeon-experimenter and Mary Rafferty

   2. Human brain surgery
      a. The motor center (film)
      b. The sensory center
      c. The temporal lobe: memories and dreams
      d. Hemispherectomy:
         Redundancy of memories
         Mass action and equipotentiality revisited

   3. Subcortical control centers of emotion and consciousness
      a. Accidents and the frontal lobes: Phineas Gage's iron rod
      b. Prefrontal lobotomy: Moniz; Hess and the 1949 Nobel Prize
      c. Recent evidence on effects
      d. Hess, French and McGoun: the reticular activating system; implantation studies of arousal
      e. Olds: are there pleasure centers in the brain?
      f. Miller: hunger and fear centers in animal brains
      g. Delgado: the amygdala and rage
         the thalamus as an aggression inhibition center
      h. Human subcortical stereotaxic implantations and surgery
         (1) Physiological: electrical stimulation of the thalamus for pain inhibition
         (2) Psychological: cingulotomy for manic-depressive psychotics
             cryosurgery for the violence-prone: amygdala lesions

CORTICAL LOCALIZATION

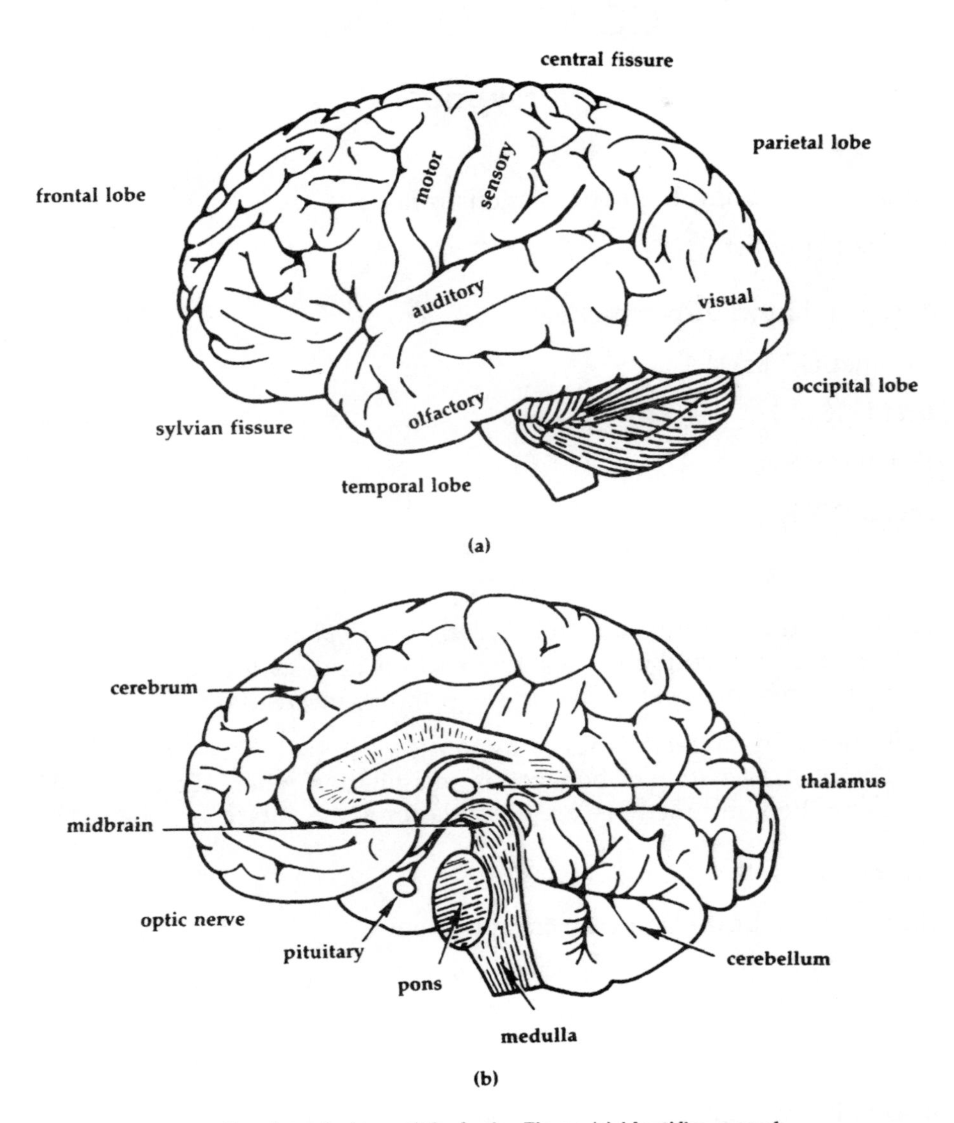

Two lateral views of the brain. Figure (a) identifies several of the important lobes and also motor, sensory, auditory, and visual areas. Figure (b) shows in schematic form the brain as it might look sliced down through the middle.

synaptic junctions in neurons

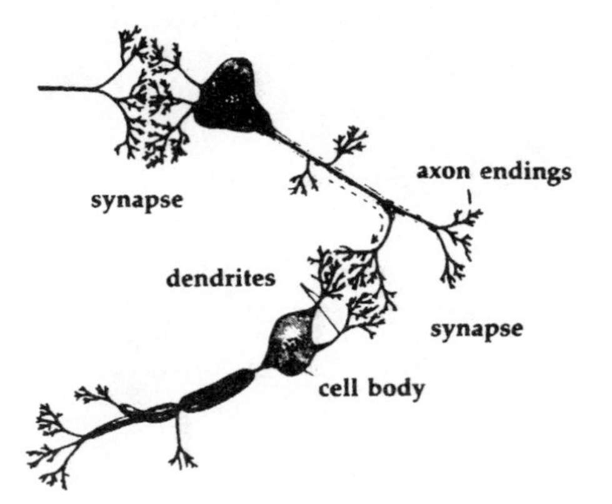

ALTERED STATES OF CONSCIOUSNESS

Hypnosis

A. Overview: witnessing hypnotic demonstrations

The stage hypnotist

B. Hypnosis in historical perspective

1. Mesmer (1770s)
2. Braid (1840s)
3. Esdaile (1880s)
4. Freud (1885)

C. Hypnotic behaviors and experiences

1. The modern day outlook; (film); *Deeper into Hypnosis*
   a look at susceptibility; negative and positive hallucinations;
   age regression; post-hypnotic suggestions; insensitivity to pain
2. Definition and characteristics of hypnosis
   Hypnosis is a state of believed-in imagination where distortions of
   perception and memory are possible for some subjects

D. Uses of hypnosis

1. Learning; test anxiety; sports; criminal justice
2. Depression; migraines; smoking and weight control; sexual dysfunction;
   surgery; birthing; body development

E. Who can be hypnotized?

1. Susceptibility tests
   The Harvard Test of Susceptibility
   The Creative Imagination Scale (Barber)
2. Dangers of hypnosis: imagined and real

PERCEPTION I & II —
PERCEPTUAL ORGANIZATION

A. Perceiving differences in the physical world

1. Distal and proximal stimuli
2. Figure-ground
   a. The phenomenon
   b. The role of contour

B. Organization of several figures

1. The laws of organization — Gestalt psychology
   a. Proximity
   b. Similarity
   c. Good continuation
   d. Closure
   e. Custom or past experience
2. Camouflage — an application of Gestalt psychology

C. The Illusions

1. Examples and demonstrations
2. Theories of illusions
3. Demonstrations
   a. Emmert's Law and the size of negative after-images
   b. The Moon illusion — Rock

D. Perception of distance and depth

1. Primary (physical) cues
   a. Accommodation
   b. Convergence
   c. Retinal disparity
2. Secondary (psychological) cues
   a. Depth cues in paintings—historical "perspective"
   b. The secondary cues:
      Linear perspective
      Aerial perspective (haze)
      Relative size
      Familiar size
      Interposition
      Patterns of light and shade
      Texture gradients (Gibson)
      Relative motion

E. The constancies
   1. Size constancy
   2. Shape constancy
   3. Lightness constancy
      a. Brightness ratio: Wallach
      b. Constancy disrupted: Gelb

F. Motion perception (if time)
   1. Two-dimensional motion perception (film)
   2. Three-dimensional motion perception (film)

G. Theoretical issues in perception—nativism and empiricism
   1. The nature-nurture issue
      Definition of the issues—Descartes and Bishop Berkeley
   2. The experimental evidence for nativism
      a. The visual cliff experiments: Gibson and Walk (film)
      b. Innate spatial localization in chickens
   3. The experimental evidence for empiricism
      a. Living in a reversed world (film)
      b. Sensory deprivation in infancy
      c. The kitten carousel
      d. Initial visual localization after cataract removal in the congenitally blind

PERCEPTION III — FACTORS INFLUENCING PERCEPTION

A. Experimental hypothesis: what common sense would dictate

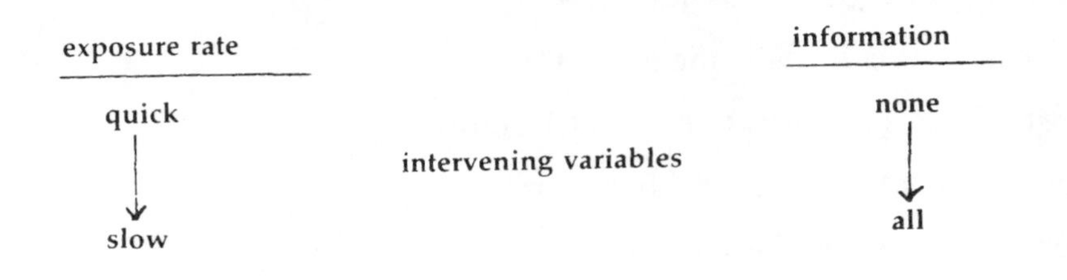

B. Experiments demonstrating intervening variables that influence the accuracy of perception

1. Instructional/mental set factors:
   Witness behavior
   Jury instructions
   War of the Worlds
   Letter Home

2. Effect of expectations on perception

3. Personal bias factors affecting event perception

   a. "They Saw a Game"—perception of shared events

   b. Rumor Transmission—memory for perceptual (and other) events and reporting of these events:
      Levelling
      Sharpening
      Assimilation

4. Needs and values as organizing factors in perception

5. Social factors influencing perception

   a. The autokinetic effect

   b. Factors influencing the perception of facial expressions

   c. Attitude and pupil size

ON THE WITNESS STAND

Specific questions:

1. In which hand did the first robber carry his gun?
2. Into which pocket did he put the money?
3. Was the woman's suit light or dark colored?
4. Was she wearing gloves? If so, one or two?
5. Were the first robber's trousers light or dark colored?
6. Of what material was the second robber's hat?
7. Did the second robber wear glasses?
8. Where was the extra tire on the getaway car?

SUBLIMINAL PERCEPTION

A. The subliminal concept
   1. The statistical approach
      a. Absolute threshold
      b. Subliminal perception
   2. Tachistoscopic presentations
   3. Happy-angry study: Klein

B. Personal values as selective factors in perception: Bruner, Postman, and McGinnies

C. Emotionality and perceptual defense: some notions about a critical word experiment by McGinnies

D. A *better* explanation: word length and frequency in subception studies; Howes and Solomon
   1. The theory of partial cues
   2. Example: past experience and subliminal perception: history of art film

E. The Vicary "experiment"—subliminal perception in advertising

F. Practical implications and conclusions

LEARNING I—CLASSICAL CONDITIONING

A. Classical conditioning
   1. Lemon and whistle demonstration
   2. Pavlov's classical experiment
   3. The classical conditioning paradigm

Major components:
  Unconditioned stimulus (UCS)
  Unconditioned response (UCR)
  Conditioned stimulus (CS)
  Conditioned response (CR)

Learning occurs as a result of an S-S bond (between CS and UCS).

B. Experimental extinction
   1. The extinction curve

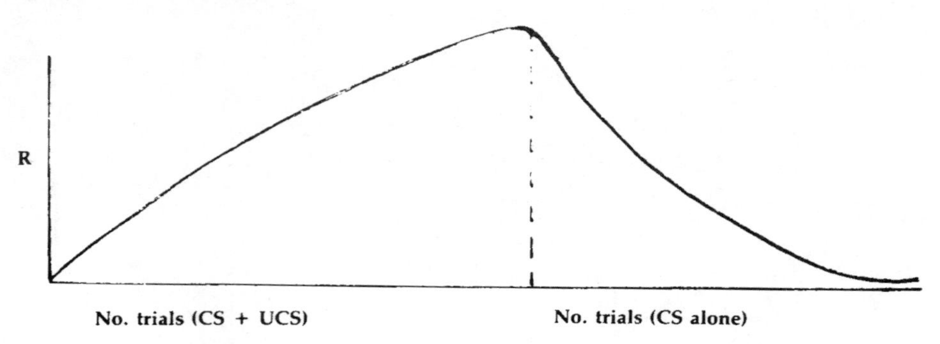

   2. Spontaneous recovery after experimental extinction
      a. The effect: After experimental extinction and rest, upon presentation of the CS alone, CR appears.

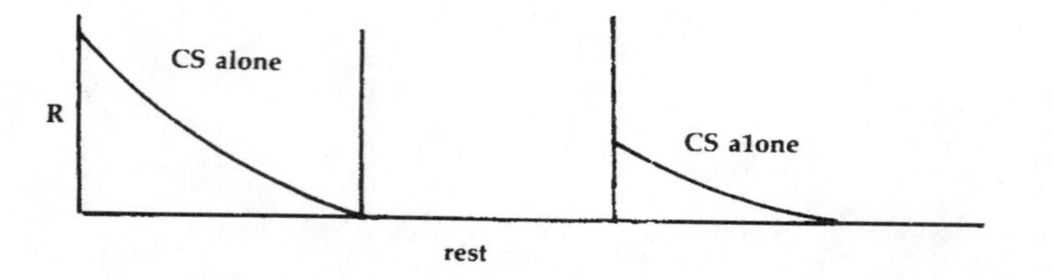

      b. Complete extinction requires repeated trials of CS alone.

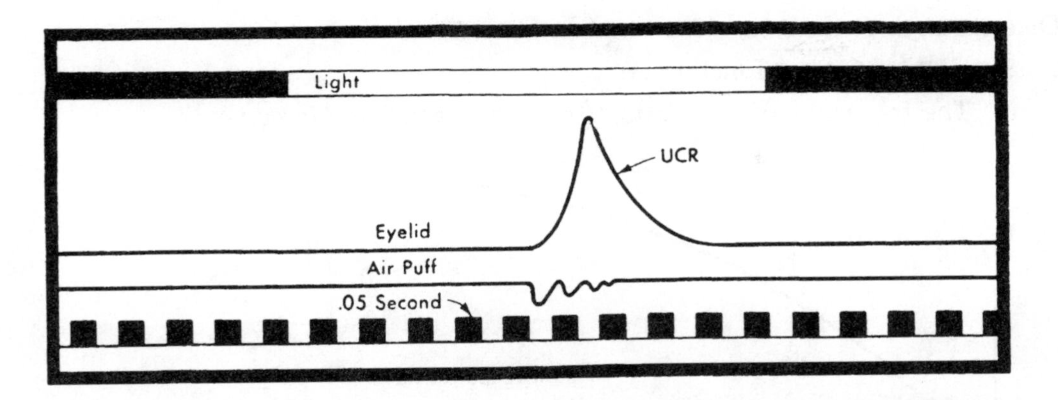

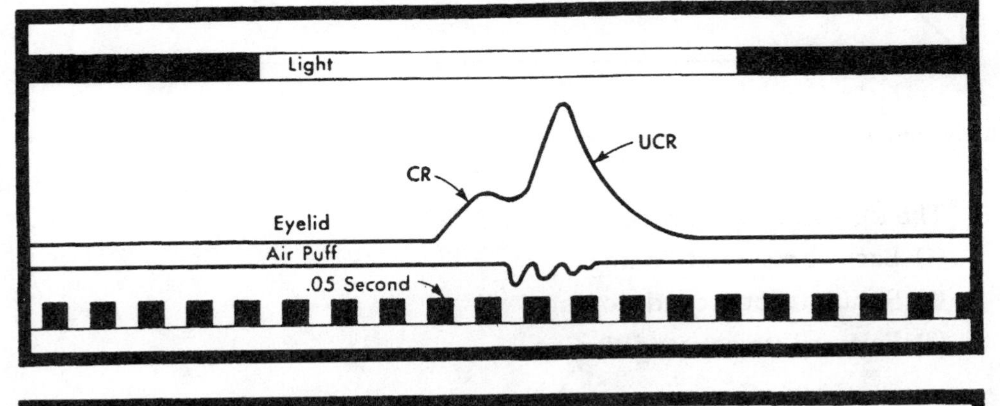

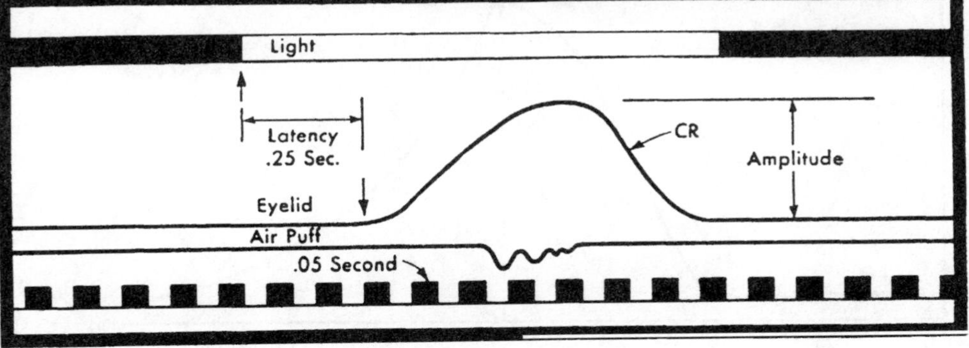

Tracings of photographic records of an eyelid response in an eyelid conditioning experiment. The CS is on when the top line of each tracing is white. The lower lines record the eyelid response and the occurrence of the air puff. The bottom line is a time line. The top record shows the appearance of a UCR, which begins after the air puff. In the second record, a small CR begins before the air puff; and the UCR is superimposed upon it. In the bottom record, the CR and UCR blend into a single response. The bottom record also illustrates the meaning of latency and amplitude. After Hilgard (1936). Courtesy, Ronald Press Company, New York.

C. Determinants of the rate of learning

1. Strength of CR is a function of:

   a. The frequency of association (total and partial reinforcement)

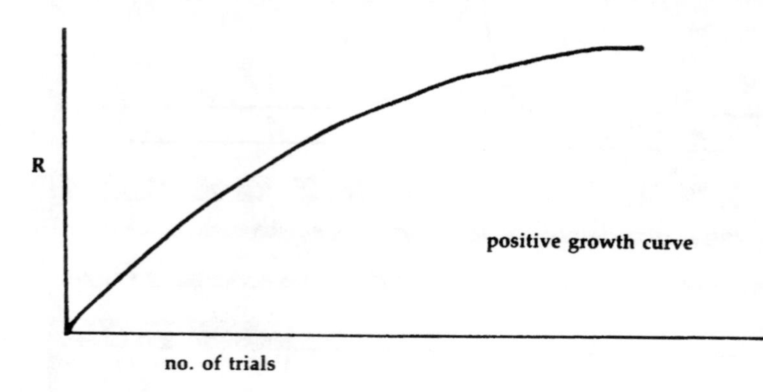

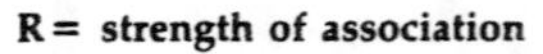

   b. The time interval between CS and UCS

      (1) Backwards conditioning

      (2) Simultaneous conditioning

      (3) Forward (trace) conditioning

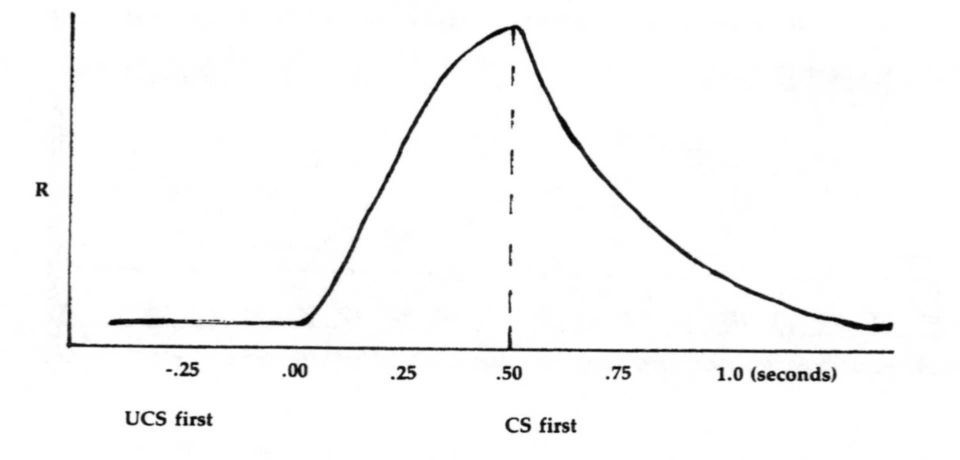

D. Generalization and generalization gradients

1. Lemon-whistle demonstration
2. Pavlov's demonstration of stimulus generalization

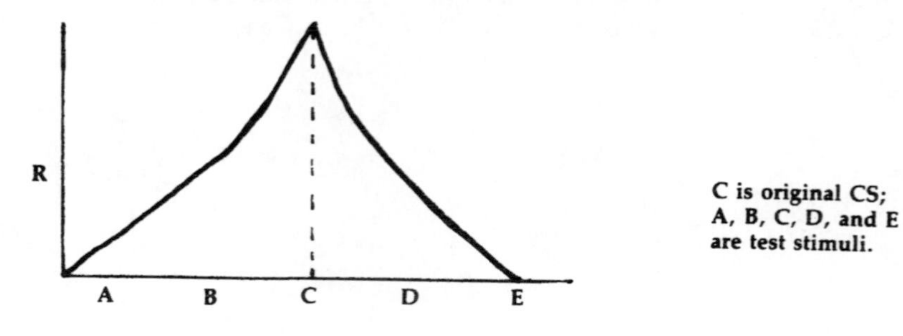

C is original CS; A, B, C, D, and E are test stimuli.

E. Applications of classical conditioning
   1. Conditioning and extinguishing emotional reactions
      a. "Little Albert" (Watson and Rayner)
         (1) Conditioning a fear response
         (2) Hypotheses for extinguishing fear responses
            a) Habituation (implosion)
            b) Reciprocal inhibition psychotherapy: (film): *Little Francis*
      b. Implications for curing neuroses (phobias)
         (1) The conditioning psychotherapies (J. Wolpe)
         (2) Ideational gradients and systematic desensitization

F. Summary of classical conditioning

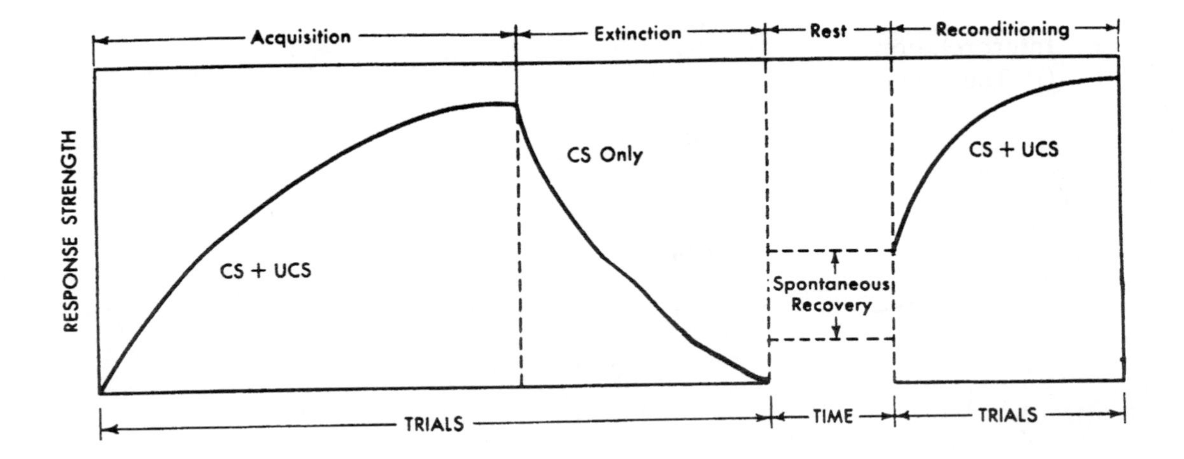

LEARNING II—INSTRUMENTAL CONDITIONING

A. The work of E. L. Thorndike
  1. Do animals understand, or do they acquire S-R connections?
    a. Methodology: the puzzle (problem) box
    b. Results: trial-and-error learning

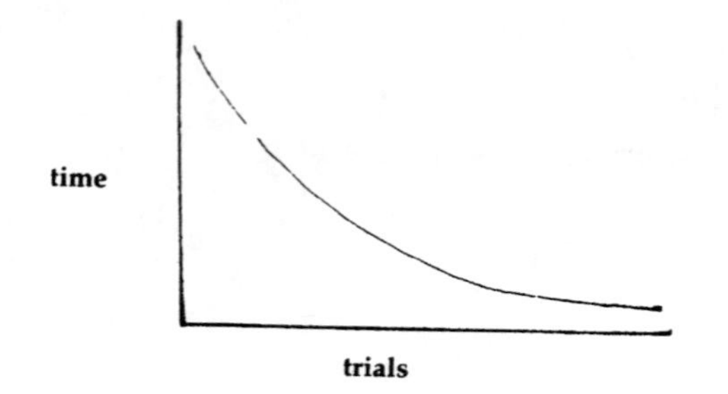

    c. Interpretation
      (1) The Law of Effect

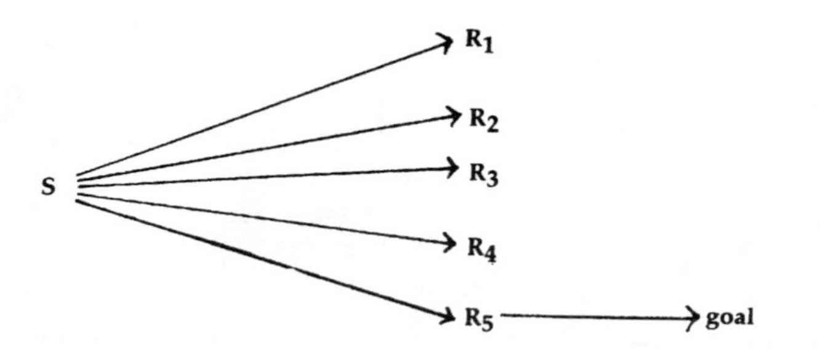

      (2) Corollary to the Law of Effect:
          The gradient of reinforcement
          example: the goal gradient
      (3) Problem solving occurs gradually
          a) the last response is cemented first;
          b) backward elimination of errors in a maze

B. The work of B.F. Skinner and his disciples (operant conditioning)
  1. Modern procedures in studying instrumental conditioning
    a. The "free operant"—a change in terms from Thorndike
      (1) The apparatus: the Skinner Box
      (2) The methodology: the operant paradigm

An R-R bond is established between the response and the reward.

(3) Getting animals and humans to learn
Shaping the operant through successive approximations

(4) Further examples
Politics and attitude change
Teaching machines and programmed texts
PSI, Audio-Tutorial, CAI
Infantile autism (film)

2. Parameters of reinforcement
   a. Frequency of reinforcement and the partial reinforcement paradox
   b. Schedules of reinforcement
   c. Application of reinforcement schedules
   d. Amount of reinforcement as a determinant of performance

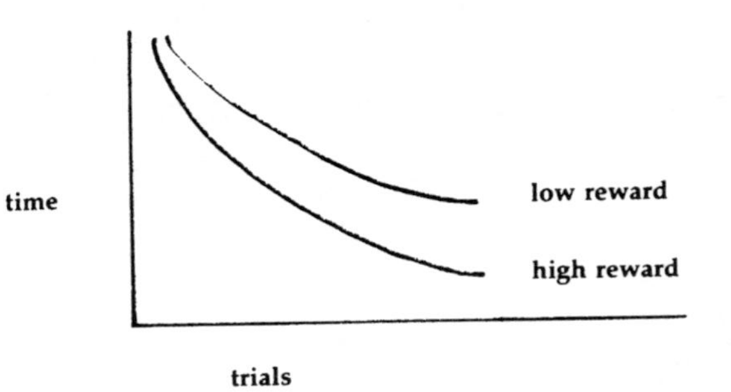

   e. The contrast effect of reinforcement
      (1) Depression and elation (Crespi)—contrast in amount

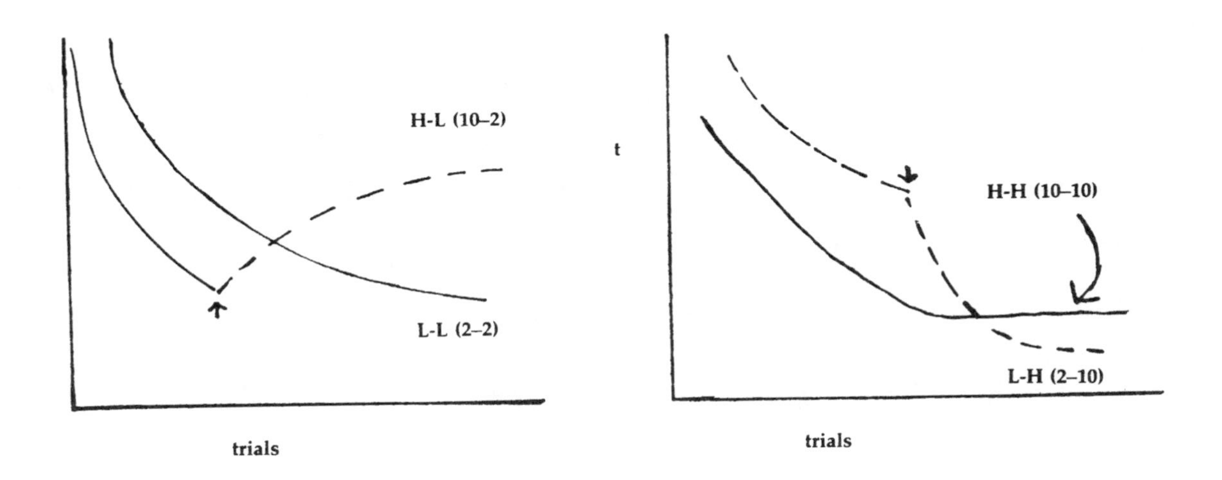

      (2) Tinklepaugh's studies—contrast in kind

3. Is reinforcement necessary for learning?
   a. Latent learning—Blodgett
      (1) Basic effect

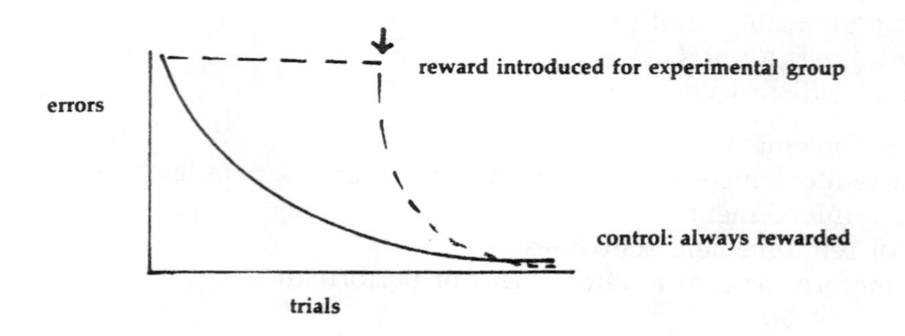

      (2) Significance: distinction between learning and performance

4. Instrumental escape
   a. Methodology and examples

5. Avoidance conditioning
   a. Methodology and examples
   b. *A Monkey Named Hellion* (film)

6. Management Training

7. Classical and instrumental (operant) conditioning compared

TELEVISION AND SOCIETY

A. The effects of television on society
   1. The audience
   2. Indirect and direct effects on behavior

B. Motivation research and the psychology of advertising
   1. Introduction to the problems of advertising research
      a. Consumer statements versus consumer behavior
      b. Definition of motivation research
      c. Examples of consumer behavior in the market situation
   2. Tools of the motivational researcher
      a. The psychiatric interview—the depth interview
      b. The use of projective tests: Rorschach, TAT, Rosenzweig Picture-Frustration Study
   3. Advertising and motivation research
      a. The four basic questions motivation research answers for advertising
      b. The eight basic "advertising wants"
      c. The nine secondary "advertising wants"

CONFLICT AND FRUSTRATION

A. The adjusting individual

B. Conflict
   1. Types of conflict
      a. Approach-approach
      b. Approach-avoidance
      c. Avoidance-avoidance
      d. Double approach-avoidance
   2. Experimental evidence
      a. Motor conflict
      b. Resolution of motor conflict

C. Frustration
   1. Conditions for frustration
   2. Obstacles: sources of frustration
   3. Reactions to frustration
      a. Successful resolution
      b. Alternative goal selection
      c. Fixation
      d. Aggression
      e. The use of defense mechanisms

D. The defense mechanisms
   1. RATIONALIZATION—the process of giving rational order or interpretation to what was previously a vague intuition, or chaotic, or confused; the process of concocting plausible reasons to account for one's practices or beliefs when these are challenged by oneself or others
   2. PROJECTION—the process of unwittingly attributing one's own traits, attitudes or subjective processes to others
   3. IDENTIFICATION—the process of seeing another person as an extension of oneself; hence seeking satisfactions through that other, and sharing the other's griefs and triumphs
   4. REACTION-FORMATION—establishment of a trait or a regular pattern of behavior that is directly opposed to a strong unconscious trend
   5. REPRESSION—the exclusion of specific psychological activities or contents from conscious awareness by a process of which the individual is not directly aware
   6. DISPLACEMENT—a substitute activity resorted to when the usual response is prevented; the attachment of an emotion to something or someone other than its proper object

7. SUBSTITUTION—replacement of approved goals for unapproved ones, and activities that can be carried out successfully for activities doomed to failure.
    a. Sublimation—redirection of energy toward behavior that will be within the boundaries of conventional approval, yet allow partial satisfaction
    b. Compensation—action that achieves partial satisfaction when direct satisfaction is blocked; striving to develop a substitute activity/ability to make up for a perceived or actual weakness/failure
8. DENIAL—the process of not recognizing the existence of an intolerable reality
9. FANTASY—vicariously seeking solutions to problems through daydreaming and imagination
10. REGRESSION—a return to earlier and less mature behavior; manifestations of more primitive behaviors after having learned mature forms, whether or not the immature or primitive behavior had actually formed part of the person's earlier behavior

PAINTINGS AS A MIRROR OF THE MIND

Two Lectures

These lectures portray the complexity of the human mind and are designed to set the framework for the empirical investigations that constitute the core of the unit on psychiatry.

A. Introduction to psychiatric art

B. Paintings used as diagnostic material

C. Paintings showing expression of thought and feeling: (film): *The Maze*: The life of William Kurelek

D. Paintings reflecting behavioral change
   Edvard Munch
   Louis Wain
   Vincent Van Gogh; (film): *Van Gogh Self-Portraits*

FILM—THE MAZE

This documentary simultaneously conveys information at five different levels: (1) aesthetic; (2) technical; (3) life-historical; (4) interactional; (5) graphic.

(1) *Aesthetic*—This film is a portrayal of critical episodes in an individual's life. It features various descriptions from his family, physician, priest, etc., but primarily emphasizes his own version of what happened to him. The juxtaposition of this patient's artistic products, next to the persons and places in his life, lends an aesthetic depth to the presentation of him as a human being.

(2) *Technical*—At a technical level (psychiatric, psychological), this film accurately portrays issues relating to both the developmental history of the hero as well as to his treatment and rehabilitation.

(a) Developmental and Familial Issues:

Confusion with gender identity. Problems of relating to parents. Difficulties of adaptation of immigrant families to a new country. Differences between generations accentuated by the fact of immigration. Anxieties of adulthood related to infantile fears (to relationships with hostile father, rejecting mother).

(b) "Psychological" Issues:

Feelings of weakness, bitterness, loneliness. The world seen as a hostile, cruel place. Feelings of need to achieve. Tremendous fears and hate of father. Pessimism, sense of failure, feelings of hopelessness. Needs for punishment.

(c) Treatment (and Rehabilitation) Issues:

Onset of depression. Hospitalization. View of electroshock treatment. Suicide attempt. Relationship to doctors and others in the hospital. The central importance of the religious conversion experience as his explanation of recovery. ("Lose yourself in religion in order to find yourself.") The taking on of new meaning. The (apparent) mastery of destructive introversion. The mastering of previous hostility.

(3) *Life Historical*—In contrast to many films of "clinical conditions," this film captures a good deal of the patient's life as an historical experience. Instead of being a "case" (i.e. an instance of "disease"), the patient emerges as a *person* whose current existential difficulties are sympathetically related to his past.

(4) *Interactional*—The relationships this man had (over time) with his father, mother, sister, physician, etc., are developed both in terms of his own recollections (and drawings) as well as in poignant descriptions given by various persons to whom he has related:

(a) Father: Father describes his son as, both in the past and present, being a disappointment. The father's remarks are not only hostile in their content but he comes across as an abundantly angry individual. Aside from the criticism of his son, it is clear that he has never understood William. In some of the dinner table scenes, the father is belatedly doing his best to relate to the grandchildren in a somewhat benign way. (The insincerity of this is shown by inserted flashbacks of William's recollections of mealtimes.)

(b) Mother: The mother's subordination to her husband is very evident. Her view of William, while not as harsh as the father's, is hostile. Her lack of sentimentality is not, however, complete. She does show some definite guilt and sadness about how she treated her children (but is unable to get the father to agree).

(c) Sister: Bill's sister documents her view of him as a severely misunderstood, withdrawn, and pitiful boy during adolescence and early adulthood.

(d) Wife: Her description of "Bill" seems at once very realistic and affectionate. She defines his perfectionism and problems in expressing emotionality as posing difficulties for her.

(e) Children: Although his children do not explicitly "speak" about him, they show a degree of spontaneity that he never enjoyed as a child. It is evident that Bill has had some problems being physically close to his kids.

(f) Priest: His spiritual counselor seems slightly worried about Bill's overzealous absorption in Catholicism (similar to his wife's concern about perfectionism).

(g) Psychiatrist and Occupational Therapist: The psychiatrist in the film is more a bystander and probably was not directly responsible for Bill's case. Interestingly, however, he avoids describing Bill as a "specimen." His occupational therapist is a somewhat virginal woman who recounts the "crush" that Bill had on her during his recovery.

(5) *Graphic*—This film is quite unique in providing a series of drawings done by the patient during various times of his life, which provide a rich (projective) documentation of his subjective experiences. These graphic representations are interspersed throughout the motion picture, alongside the actual people who were important to him. This provides an unusually deep understanding of this man's subjective reality.

INTRODUCTION TO PSYCHIATRIC DISORDERS

A. The prevalence of mental illness in America

B. Abnormal behavior
   1. Problems of definition and classification
   2. Distinction between neuroses and psychoses (see following pages)
      a. Intensity
      b. Nature
      c. Orientation
      d. Insight
      e. Social aspects
      f. Treatment
      g. Legal

C. The neuroses (DSM II); somatoform, anxiety and dissociative disorders (DSM III): symptoms, causes, and treatments
   1. In general
   2. Somatoform disorders
      a. Visceral symptoms: hypochondriasis; fatigue (neurasthenia)
      b. Motor symptoms: paralysis (conversion reaction/hysteria)
   3. Anxiety disorders
   4. Dissociative disorders
      a. Psychogenic amnesia
      b. Psychogenic fugue
      c. Multiple personality

D. The psychoses in general
   1. General symptomology
   2. Delusions: definitions and variants
   3. Hallucinations: definitions and variants

E. Paranoia
   1. Definition
   2. Symptoms
   3. Modes of adjustment
   4. Causes and prognosis

SOME FACTORS THAT DISTINGUISH BETWEEN PSYCHONEUROSES AND PSYCHOSES

Factor	Neuroses	Psychoses
1) Intensity of symptoms	Relatively mild; limited to certain areas of personality; individual maintains reality contact and capacity for social functioning.	Severe disorganization of the personality; reality testing impaired, as is social functioning.
2) Nature of symptoms	May exhibit a wide range of psychic and psychosomatic complaints, but patient isn't hallucinatory, delusional, or markedly deviant in behavior. Speech disturbances infrequent. Symptoms are usually not totally incapacitating for social interaction.	Often long-lasting; may be progressive; hallucinations and delusions are not uncommon. Speech disturbances frequently occur; symptoms often incapacitating for social interaction.
3) Orientation	Patient rarely loses orientation to environment.	Frequent loss of orientation.
4) Insight	Patient often has some insight into his problem.	Rarely has insight into nature of his or her behavior.
5) Social aspects	Behavior rarely injurious or dangerous to patient and society.	Behavior may be injurious to patient and society.
6) Treatment	Usually not hospitalized; psychotherapy often the prescribed treatment.	Usually requires hospitalization with wide range of somatic (drug, electric shock) therapies used in conjunction with psychotherapy.
7) Legal	Can't be committed against will.	Can be committed upon agreement of board of psychiatrists (3 concurring in most states).

F. The affective disorders
   1. Mania
   2. Unipolar depression
   3. Suicide (mood disorder)
   4. Bipolar affective disorder
   5. Causes (theories)
   6. Treatments

G. Schizophrenia
   1. Simple
   2. Catatonic
   3. Paranoid
   4. Hebephrenic
   5. Schizo-affective reaction
   6. Causes (theories)
   7. Treatments

H. Childhood psychoses (optional)
   Infantile autism and childhood schizophrenia

I. The Organic psychoses
   Senile and alcoholic psychoses

J. Social psychiatry: alcoholism and drunken driving (film): *Until I Get Caught*

PARENTING

The Psychology of Parenting

Some words of wisdom for your future

SAMPLE EXAM INSTRUCTIONS

In order to receive credit for any examination:

1. Use only a number 2 pencil and make dark dots.
2. Print your LAST NAME (space) then FIRST NAME in the blocks provided and darken the corresponding letters in each grid.
3. Where it says IDENTIFICATION NUMBER on the answer sheet, print your SEVEN DIGIT student identification number in columns A through G and darken the corresponding letters in each grid.

SIDE 1

GENERAL PURPOSE - PEARSON NCS - ANSWER SHEET

SEE IMPORTANT MARKING INSTRUCTIONS ON SIDE 2

NAME (Last, First, M.I.)

SEX: Ⓜ Ⓕ

GRADE OR EDUC: ⓪ ① ② ③ ④ ⑤ ⑥ ⑦ ⑧ ⑨ ⑩ ⑪ ⑫ ⑬ ⑭ ⑮ ⑯

BIRTHDATE			IDENTIFICATION NUMBER										SPECIAL CODES					
MO.	DAY	YR.	A	B	C	D	E	F	G	H	I	J	K	L	M	N	O	P

Jan. Feb. Mar. Apr. May Jun. Jul. Aug. Sep. Oct. Nov. Dec.

Question	A	B	C	D	E
1	1	2	3	4	5
2	1	2	3	4	5
3	1	2	3	4	5
4	1	2	3	4	5
5	1	2	3	4	5
6	1	2	3	4	5
7	1	2	3	4	5
8	1	2	3	4	5
9	1	2	3	4	5
10	1	2	3	4	5
11	1	2	3	4	5
12	1	2	3	4	5
13	1	2	3	4	5
14	1	2	3	4	5
15	1	2	3	4	5
16	1	2	3	4	5
17	1	2	3	4	5
18	1	2	3	4	5
19	1	2	3	4	5
20	1	2	3	4	5
21	1	2	3	4	5
22	1	2	3	4	5
23	1	2	3	4	5
24	1	2	3	4	5
25	1	2	3	4	5
26	1	2	3	4	5
27	1	2	3	4	5
28	1	2	3	4	5
29	1	2	3	4	5
30	1	2	3	4	5
31	1	2	3	4	5
32	1	2	3	4	5
33	1	2	3	4	5
34	1	2	3	4	5
35	1	2	3	4	5
36	1	2	3	4	5
37	1	2	3	4	5
38	1	2	3	4	5
39	1	2	3	4	5
40	1	2	3	4	5
41	1	2	3	4	5
42	1	2	3	4	5
43	1	2	3	4	5
44	1	2	3	4	5
45	1	2	3	4	5
46	1	2	3	4	5
47	1	2	3	4	5
48	1	2	3	4	5
49	1	2	3	4	5
50	1	2	3	4	5
51	1	2	3	4	5
52	1	2	3	4	5
53	1	2	3	4	5
54	1	2	3	4	5
55	1	2	3	4	5
56	1	2	3	4	5
57	1	2	3	4	5
58	1	2	3	4	5
59	1	2	3	4	5
60	1	2	3	4	5
61	1	2	3	4	5
62	1	2	3	4	5
63	1	2	3	4	5
64	1	2	3	4	5
65	1	2	3	4	5
66	1	2	3	4	5
67	1	2	3	4	5
68	1	2	3	4	5
69	1	2	3	4	5
70	1	2	3	4	5
71	1	2	3	4	5
72	1	2	3	4	5
73	1	2	3	4	5
74	1	2	3	4	5
75	1	2	3	4	5
76	1	2	3	4	5
77	1	2	3	4	5
78	1	2	3	4	5
79	1	2	3	4	5
80	1	2	3	4	5
81	1	2	3	4	5
82	1	2	3	4	5
83	1	2	3	4	5
84	1	2	3	4	5
85	1	2	3	4	5
86	1	2	3	4	5
87	1	2	3	4	5
88	1	2	3	4	5
89	1	2	3	4	5
90	1	2	3	4	5
91	1	2	3	4	5
92	1	2	3	4	5
93	1	2	3	4	5
94	1	2	3	4	5
95	1	2	3	4	5
96	1	2	3	4	5
97	1	2	3	4	5
98	1	2	3	4	5
99	1	2	3	4	5
100	1	2	3	4	5

Supplementary Readings for Psychology 101—Fall, 2007

PREFACE

Frontiers of Psychology – 2007 is a collection of classic and recently published articles on research in the field of psychology. This material supplements the lectures and films by exploring related issues in depth. The articles have been taken directly from the professional journal literature, while others have first appeared in lay publications. Regardless of the source, each "scientific claim" should be read with a critical eye toward what is being espoused as "evidence."

The order of the readings parallels the presentation of lecture material, beginning with articles on the nature of psychological inquiry and research design, followed by material on neuropsychology, perception, learning, motivation, personality and social psychology, abnormal psychology, and psychotherapy.

In addition to Myers' *Psychology in Modules (9th edition),* the reader constitutes the core of the reading assignments for Psychology 101. For each reading assignment you should be able to identify the major theories and concepts, research hypotheses, research methodology employed to investigate the problem, results, conclusions, and general readings. Therefore, it is important that you complete reading assignments as scheduled on the course syllabus. Understanding the material and all its ramifications will be possible only through careful assimilation of the articles in the book.

I am particularly interested in your reactions to the readings I have selected this year. Some have been utilized in the previous semesters and have withstood the test of time; others are new.

Ithaca, New York
September 2007

Jim Maas

Contents

Copyright Acknowledgments

Grateful acknowledgment is made to the following sources for permission to reprint material copyrighted or controlled by them:

"You Know What They Say," by Alfie Kohn, reprinted from *Psychology Today* (1988).

"Behavioral Study of Obedience," by Stanley Milgram, reprinted from *Abnormal and Social Psychology* 67, no. 4 (1963).

"The Mind Is a Formidable Jailer: A Pirandellian Prison," by Philip G. Zimbardo, W. Curtis Banks, Craig Haney, and David Jaffe, the *New York Times Magazine* (1973), The New York Times Company.

"Resisting Mind Control," by Susan M. Anderson and Philip Zimbardo, reprinted from *USA Today Magazine*, November 1989.

"The Perils of Higher Education," by Steven Kotler, reprinted from *Psychology Today* (April 2005), by permission of Sussex Publishers, Inc.

"Candid Camera," by Stanley Milgram and John Sabini, reprinted from *Society* 16, no. 6 (Sept—Oct 1979), Springer Science and Business Media.

"Parapsychology–Andrew Weil's Search for the True Geller, Part II: The Let Down," by Andrew Weil, reprinted from *Psychology Today* (1974), Sussex Publishers, Inc.

"Two Ballgames," by Douglas A. Kleiber and Edward C. Devereux (1988), reprinted by permission of Douglas A. Kleiber.

"Do Black Shirts Make Bad Guys," by Jack C. Horn, reprinted from *Psychology Today* 22, no. 11 (November 1988), Sussex Publishers, Inc.

"Who Likes Whom and Why," by Elliot Aronson, reprinted from *Psychology Today* (1970).

"The Pygmalion Effect Lives," by Robert Rosenthal, reprinted from *Psychology Today* (1973), Sussex Publishers, Inc.

"The Trouble with Hypnosis," by Keith Harary, reprinted from *Psychology Today* 25 no. 2 (March—April 1992), Sussex Publishers, Inc.

"Flights of Memory," by Minouche Kandel and Eric Kandel, reprinted from *Discover*, May 1994.

"Hidden Messages," reprinted by permission from the University of California at Berkely Wellness Letter (1991).

"How to . . . uh . . . Remember," by Gordon Bower, reprinted from *Psychology Today* (1973), Sussex Publishers, Inc.

"Extraordinary People," by Darold Treffert, reprinted from *Extraordinary People: Redefining the "Idiot Savant,"* by permission of the author.

"The Truth About TV," by Phil Catalfo, reprinted from *Sesame Street Parents*, March 1995.

"Adolescence: Whose Hell Is It?" by Virginia Rutter, reprinted from *Psychology Today* (Jan—Feb 1995), Sussex Publishers, Inc.

"Beating Depression," by Erica E. Goode, Nancy Linnon, and Sarah Burke, reprinted from *U.S. News & World Report*, July 1993.

"The Crime of Commitment: Do We Banish Them to Bed for Society's Convenience?" by Thomas Szasz, reprinted from *Psychology Today* (1986), Sussex Publishers, Inc.

"On Being Sane in Insane Places," by David L. Rosenhan, reprinted from *Science 87 Magazine* 179 (1973), American Association for the Advancement of Science.

"The Three Faces of Love," by Robert J. Trotter, reprinted from *Psychology Today* (1986), Sussex Publishers, Inc.

"Making the Grade as Parents," by Michael Meyerhoff & Burton L. White, reprinted from *Science 87 Magazine* 3, no. 6 (July—August 1982), The Epicenter, Inc.

"How to Manage Your Kids," by Frank Pittman, M.D., reprinted from *Psychology Today* (May—June 1995), Sussex Publishers, Inc.

You Know What They Say

Alfie Kohn

Proverbs are heirlooms, treasured and passed on from generation to generation. These pithy, unforgettable phrases seem to sum up timeless wisdom about human nature. But are the truisms really true? Stacked up against the results of psychological research, they're pretty hit-and-miss: Some home-grown adages hit; some maxims miss.

Cry and you cry alone.

Misery may love company (depressed people are more likely to seek emotional support than are people who are not depressed), but company clearly does not love misery. In 1976, psychologist James C. Coyne, while at Miami University, asked 45 female college students to talk on the phone for 20 minutes with other women, some of whom were depressed—although the students weren't told that. Later, the students indicated they had much less interest in spending time with the depressed women than with the others.

Such reactions are part of a vicious circle that is all too common among unhappy people: Their behavior drives away the very people whose support and acceptance they need, thereby worsening their depression and intensifying their need for support. These findings are also important because they suggest that when depressed people say others view them negatively, they may well be right.

Spare the rod and spoil the child.

Few proverbs have been so thoroughly disproved—or have caused so much harm—as this one. Nearly 40 years of research have shown conclusively that the "rod" produces children who are more aggressive than their peers. "Physical punishment teaches that the way to solve problems is to beat up others," says Leonard Eron, a research psychologist at the University of Illinois at Chicago. He and others explain that having children focus on what they did wrong and why it was wrong encourages them to internalize control of their own actions. But physical punishment, while suppressing misbehavior in the short run, ultimately promotes nothing more than a determination to avoid getting caught.

In 1960 Eron and his colleagues studied 870 8-year-olds in rural New York and found a clear-cut relationship between the severity of the physical punishment they received—ranging from none at all to slaps and spankings—and how aggressive other children judged them to be. Twenty-two years later, the researchers tracked down some of these same people and found that the aggressive kids were now aggressive adults. And those adults now had aggressive children of their own.

The squeaky wheel gets the grease.

Obviously we don't get everything we ask for, but many people get more than others just by demanding it. Salaries are a case in point. Psychologist Brenda Major and her colleagues at the State University of New York at Buffalo asked management students, most of whom had real-world work experience under their belts, to play the role of a personnel supervisor at a department store. Folders from mock applicants indicated what salary levels were expected—some of them below, some at and some above the range advertised.

The result? Pay expectations didn't affect who was offered a job. But of the applicants who were hired, those who squeaked louder got more grease—in their palms. "Although applicants did not receive exactly what they asked for," the researchers say, "the more pay an applicant requested, the more pay he or she was offered."

Actions speak louder than words.

Common sense suggests that our impressions of people are shaped more by how they act than by what they say about themselves. But Brandeis University psychologist Teresa M. Amabile and her student Loren G. Kabat tested this idea by videotaping women while they deliberately acted either introverted or extroverted in conversations and while they described themselves as having one or the other personality trait.

Then, 160 students watched the videotapes and evaluated how "outgoing," "friendly," "shy" or "withdrawn" the women were. When the women's self-descriptions and actual behavior conflicted, the students usually gave more credence to behavior. In general, the students' judgments were influenced about 20 times more strongly by what the women did than by what they said about themselves.

Actions speak louder than words not only when we judge the character of adults but when we try to shape the character of children. Adults who want to encourage children to be generous should practice what they preach, according to psychologists James H. Bryan and Nancy Hodges Walbek of Northwestern University. These researchers awarded gift certificates to fourth-graders for playing a miniature bowling game and offered them a chance to put some of their winnings in a box "for the poor children" if they chose. The children had previously seen adults who either donated or didn't and who preached either generosity or selfishness. When the adults' actions didn't match their advice, the researchers found, the children were more likely to pay attention to the deeds than to the words.

Beauty is only skin deep.

Psychologists Karen Dion, Ellen Berscheid and Elaine Hatfield found in 1972 that when people are good-looking, we assume many other good things about them. These researchers asked 60 students to describe people's character solely on the basis of their photographs. The more attractive people were rated as more socially desirable and likely to have more prestigious jobs and happier marriages than those who were less attractive.

This study, entitled "What is Beautiful is Good," unleashed a torrent of social psychological studies on attractiveness. Scores of researchers since then have uncovered a major self-fulfilling prophecy: Because attractive people are treated as if they have more to offer, they live up to our positive expectations. Sadly, those less pleasing to look at live down to our negative expectations.

In studies looking at the relationship between attractiveness and personality, good-looking people turn out to have higher self-esteem and to be happier, less neurotic and more resistant to peer pressure than those who are less attractive. The list goes on. Those blessed with good looks also have more influence on others, get higher salaries, receive more lenient decisions in court, are thought by their students to be superior teachers and are more valued as friends, colleagues and lovers. The general pattern is true of both men and women.

One of the most distressing findings is that attractiveness is related to the perception—and perhaps even the reality—of serious mental disorders. Psychologist Warren H. Jones and his colleagues at the University of Tulsa found that it was assumed that ugly people were more likely to be psychologically disturbed than were good-looking ones. Even when Jones and his coworkers made a point of telling people to disregard attractiveness, they still rated the unattractive people as more troubled.

When Kevin O'Grady, a psychologist at the University of New Mexico, stopped people on the street and asked them to fill out a questionnaire assessing their chances of ever developing psychological disorders, he found that the better looking people were, the more remote seemed their chances of becoming mentally ill.

The trouble is, these predictions may be right. A study by psychologist Amerigo Farina and colleagues at the University of Connecticut showed that female psychiatric patients were relatively unattractive compared with other women—and not simply because their troubles had spoiled their looks. A study of a similar group of female patients showed that, judging by yearbook photographs, they were less attractive than their peers even back in high school, before they were hospitalized.

"The way we treat attractive versus unattractive people shapes the way they think about themselves," says University of Hawaii psychologist Hatfield, "and, as a consequence, the kind of people they become." Beauty in our culture is clearly more than a superficial matter.

Beauty is as beauty does.

The central finding of the research on attractiveness is that what is beautiful is indeed good. But psychologist Alan E. Gross and colleague Christine Crofton of the University of Missouri at St. Louis wondered whether the reverse is also true: Is what is good beautiful? In other words, do our judgments of people's attractiveness rest partly on how we view their character?

Gross and Crofton sorted photos of women by their attractiveness and attached them to invented personality descriptions. Some were presented as good students, friendly, energetic and so on; others as average, and a third group as losers. People were asked to evaluate how attractive they found these people. It turned out that the more favorably described they were, the better-looking they were judged to be, regardless of how physically attractive they really were. (Other researchers have found that character descriptions affect how women's attractiveness is judged but not men's.)

Marry in haste, repent at leisure.

Any way you look at it, this proverb is true. If "marrying in haste" means marrying young, then many studies support the adage. People who wed as teenagers are twice as likely to get divorced as those who wed in their 20s.

If "haste" means a whirlwind romance before marriage—at whatever age—that, too, can lead to marital problems. A large-scale British study from the 1970s revealed that 20 percent of those who were divorced—as opposed to only 8 percent of those still married—had known their partner for less than a year before tying the knot.

Familiarity breeds contempt.

Yes, intimate knowledge can lead to passionate hatred, but familiarity is usually more likely to breed liking than contempt. In a classic series of studies, psychologist Robert Zajonc of the University of Michigan showed people a set of seven-letter Turkish words. They didn't know what the words meant, but the more often people saw certain words, the more likely they were to say they meant something good. Likewise, after being shown yearbook photographs of men they didn't know, people said they liked the men whose photos they had seen more often.

If you already have reason to dislike something or someone strongly, greater exposure probably won't change your feelings. But most of us seem to find things and people more likable as we get used to them—at least up to a point. David J. Hargreaves, a psychologist at the University of Leicester, in England, believes that after enough exposure to a piece of music, say, or a work of art, a person will find it less pleasant. Too much familiarity, Hargreaves contends, can leave us wanting less.

He who lives by the sword dies by the sword.

If the contemporary "sword" is a handgun, then this maxim seems to be true. A study of more than 700 gunshot deaths in the Seattle area from 1978 to 1983 showed that most of them had occurred in homes where a gun was kept. Moreover, the guns were far more likely to kill a resident than an intruder. In only two cases was a stranger killed: the rest were accidental deaths, suicides or homicides in which the victim was either a friend of the gun owner or a member of the family.

Many proverbs, like muscles and expert witnesses, come in opposing pairs. For every adage counseling caution, such as "Look before you leap," there is one exhorting us to throw caution to the winds, such as, "He who hesitates is lost." We are told that "Too many cooks spoil the broth" but also advised that "Many hands make light work." People tell us that "Variety is the spice of life," but they also say that "Old shoes are easiest."

Intrigued by the way we react to such conflicting advice, psychologist Karl Halvor Teigen of the University of Bergen, Norway, devised a clever experiment in 1986. He transformed 24 proverbs into their opposites. Thus, for example,. "Fear is stronger than love" became "Love is stronger than fear," and "Truth needs no colors" became "Truth needs colors."

Teigen gave his students lists that contained some authentic sayings and some that he had just reversed, asking them to rate how original and true the proverbs were. The result: no significant difference between the wisdom of the ages and Teigen's newly minted counterfeits.

When proverbs conflict, which ones should we believe? You can pick the one that suits the moment, or you can lean on the psychological experts. Here's how three pairs of proverbs stack up against the research.

You're never too old to learn vs. You can't teach an old dog new tricks.

People learn new things their whole lives through, but aging does make the process somewhat harder. As a rule, older adults have more difficulties with intellectual functioning than do younger adults. For example, some studies suggest that beyond age 60, people find it more difficult to remember texts they read or hear and have trouble distinguishing between more- and less-important ideas in the text. But since there is considerable variation among people of any given age, there are a good number of elderly exceptions to the rule.

Psychologists Warner Schaie and Christopher Hertzog of Pennsylvania State University have been testing a group of 162 people at seven-year intervals since 1956 to see how their intelligence changes. A number of measures have shown a decline in ability that becomes evident after age 60. But Schaie and other researchers have found that, up to a point, older people can be taught skills that will compensate for or reverse this decline.

Many types of training seem to help in the short run, although the effects don't always last. Psychologist Paul Baltes and his colleagues at the Max Planck Institute in Berlin, for example, put more than 200 older people through a training program that helped them to identify rules and concepts useful in solving problems on intelligence tests. The people's scores did improve. Although they had begun to fall back after six months, they were still ahead of where they were before the training began.

In a study conducted by Schaie and psychologist Sherry L. Willis, a group of people whose average age was over 72 were given five one-hour training sessions similar to those used by Baltes, then tested and compared with their own levels of cognitive ability of 14 years earlier. The training brought 40 percent back to their previous mark and helped many others to a less dramatic extent.

A "substantial proportion" of older people, Schaie and Willis conclude, were victims of the "use it or lose it" rule: Their intellectual abilities probably declined due to disuse. But those abilities are not really lost, they say. They can be regained, at least in part, through "relatively simple and inexpensive educational training techniques."

Absence makes the heart grow fonder vs Out of sight, out of mind.

The effect of absence depends on how you felt to begin with. If a lover is absent (assuming you aren't distracted by someone new), separation is likely to intensify whatever you felt before you were torn apart. If you felt positively, absence will allow you to cling to an idealized version of your beloved that can't be contradicted by real-life imperfections.

That's the conclusion of Abraham Tesser, a psychologist at the University of Georgia, based on more than a decade of work with attitudes toward everything from people to paintings. "Absence has the *potential* for making the heart grow fonder," he says, but if your feelings start out negative, "absence will make the heart grow colder."

Psychologist Phillip Shaver and his colleagues at the University of Denver came up with a similar conclusion. They asked 400 college freshmen what they felt about the people they left back home. It turned out that their relationships with family members had improved, but high school romances tended to disintegrate with distance. High school loves weren't necessarily forgotten; they just weren't remembered as being all that great after all.

Birds of a feather flock together vs. Opposites attract.

People are more like birds than magnets. After lots of research, the idea that opposites attract still has gained little experimental support, according to psychologist Richard W. Lewak of the Del Mar Psychiatric Clinic and his coworkers in California. Many studies have shown that people who share the same racial, religious and economic backgrounds usually flock together, as do those with similar political views. And when it comes to attraction powerful enough to draw people into wedlock, "Marriage partners tend to be more alike than different," the researchers say. Lewak's own work shows that we tend to marry people whose IQ's are more or less similar to our own. And, as psychologist Bernard Murstein of Connecticut College and other researchers have found, despite our fantasies of marrying the most magnificent-looking person possible, we're likely to wind up with someone about as attractive as we are. According to University of Michigan psychologist David M. Buss, the principle that people are attracted to those similar to themselves is "one of the most well established replicable findings in the psychology and biology of human mating."

Behavioral Study of Obedience

Stanley Milgram

Obedience is as basic an element in the structure of social life as one can point to. Some system of authority is a requirement of all communal living, and it is only the man dwelling inisolation who is not forced to respond, through defiance or submission, to the commands of others. Obedience, as a determinant of behavior, is of particular relevance to our time. It has been reliably established that from 1933–45 millions of innocent persons were systematically slaughtered on command. Gas chambers were built, death camps were guarded, daily quotas of corpses were produced with the same efficiency as the manufacture of appliances. These inhumane policies may have originated in the mind of a single person, but they could only be carried out on a massive scale if a very large number of persons obeyed orders.

Obedience is the psychological mechanism that links individual action to political purpose. It is the dispositional cement that binds men to systems of authority. Facts of recent history and observation in daily life suggest that for many persons obedience may be a deeply ingrained behavior tendency, indeed, a prepotent impulse overriding training in ethics, sympathy, and moral conduct. C. P. Snow points to its importance when he writes:

> When you think of the long and gloomy history of man, you will find more hideous crimes have been committed in the name of obedience than have ever been committed in the name of rebellion. If you doubt that, read William Shirer's "Rise and Fall of the Third Reich." The German Officer Corps were brought up in the most rigorous code of obedience . . . in the name of obedience they were party to, and assisted in, the most wicked large scale actions in the history of the world.[1]

While the particular form of obedience dealt with in the present study has its antecedents in these episodes, it must not be thought all obedience entails acts of aggression against others. Obedience serves numerous productive functions. Indeed, the very life of society is predicated on its existence. Obedience may be ennobling and educative and refer to acts of charity and kindness, as well as to destruction.

General Procedure

A procedure was devised which seems useful as a tool for studying obedience.[2] It consists of ordering a naive subject to administer electric shock to a victim. A simulated shock generator is used, with 30 clearly marked voltage levels that range from 15 to 450 volts. The instrument bears verbal designations that range from Slight Shock to Danger: Severe Shock. The responses of the victim, who is a trained confederate of the experimenter, are standardized. The orders to adminster shocks are given to the naive subject in the context of a "learning experiment" ostensibly set up to study the effects of punishment on memory. As the experiment proceeds the naive subject is commanded to administer increasingly more intense shocks to the victim, even to the point of reaching the level marked Danger: Severe Shock. Internal resistances become stronger, and at a certain point the subject refuses to go on with the experiment. Behavior prior to this rupture is considered "obedience," in that the subject complies with the commands of the experimenter. The point of rupture is the act of disobedience. A quantitative value is assigned to the subject's performance based on the maximum intensity shock he is willing to administer before he refuses to participate further. Thus for any particular subject and for any particular experimental condition the degree of obedience may be specified with a numerical value. The crux of the study is to systematically vary the factors believed to alter the degree of obedience to the experimental commands.

The technique allows important variables to be manipulated at several points in the experiment. One may vary aspects of the source of command, content and form of command, instrumentalities for its execution, target object, general social setting, etc. The problem, therefore, is not one of designing increasingly more numerous experimental conditions, but of selecting those that best illuminate the *process* of obedience from the sociopsychological standpoint.

Related Studies

The inquiry bears an important relation to philosophic analyses of obedience and authority (Arendt,[3] Friedrich,[4] Weber[5]), an early experimental study of obedience by Frank,[6] studies in "authoritarianism" (Adorno, Frenkel-Brunswik, Levinson, and Sanford,[7] Rokeach[8]), and a recent series of analytic and empirical studies in social power (Cartwright[9]). It owes much to the long concern with *suggestion* in social psychology, both in its normal forms (e.g., Binet[10]) and in its clinical manifestations (Charcot[11]). But it derives, in the first instance, from direct observation of a social fact; the individual who is commanded by a legitimate authority ordinarily obeys. Obedience comes easily and often. It is a ubiquitous and indispensable feature of social life.

Method

Subjects

The subjects were 40 males between the ages of 20 and 50, drawn from New Haven and the surrounding communities. Subjects were obtained by a newspaper advertisement and direct mail solicitation. Those who responded to the appeal believed they were to participate in a study of memory and learning at Yale University. A wide range of occupations is represented in the sample. Typical subjects were postal clerks, high school teachers, salesmen, engineers, and laborers. Subjects ranged in educational level from one who had not finished elementary school, to those who had doctorate and other professional degrees. They were paid $4.50 for their participation in the experiment. However, subjects were told that payment was simply for coming to the laboratory, and that the money was theirs no matter what happened after they arrived. Table 1 shows the proportion of age and occupational types assigned to the experimental condition.

Personnel and locale

The experiment was conducted on the grounds of Yale University in the

Table 1
Distribution of age and occupational types in the experiment

Occupations	*20–29 years* *n*	*30–39 years* *n*	*40–50 years* *n*	*Percentage of total (occupations)*
Workers, skilled and unskilled	4	5	6	37.5
Sales, business, and white-collar	3	6	7	40.0
Professional	1	5	3	22.5
Percentage of total (age)	20	40	40	

Note: Total n = 40.

elegant interaction laboratory. (This detail is relevant to the perceived legitimacy of the experiment. In further variations, the experiment was dissociated from the university, with consequences for performance.) The role of experimenter was played by a 31-year-old high school teacher of biology. His manner was impassive, and his appearance somewhat stern throughout the experiment. He was dressed in a gray technician's coat. The victim was played by a 47-year-old accountant, trained for the role; he was of Irish-American stock, whom most observers found mild-mannered and likable.

Procedure

One naive subject and one victim (an accomplice) performed in each experiment. A pretext had to be devised that would justify the administration of electric shock by the naive subject. This was effectively accomplished by the cover story. After a general introduction on the presumed relation between punishment and learning, subjects were told:

> But actually, we know *very little* about the effect of punishment on learning, because almost no truly scientific studies have been made of it in human beings.
>
> For instance, we don't know how *much* punishment is best for learning—and we don't know how much difference it makes as to who is giving the punishment, whether an adult learns best from a younger or an older person than himself—or many things of that sort.
>
> So in this study we are bringing together a number of adults of different occupations and ages. And we're asking some of them to be teachers and some of them to be learners.
>
> We want to find out just what effect different people have on each other as teachers and learners, and also what effect *punishment* will have on learning in this situation.
>
> Therefore, I'm going to ask one of you to be the teacher here tonight and the other one to be the learner.
>
> Does either of you have a preference?

Subjects then drew slips of paper from a hat to determine who would be the teacher and who would be the learner in the experiment. The drawing was rigged so that the naive subject was always the teacher and the accomplice always the learner. (Both slips contained the word "Teacher.") Immediately after the drawing, the teacher and learner were taken to an adjacent room and the learner was strapped into an "electric chair" apparatus.

The experimenter explained that the straps were to prevent excessive movement while the learner was being shocked. The effect was to make it impossible for him to escape from the situation. An electrode was attached to the learner's wrist, and electrode paste was applied "to avoid blisters and burns." Subjects were told that the electrode was attached to the shock generator in the adjoining room.

In order to improve credibility the experimenter declared, in response to a question by the learner: "Although the shocks can be extremely painful, they cause no permanent tissue damage."

Learning task. The lesson administered by the subject was a paired-associate learning task. The subject read a series of word pairs to the learner, and then read the first word of the pair along with four terms. The learner was to indicate which of the four terms had originally been paired with the first word. He communicated his answer by pressing one of four switches in front of him, which in turn lit up one of four numbered quadrants in an answer-box located atop the shock generator.

Shock generator. The instrument panel consists of 30 lever switches set in a horizontal line. Each switch is clearly labeled with a voltage designation that ranges from 15 to 450 volts. There is a 15-volt increment from one switch to the next going from left to right. In addition, the following verbal designations are clearly indicated for groups of four switches going from left to right: Slight Shock, Moderate Shock, Strong Shock, Very Strong Shock, Intense Shock, Extreme Intensity Shock, Danger: Severe Shock. (Two switches after this last designation are simply marked XXX.)

Upon depressing a switch; a pilot light corresponding to each switch is illuminated in bright red; an electric buzzing is heard; an electric blue light, labeled "voltage energizer," flashes; the dial on the voltage meter swings to the right; various relay clicks are sounded.

The upper left-hand corner of the generator is labeled Shock Generator, Type ZLB, Dyson Instrument Company, Waltham, Mass. Output 15 Volts–450 Volts.

Details of the instrument were carefully handled to insure an appearance of authenticity. The panel was engraved by precision industrial engravers, and all components were of high quality. No subject in the experiment suspected that the instrument was merely a simulated shock generator.

Sample shock. Each naive subject is given a sample shock on the shock generator, prior to beginning his run as teacher. This shock is always 45 volts, and is applied by pressing the third switch of the generator. The shock is applied to the wrist of the naive subject, and has its source in a 45-volt battery wired into the generator. This further convinces the subject of the authenticity of the generator.

Shock instructions. The subject is told to administer a shock to the learner each time he gives a wrong response. Moreover—and this is the key command—the subject is instructed to "move one level higher on the shock generator each time the learner flashes a wrong answer." He is also instructed to announce the voltage level before administering a shock. This serves to continually remind subjects of the increasing intensity of shocks administered to the learner.

Preliminary and regular run. Pretests revealed that the procedure of reading words and administering shocks requires some practice before it can be handled smoothly. Therefore, immediately preceding the regular run, the teacher is given a preliminary series of 10 words to read to the learner. There are 3 neutral words in the practice series (i.e., words that the learner answers correctly), so that shocks are administered for 7 of the words, with the maximum shock at 105 volts (moderate shock). Almost all subjects master the procedure by the time the preliminary run is over.

Subjects are then presented with a second list, and are told that the procedure is is the same as for the first list; the experimenter adds, however: "When you get to the bottom of the list, repeat it over again, and continue giving shocks, until the learner has learned all the pairs correctly." The experimenter instructs the subject to, "start from 15 volts and increase the shock level one step each time the learner gives a wrong answer."

Feedback from the victim. In all conditions the learner gives a predetermined set of responses to the word pair test, based on a schedule of approximately three wrong answers to one correct answer. In the present experimental condition no vocal response or other sign of protest is heard from the learner until Shock Level 300 is reached. When the 300-volt shock is administered, the learner pounds on the wall of the room in which he is bound to the electric chair. The pounding can be heard by the subject. From this point on, the learner's answers no longer appear on the four-way panel.

At this juncture, subjects ordinarily turn to the experimenter for guidance. The experimenter instructs the subject to treat the absence of a response as wrong answer, and to shock the subject according to the usual schedule. He advises the subjects to allow 5–10 seconds before considering no response as a wrong answer, and to increase the shock level one step each time the learner fails to respond correctly. The learner's pounding is repeated after the 315-volt shock is administered; afterwards he is not heard from, nor do his answers reappear on the four-way signal box.

Experimenter feedback. At various points in the experiment the subject may turn to the experimenter for advice on whether he should continue to administer shocks. Or he may indicate that he does not wish to go on. It was important to standardize the experimenter's responses to these inquiries and reactions.

If the subject indicated his unwillingness to go on, the experimenter responded with a sequence of "prods," using as many as necessary to bring the subject into line.

Prod 1: Please continue, *or* Please go on.
Prod 2: The experiment requires that you continue.
Prod 3: It is absolutely essential that you continue.
Prod 4: You have no other choice, you *must* go on.

The prods were always made in sequence: Only if Prod 1 had been unsuccessful could Prod 2 be used. If the subject refused to obey the experimenter after Prod 4, the experiment was terminated. The experimenter's tone of voice was at all times firm, but not impolite. The sequence was begun anew on each occasion that the subject balked or showed reluctance to follow orders.

Special prods. If the subject asked if the learner was liable to suffer permanent physical injury, the experimenter said: "Although the shocks may be painful, there is no permanent tissue damage, so please go on." [Followed by Prods 2, 3, and 4 if necessary.]

If the subject said that the learner did not want to go on, the experimenter replied: "Whether the learner likes it or not, you must go on until he has learned all the word pairs correctly. So please go on." [Followed by Prods 2, 3, and 4 if necessary.]

Dependent measures

The primary dependent measure for any subject is the maximum shock he administers before he refuses to go any further. In principle this may vary from 0 (for a subject who refuses to administer even the first shock) to 30 (for a subject who administers the highest shock on the generator). A subject who breaks off the experiment at any point prior to administering the thirtieth shock level is termed a *defiant* subject. One who complies with experimental commands fully, and proceeds to administer all shock levels commanded, is termed an *obedient* subject.

Further records. With few exceptions, experimental sessions were recorded on magnetic tape. Occasional photographs were taken through one-way mirrors. Notes were kept on any unusual behavior occurring during the course of the experiments. On occasion, additional observers were directed to write objective descriptions of the subjects' behavior. The latency and duration of shocks were measured by accurate timing devices.

Interview and dehoax. Following the experiment, subjects were interviewed; open-ended questions, projective measures, and attitude scales were employed. After the interview, procedures were undertaken to assure that the subject would leave the laboratory in a state of well being. A friendly reconciliation was arranged between the subject and the victim, and an effort was made to reduce any tensions that arose as a result of the experiment.

Results

Preliminary notions

Before giving an account of the experimental results, it is instructive to consider how persons predict others will perform when commanded to administer powerful shocks to another person. Fourteen Yale seniors, all psychology majors, were provided with a detailed description of the experimental situation. They were asked to reflect carefully on it, and to predict the behavior of 100 hypothetical subjects. More specifically, they were instructed to plot the distribution of obedience of "100 Americans of diverse occupations, and ranging in age from 20 to 50 years," who were placed in the experimental situation.

There was considerable agreement among the respondents on the expected behavior of hypothetical subjects. All respondents predicted that only an insignificant minority would go through to the end of the shock series. (The estimates ranged from 0 to 3 percent; i.e., the most "pessimistic" member of the class predicted that of 100 persons, 3 would continue through to the most potent shock available on the shock generator—450 volts.) The class mean was 1.2 percent. The question was also posed informally to colleagues of the author, and the most general feeling was that few if any subjects would go beyond the designation Very Strong Shock.

Result of experiment I

Subjects accept situation. With few exceptions subjects were convinced of the reality of the experimental situation, that they were administering shocks to another person, and the most potent shocks were extremely painful. In the postexperimental interview subjects were asked: "How painful to the learner were the last few shocks that you administered to him?" Subjects were instructed to indicate their answers on a printed 14-point scale ranging from "Not at all painful" to "Extremely painful." The modal response was 14 (Extremely painful) with the mean at 13.42.

Signs of extreme tension. Many subjects showed signs of nervousness in the experimental situation, and especially upon administering the more powerful shocks. In a large number of cases the degree of tension reached extremes that are rarely seen in sociopsychological laboratory studies. Subjects were observed to sweat, tremble, stutter, bite their lips, groan, and dig their fingernails into their flesh. These were characteristic rather than exceptional reponses to the experiment.

One sign of tension was the regular occurrence of nervous laughing fits. Fourteen of the 40 subjects showed definite signs of nervous laughter and smiling. The laughter seemed entirely out of place, even bizarre. Full-blown, uncontrollable seizures were observed for 3 subjects. On one occasion we observed a seizure so violently convulsive that it was necessary to call a halt to the experiment. The subject, a 46-year-old encyclopedia salesman, was seriously embarrassed by his untoward and uncontrollable behavior. In the postexperimental interviews subjects took pains to point out that they were not sadistic types, and that the laughter did not mean they enjoyed shocking the victim.

Distribution of scores. It had been conjectured that persons would not, in general, agree to administer shocks beyond the level designated as Very Strong Shock. The distribution of maximum shocks for this experiment is shown in Table 2. The obtained distribution of scores deviates radically from the prediction.

Upon command of the experimenter, each of the 40 subjects went beyond the expected breakoff point. No subject stopped prior to administering Shock Level 20. (At this level—300 volts—the victim kicks on the wall and no longer provides answers to the teacher's multiple-choice questions.)

Of the 40 subjects, 5 refused to obey the experimental commands beyond the 300-volt level. Four more subjects administered one further shock, and then refused to go on. Two broke off at the 330-volt level, and 1 each at 345, 360, and 375 volts. Thus a total of 14 subjects defied the experimenter. It is instructive to reprint their remarks at the point of defiance, as transcribed from the tape recordings:

[0124] I think he's trying to communicate, he's knocking. . . . Well it's not fair to shock the guy . . . these are terrific volts. I don't think this is very humane. . . . Oh, I can't go on with this; no, this isn't right. It's a hell of an experiment. The guy is suffering in there. No, I don't want to go on. This is crazy. [Subject refused to administer more shocks.]

Table 2
Distribution of breakoff points

Verbal designation and voltage indication	*Number of subjects for whom this was maximum shock*
Slight Shock:	
15	0
30	0
45	0
60	0
Moderate Shock:	
75	0
90	0
105	0
120	0
Strong Shock:	
135	0
150	0
165	0
180	0
Very Strong Shock:	
195	0
210	0
225	0
240	0
Intense Shock:	
255	0
270	0
285	0
300	5
Extreme Intensity Shock:	
315	4
330	2
345	1
360	1
Danger: Severe Shock:	
375	1
390	0
405	0
420	0
XXX	
435	0
450	26

[0123] He's banging in there. I'm gonna chicken out. I'd like to continue, but I can't do that to a man. . . . I'm sorry I can't do that to a man. I'll hurt his heart. You take your check. . . . No really, I couldn't do it.

These subjects were frequently in a highly agitated and even angered state. Sometimes, verbal protest was at a minimum, and the subject simply got up from his chair in front of the shock generator, and indicated that he wished to leave the laboratory.

Of the 40 subjects, 26 obeyed the orders of the experimenter to the end, proceeding to punish the victim until they reached the most potent shock available on the shock generator. At that point, the experimenter called a halt to the session. (The maximum shock is labeled 450 volts, and is two steps beyond the designation: Danger: Severe Shock.) Although obedient subjects continued to administer shocks, they often did so under extreme stress. Some expressed reluctance to administer shocks beyond the 300-volt level, and displayed fears similar to those who defied the experimenter; yet they obeyed.

After the maximum shocks had been delivered, and the experimenter called a halt to the proceedings, many obedient subjects heaved sighs of relief, mopped their brows, rubbed their fingers over their eyes, or nervously fumbled cigarettes. Some shook their heads, apparently in regret. Some subjects had remained calm throughout the experiment, and displayed only minimal signs of tension from beginning to end.

Discussion

The experiment yielded two findings that were surprising. The first finding concerns the sheer strength of obedient tendencies manifested in this situation. Subjects have learned from childhood that it is a fundamental breach of moral conduct to hurt another person against his will. Yet, 26 subjects abandon this tenet in following the instructions of an authority who has no special powers to enforce his commands. To disobey would bring no material loss to the subject; no punishment would ensue. It is clear from the remarks and outward behavior of many participants that in punishing the victim they are often acting against their own values. Subjects often expressed deep disapproval of shocking a man in the face of his objections, and others denounced it as stupid and senseless. Yet the majority complied with the experimental commands. This outcome was surprising from two perspectives: first, from the standpoint of predictions made in the questionnaire described earlier. (Here, however, it is possible that the remoteness of the respondents from the actual situation, and the difficulty of conveying to them the concrete details of the experiment, could account for the serious underestimation of obedience.)

But the results were also unexpected to persons who observed the experiment in progress, through one-way mirrors. Observers often uttered expressions of disbelief upon seeing a subject administer more powerful shocks to the victim. These persons had a full acquaintance with the details of the situation, and yet systematically underestimated the amount of obedience that subjects would display.

The second unanticipated effect was the extraordinary tension generated by the procedures. One might suppose that a subject would simply break off or continue as his conscience dictated. Yet, this is very far from what happened. There were striking reactions of tension and emotional strain. One observer related:

> I observed a mature and initially poised businessman enter the laboratory smiling and confident. Within 20 minutes he was reduced to a twitching, stuttering wreck, who was rapidly approaching a point of nervous collapse. He constantly pulled on his earlobe, and twisted his hands. At one point he pushed his fist into his forehead and muttered: "Oh God, let's stop it." And yet he continued to respond to every word of the experimenter, and obeyed to the end.

Any understanding of the phenomenon of obedience must rest on an analysis of the particular conditions in which it occurs. The following features of the experiment go some distance in explaining the high amount of obedience observed in the situation.

1. The experiment is sponsored by and takes place on the grounds of an institution of unimpeachable reputation, Yale University. It may be reasonably presumed that the personnel are competent and reputable. The importance of this background authority is now being studied by conducting a series of experiments outside of New Haven, and without any visible ties to the university.

2. The experiment is, on the face of it, designed to attain a worthy purpose—advancement of knowledge about learning and memory. Obedience occurs not as an end in itself, but as an instrumental element in a situation that the subject construes as significant, and meaningful. He may not be able to see its full significance, but he may properly assume that the experimenter does.

3. The subject perceives that the victim has voluntarily submitted to the authority system of the experimenter. He is not (at first) an unwilling captive impressed for involuntary service. He has taken the trouble to come to the laboratory presumably to aid the experimental research. That he later becomes an involuntary subject does not alter the fact that, initially, he consented to participate without qualification. Thus he has in some degree incurred an obligation toward the experimenter.

4. The subject, too, has entered the experiment voluntarily, and perceives

himself under obligation to aid the experimenter. He has made a commitment, and to disrupt the experiment is a repudiation of this initial promise of aid.

5. Certain features of the procedure strengthen the subject's sense of obligation to the experimenter. For one, he has been paid for coming to the laboratory. In part this is canceled out by the experimenter's statement that: "Of course, as in all experiments, the money is yours simply for coming to the laboratory. From this point on, no matter what happens, the money is yours."[12]

6. From the subject's standpoint, the fact that he is the teacher and the other man the learner is purely a chance consequence (it is determined by drawing lots) and he, the subject, ran the same risk as the other man in being assigned the role of learner. Since the assignment of positions in the experiment was achieved by fair means, the learner is deprived of any basis of complaint on this count. (A similar situation obtains in Army units, in which—in the absence of volunteers—a particularly dangerous mission may be assigned by drawing lots, and the unlucky soldier is expected to bear his misfortune with sportsmanship.)

7. There is, at best, ambiguity with regard to the prerogatives of a psychologist and the corresponding rights of his subject. There is a vagueness of expectation concerning what a psychologist may require of his subject, and when he is overstepping acceptable limits. Moreover, the experiment occurs in a closed setting, and thus provides no opportunity for the subject to remove these ambiguities by discussion with others. There are few standards that seem directly applicable to the situation, which is a novel one for most subjects.

8. The subjects are assured that the shocks administered to the subject are "painful but not dangerous." Thus they assume that the discomfort caused the victim is momentary, while the scientific gains resulting from the experiment are enduring.

9. Through Shock Level 20 the victim continues to provide answers on the signal box. The subject may construe this as a sign that the victim is still willing to "play the game." It is only after Shock Level 20 that the victim repudiates the rules completely, refusing to answer further.

These features help to explain the high amount of obedience obtained in this experiment. Many of the arguments raised need not remain matters of speculation, but can be reduced to testable propositions to be confirmed or disproved by further experiments.[13]

The following features of the experiment concern the nature of the conflict which the subject faces.

10. The subject is placed in a position in which he must respond to the competing demands of two persons: the experimenter and the victim. The conflict must be resolved by meeting the demands of one or the other; satisfaction of the victim and the experimenter are mutually exclusive. Moreover, the resolution must take the form of a highly visible action, that of continuing to shock the victim or breaking off the experiment. Thus the subject is forced into a public conflict that does not permit any completely satisfactory solution.

11. While the demands of the experimenter carry the weight of scientific authority, the demands of the victim spring from his personal experience of pain and suffering. The two claims need not be regarded as equally pressing and legitimate. The experimenter seeks an abstract scientific datum; the victim cries out for relief from physical suffering caused by the subject's actions.

12. The experiment gives the subject little time for reflection. The conflict comes on rapidly. It is only minutes after the subject has been seated before the shock generator that the victim begins his protests. Moreover, the subject perceives that he has gone through but two-thirds of the shock levels at the time the subject's first protests are heard. Thus he understands that the conflict will have a persistent aspect to it, and may well become more intense as increasingly more powerful shocks are required. The rapidity with which the conflict descends on the subject and his realization that it is predictably recurrent may well be sources of tension to him.

13. At a more general level, the conflict stems from the opposition of two deeply ingrained behavior dispositions: first, the disposition not to harm other people, and second, the tendency to obey those whom we perceive to be legitimate authorities.

---

[1] C. P. Snow, "Either/Or," *Progressive*, Feb., 1961, p. 24.

[2] S. Milgram, "Dynamics of Obedience" (Washington, D.C.: National Science Foundation, January 25, 1961), mimeo.

[3] H. Arendt, "What Was Authority?" in *Authority*, C. J. Friedrich (ed.) (Cambridge: Harvard Univ. Press, 1958), pp. 81–112.

[4] C. J. Friedrich (ed.), *Authority* (Cambridge: Harvard Univ. Press, 1958).

[5] M. Weber, *The Theory of Social and Economic Organization* (Oxford: Oxford Univ. Press, 1947).

[6] J. D. Frank, "Experimental Studies of Personal Pressure and Resistance," *J. Gen. Psychol.*, Vol. 30 (1944), pp. 23–64.

[7] T. Adorno, Else Frenkel-Brunswik, D. J. Levinson, and R. N. Sanford, *The Authoritarian Personality* (New York: Harper, 1950).

[8] M. Rokeach, "Authority, Authoritarianism, and Conformity," in *Conformity and Deviation*, I. A. Berg and B. M. Bass (eds.) (New York: Harper, 1961), pp. 230–57.

[9] D. Cartwright (ed.), *Studies in Social Power* (Ann Arbor: Univ. of Michigan Institute for Social Research, 1959).

[10] A. Binet, *La Suggestibilité* (Paris: Schleicher, 1900).

[11] J. M. Charcot, *Oeuvres Complètes* (Paris: Bureaux du Progrès Médical, 1881).

[12] Forty-three subjects, undergraduates at Yale University, were run in the experiment without payment. The results are very similar to those obtained with paid subjects.

[13] A series of recently completed experiments employing the obedience paradigm is reported in S. Milgram "Some Conditions of Obedience and Disobedience to Authority," *Human Relations*, 1964.

The Mind Is a Formidable Jailer: A Pirandellian Prison

Philip Zimbardo, W. Curtis Banks, Craig Haney and David Jaffe

In prison, those things withheld from and denied to the prisoner become precisely what he wants most of all.

—Eldridge Cleaver, *Soul on Ice*

Our sense of power is more vivid when we break a man's spirit than when we win his heart.

—Eric Hoffer, *The Passionate State of Mind*

Every prison that men build is built with bricks of shame,/and bound with bars lest Christ should see how men their brothers maim.

—Oscar Wilde, "The Ballad of Reading Gaol"

Wherever anyone is against his will that is to him a prison.

—Epictetus, *Discourses*

The quiet of a summer morning in Palo Alto, Calif., was shattered by a screeching squad car siren as police swept through the city picking up college students in a surprise mass arrest. Each suspect was charged with a felony, warned of his constitutional rights, spread-eagled against the car, searched, handcuffed and carted off in the back seat of the squad car to the police station for booking.

After fingerprinting and the preparation of identification forms for his "jacket" (central information file), each prisoner was left isolated in a detention cell to wonder what he had done to get himself into this mess. After a while, he was blindfolded and transported to the "Stanford County Prison." Here he began the process of becoming a prisoner—stripped naked, skin-searched, deloused and issued a uniform, bedding, soap and towel.

The warden offered an impromptu welcome:

"As you probably know, I'm your warden. All of you have shown that you are unable to function outside in the real world for one reason or another—that somehow you lack the responsibility of good citizens of this great country. We of this prison, your correctional staff, are going to help you learn what your responsibilities as citizens of this country are. Here are the rules. Sometime in the near future there will be a copy of the rules posted in each of the cells. We expect you to know them and to be able to recite them by number. If you follow all of these rules and keep your hands clean, repent for your misdeeds and show a proper attitude of penitence, you and I will get along just fine.

There followed a reading of the 16 basic rules of prisoner conduct: "Rule Number One: Prisoners must remain silent during rest periods, after lights are out, during meals and whenever they are outside the prison yard. Two: Prisoners must eat at mealtimes and only at mealtimes. Three: Prisoners must not move, tamper, deface or damage walls, ceilings, windows, doors, or other prison property. . . . Seven: Prisoners must address each other by their ID number only. Eight: Prisoners must address the guards as 'Mr. Correctional Officer.' . . . Sixteen: Failure to obey any of the above rules may result in punishment."

By late afternoon these youthful "first offenders" sat in dazed silence on the cots in their barren cells trying to make sense of the events that had transformed their lives so dramatically.

If the police arrests and processing were executed with customary detachment, however, there were some things that didn't fit. For these men were now part of a very unusual kind of prison, an experimental mock prison, created by social psychologists to study the effects of imprisonment upon volunteer research subjects. When we planned our two-week-long simulation of prison life, we sought to understand more about the process by which people called "prisoners" lose their liberty, civil rights, independence and privacy, while those called "guards" gain social power by accepting the responsibility for controlling and managing the lives of their dependent charges.

Why didn't we pursue this research in a real prison? First, prison systems are fortresses of secrecy, closed to impartial observation, and thereby immune to critical analysis from anyone not already part of the correctional authority. Second, in any real prison, it is impossible to separate what each individual brings into the prison from what the prison brings out in each person.

We populated our mock prison with a homogeneous group of people who could be considered "normal-average" on the basis of clinical interviews and personality tests. Our participants (10 prisoners and 11 guards) were selected from more than 75 volunteers recruited through ads in the city and campus newspapers. The applicants were mostly college students from all over the United States and Canada who happened to be in the Stanford area during the summer and were attracted by the lure of earning $15 a day for participating in a study of prison life. We selected only those judged to be emotionally stable, physically healthy, mature, law-abiding citizens.

This sample of average, middle-class, Caucasian, college-age males (plus one Oriental student) was arbitrarily divided by the flip of a coin. Half were randomly assigned to play the role of guards, the others of prisoners. There were no measurable differences between the guards and the prisoners at the start of the experiment. Although initially warned that as prisoners their privacy and other civil rights would be violated and that they might be subjected to harassment, every subject was completely confident of his ability to endure whatever the prison had to offer for the full two-week experimental period. Each subject unhesitatingly agreed to give his "informed consent" to participate.

The prison was constructed in the basement of Stanford University's psychology building, which was deserted after the end of the summer-school session. A long corridor was converted into the prison "yard" by partitioning off both ends. Three small laboratory rooms opening onto this corridor were made into cells by installing metal barred doors and replacing existing furniture with cots, three to a cell. Adjacent offices were refurnished as guards' quarters, interview-testing rooms and bedrooms for the "warden" (Jaffe) and the "superintendent" (Zimbardo). A concealed video camera and hidden microphones recorded much of the activity and conversation of guards and prisoners. The physical environment was one in which prisoners could always be observed by the staff, the only exception being when they were secluded in solitary confinement (a small, dark storage closet, labeled "The Hole").

Our mock prison represented an attempt to simulate the psychological state of imprisonment in certain ways. We based our experiment on an in-depth analysis of the prison situation, developed after hundreds of hours of discussion with Carlo Prescott (our ex-con consultant), parole officers, and correctional personnel, and after reviewing much of the existing literature on prisons and concentration camps.

"Real" prisoners typically report feeling powerless, arbitrarily controlled, dependent, frustrated, hopeless, anonymous, dehumanized and emasculated. It was not possible, pragmatically or ethically, to create such chronic states in volunteer subjects who realize that they are in an experiment for only a short time. Racism, physical brutality, indefinite confinement and enforced homosexuality were not features of our mock prison. But we did try to reproduce those elements of the prison experience that seemed most fundamental.

We promoted anonymity by seeking to minimize each prisoner's sense of uniqueness and prior identity. The prisoners wore smocks and nylon stocking caps; they had to use their ID numbers; their personal effects were removed and they were housed in barren cells. All of this made them appear similar to each other and indistinguishable to observers. Their smocks, which were like dresses, were worn without undergarments, causing the prisoners to be restrained in their physical actions and to move in ways that were more feminine than masculine. The prisoners were forced to obtain permission from the guard for routine and simple activities such as writing letters, smoking a cigarette or even going to the toilet; this elicited a childlike dependency.

Their quarters, though clean and neat, were small, stark and without esthetic appeal. The lack of windows resulted in poor air circulation, and persistent odors arose from the unwashed bodies of the prisoners. After 10 P.M. lockup, toilet privileges were denied, so prisoners who had to relieve themselves would have to urinate and defecate in buckets provided by the guards. Sometimes the guards refused permission to have them cleaned out, and this made the prison smell.

Above all, the "real" prisons are machines for playing tricks with the human conceptions of time. In our windowless prison, the prisoners often did not even know whether it was day or night. A few hours after falling asleep, they were roused by shrill whistles for their "count." The ostensible purpose of the count was to provide a public test of the prisoners' knowledge of the rules and of their ID numbers. But more important, the count, which occurred at least once on each of the three different guard shifts, provided a regular occasion for the guards to relate to the prisoners. Over the course of the study, the duration of the counts was spontaneously increased by the guards from their initial perfunctory 10 minutes to a seemingly interminable several hours. During these confrontations, guards who were bored could find ways to amuse themselves, ridiculing recalcitrant prisoners, enforcing arbitrary rules and openly exaggerating any dissension among the prisoners.

The guards were also "deindividualized": They wore identical khaki uniforms and silver reflector sunglasses that made eye contact with them impossible. Their symbols of power were billy clubs, whistles, handcuffs, and the keys to the cells and the "main gate." Although our guards received no formal training from us in how to be guards, for the most part they moved with apparent ease into their roles. The media had already provided them with ample models of prison guards to emulate.

Because we were as interested in the guards' behavior as in the prisoners, they were given considerable latitude to improvise and to develop strategies and tactics of prisoner management. Our guards were told that they must maintain "law and order" in this prison, that they were responsible for handling any trouble that might break out, and they were cautioned about the seriousness and potential dangers of the situation they were about to enter. Surprisingly, in most prison systems, "real" guards are not given much more psychological preparation or adequate training than this for what is one of the most complex, demanding and dangerous jobs our society has to offer. They are expected to learn how to adjust to their new employment mostly from on-the-job experience, and from contacts with the "old bulls" during a survival-of-the-fittest orientation period. According to an orientation manual for correctional officers at San Quentin, "the only way you really get to know San Quentin is through experience and time. Some of us take more time and must go through more experiences than others to accomplish this; some really never do get there."

You cannot be a prisoner if no one will be your guard, and you cannot be a prison guard if no one takes you or your prison seriously. Therefore, over time a perverted symbiotic relationship developed. As the guards became more aggressive, prisoners became more passive; assertion by the guards led to dependency in the prisoners; self-aggrandizement was met with self-deprecation, authority with helplessness, and the counterpart of the guards' sense of mastery and control was the depression and hopelessness witnessed in the prisoners. As these differences in behavior, mood and perception became more evident to all, the need for the now "righteously" powerful guards to rule the obviously inferior and powerless inmates became a sufficient reason to support almost any further indignity of man against man:

Guard K: "During the inspection, I went to cell 2 to mess up a bed which the prisoner had made and he grabbed me, screaming that he had just made it, and he wasn't going to let me mess it up. He grabbed my throat, and although he was laughing I was pretty scared . . . I lashed out with my stick and hit him in the chin (although not very hard), and when I freed myself I became angry. I wanted to get back in the cell and have a go with him, since he attacked me when I was not ready."

Guard M: "I was surprised at myself . . . I made them call each other names and clean the toilets out with their bare hands. I practically considered the prisoners cattle, and I kept thinking: 'I have to watch out for them in case they try something.'"

Guard A: "I was tired of seeing the prisoners in their rags and smelling the strong odors of their bodies that filled the cells. I watched them tear at each other on orders given by us. They didn't see it as an experiment. It was real and they were fighting to keep their identity. But we were always there to show them who was boss."

Power takes as ingratitude the writhing of its victims.

—Rabindranath Tagore, "Stray Birds"

Because the first day passed without incident, we were surprised and totally unprepared for the rebellion that broke out on the morning of the second day. The prisoners removed their stocking caps, ripped off their numbers and barricaded themselves inside the cells by putting their beds against the doors. What should we do? The guards were very much upset because the prisoners also began to taunt and curse them to their faces. When the morning shift of guards came on, they were upset at the night shift who, they felt, must have been too permissive and too lenient. The guards had to handle the rebellion themselves, and what they did was startling to behold.

At first they insisted that reinforcements be called in. The two guards who were waiting on stand-by call at home came in, and the night shift of guards voluntarily remained on duty (without extra pay) to bolster the morning shift. The guards met and decided to treat force with force. They got a fire extinguisher that shot a stream of skin-chilling carbon dioxide and forced the prisoners away from the doors; they broke into each cell, stripped the prisoners naked, took the beds out, forced the prisoners who were the ringleaders into solitary confinement and generally began to harass and intimidate the prisoners.

After crushing the riot, the guards decided to head off further unrest by creating a privileged cell for those who were "good prisoners" and then, without explanation, switching some of the troublemakers into it and some of the good prisoners out into the other cells. The prisoner ringleaders could not trust these new cellmates because they had not joined in the riot and might even be "snitches." The prisoners never again acted in unity against the system. One of the leaders of the prisoner revolt later confided:

"If we had gotten together then, I think we could have taken over the place. But when I saw the revolt wasn't working, I decided to toe the line. Everyone settled into the same pattern. From then on, we were really controlled by the guards."

It was after this episode that the guards really began to demonstrate their inventiveness in the application of arbitrary power. They made the prisoners obey petty, meaningless and often inconsistent rules, forced them to engage in tedious, useless work, such as moving cartons back and forth between closets and picking thorns out of their blankets for hours on end. (The guards had previously dragged the blankets through thorny bushes to create this disagreeable task.) Not only did the prisoners have to sing songs or laugh or refrain from smiling on command; they were also encouraged to curse and vilify each other publicly during some of the counts. They sounded off their numbers endlessly and were repeatedly made to do push-ups, on occasion with a guard stepping on them or a prisoner sitting on them.

Slowly the prisoners became resigned to their fate and even behaved in ways that actually helped to justify their dehumanizing treatment at the hands of the guards. Analysis of the tape-recorded private conversations between prisoners and of remarks made by them to interviewers revealed that fully half could be classified as nonsupportive of other prisoners. More dramatic, 85 percent of the evaluative statements by prisoners about their fellow prisoners were uncomplimentary and deprecating.

This should be taken in the context of an even more surprising result. What do you imagine the prisoners talked about when they were alone in their cells with each other, given a temporary respite from the continual harassment and surveillance by the guards? Girlfriends, career plans, hobbies or politics?

No, their concerns were almost exclusively riveted to prison topics. Their monitored conversations revealed that only 10 percent of the time was devoted to "outside" topics, while 90 percent of the time they discussed escape plans, the awful food, grievances or ingratiation tactics to use with specific guards in order to get a cigarette, permission to go to the toilet or some other favor. Their obsession with these immediate survival concerns made talk about the past and future an idle luxury.

And this was not a minor point. So long as the prisoners did not get to know each other as people, they only extended the oppressiveness and reality of their life as prisoners. For the most part, each prisoner observed his fellow prisoners allowing the guards to humiliate them, acting like compliant sheep, carrying out mindless orders with total obedience and even being cursed by fellow prisoners (at a guard's command). Under such circumstances, how could a prisoner have respect for his fellows, or any self-respect for what he obviously was becoming in the eyes of all those evaluating him?

Life is the art of being well deceived; and in order that the deception may succeed it must be habitual and uninterrupted.

—William Hazlitt, "On Pedantry," in *The Round Table*

The combination of realism and symbolism in this experiment had fused to create a vivid illusion of imprisonment. The illusion merged inextricably with reality for at least some of the time for every individual in the situation. It was remarkable how readily we all slipped into our roles, temporarily gave up our identities and allowed these assigned roles and the social forces in the situation to guide, shape and eventually to control our freedom of thought and action.

But precisely where does one's "identity" end and one's "role" begin? When the private self and the public role behavior clash, what direction will attempts to impose consistency take? Consider the reactions of the parents, relatives and friends of the prisoners who visited their forlorn sons, brothers and lovers during two scheduled visitors' hours. They were taught in short order that they were our guests, allowed the privilege of visiting only by complying with the regulations of the institution. They had to register, were made to wait half an hour, were told that only two visitors could see any one prisoner; the total visiting time was cut from an hour to only 10 minutes, they had to be under the surveillance of a guard, and before any parents could enter the visiting area, they had to discuss their son's case with the warden. Of course they complained about these arbitrary rules, but their conditioned, middle-class reaction was to work within the system to appeal privately to the superintendent to make conditions better for their prisoners.

In less than 36 hours we were forced to release prisoner 8612 because of extreme depression, disorganized thinking, uncontrollable crying and fits of rage. We did so reluctantly because we believed he was trying to "con" us—it was unimaginable that a volunteer prisoner in a mock prison could legitimately be suffering and disturbed to that extent. But then on each of the next three days another prisoner reacted with similar anxiety symptoms, and we were forced to terminate them, too. In a fifth case, a prisoner was released after a psychosomatic rash developed over his entire body (triggered by rejection of his parole appeal by the mock parole board). These men were simply unable to make an adequate adjustment to prison life. Those who endured the prison experience to the end could be distinguished from those who broke down and were released early in only one dimension—authoritarianism. On a psychological test designed to reveal a person's authoritarianism, those prisoners who had the highest scores were best able to function in this authoritarian prison environment.

If the authoritarian situation became a serious matter for the prisoners, it became even more serious—and sinister—for the guards. Typically, the guards insulted the prisoners, threatened them, were physically aggressive, used instruments (night sticks, fire extinguishers, etc.) to keep the prisoners in line and referred to them in anonymous, deprecating ways: "Hey, you," or "You [obscenity], 5401, come here." From the first to the last day, there was a significant increase in the guards' use of most of these domineering, abusive tactics.

Everyone and everything in the prison was defined by power. To be a guard who did not take advantage of this institutionally sanctioned use of power was to appear "weak," "out of it," "wired up by the prisoners," or simply a deviant from the established norms of appropriate guard behavior. Using Erich Fromm's definition of sadism, as "the wish for absolute control over another living being," all of the mock guards at one time or another during this study behaved sadistically toward the prisoners. Many of them reported—in their diaries, on critical-incident report forms and during post-experimental interviews—being delighted in the new-found power and control they exercised and sorry to see it relinquished at the end of the study.

Some of the guards reacted to the situation in the extreme and behaved with great hostility and cruelty in the forms of degradation they invented for the prisoners. But others were kinder; they occasionally did little favors for the prisoners, were reluctant to punish them, and avoided situations where prisoners were being harassed. The torment experienced by one of these good guards is obvious in his perceptive analysis of what it felt like to be responded to as a "guard":

"What made the experience most depressing for me was the fact that we were continually called upon to act in a way that just was contrary to what I really feel inside. I don't feel like I'm the type of person that would be a guard, just constantly giving out . . . and forcing people to do things, and pushing and lying—it just didn't seem like me, and to continually keep up and put on a face like that is just really one of the most oppressive things you can do. It's almost like a prison that you create yourself—you get into it, and it becomes almost the definition you make of yourself, it almost becomes like walls, and you want to break out and you want just to be able to tell everyone that 'this isn't really me at all, and I'm not the person that's confined in there—I'm a person who wants to get out and show you that I am free, and I do have my own will, and I'm not the sadistic type of person that enjoys this thing.'"

Still, the behavior of these good guards seemed more motivated by a desire to be liked by everyone in the system than by a concern for the inmates' welfare. No guard ever intervened in any direct way on behalf of the prisoners, ever interfered with the orders of the cruelest guards or ever openly complained about the subhuman quality of life that characterized this prison.

Perhaps the most devastating impact of the more hostile guards was their creation of a capricious, arbitrary environment. Over time the prisoners began to react passively. When our mock prisoners asked questions, they got answers about half the time, but the rest of the time they were insulted and punished—and it was not possible for them to predict which would be the outcome. As they began to "toe the line," they stopped resisting, questioning and, indeed, almost ceased responding altogether. There was a general decrease in all categories of response as they learned the safest strategy to use in an unpredictable, threatening environment from which there is no physical escape—do nothing, except what is required. Act not, want not, feel not and you will not get into trouble in prisonlike situations.

> And the only way to really make it with the bosses (in Texas prisons) is to withdraw into yourself, both mentally and physically—literally making yourself as small as possible. It's another way they dehumanize you. They want you to make no waves in prison and they want you to make no waves when you get out.
>
> —Mike Middleton, ex-con, *The Christian Science Monitor*

Can it really be, you wonder, that intelligent, educated volunteers could have lost sight of the reality that they were merely acting a part in an elaborate game that would eventually end? There are many indications not only that they did, but that, in addition, so did we and so did other apparently sensible, responsible adults.

Prisoner 819, who had gone into a rage followed by an uncontrollable crying fit, was about to be prematurely released from the prison when a guard lined up the prisoners and had them chant in unison, "819 is a bad prisoner. Because of what 819 did to prison property we all must suffer. 819 is a bad prisoner." Over and over again. When we realized 819 might be overhearing this, we rushed into the room where 819 was supposed to be resting, only to find him in tears, prepared to go back into the prison because he could not leave as long as the others thought he was a "bad prisoner." Sick as he felt, he had to prove to them he was not a "bad" prisoner. He had to be persuaded that he was not a prisoner at all, that this was just an experiment and not a prison and the prison staff were only research psychologists. A report from the warden notes, "While I believe that it was necessary for staff [me] to enact the warden role, at least some of the time, I am startled by the ease with which I could turn off my sensitivity and concern for others for 'a good cause.'"

Consider our overreaction to the rumor of a mass escape plot that one of the guards claimed to have overheard. It went as follows: Prisoner 8612, previously released for emotional disturbance, was only faking. He was going to round up a bunch of his friends, and they would storm the prison right after visiting hours. Instead of collecting data on the pattern of rumor transmission, we made plans to maintain the security of our institution. After putting a confederate informer into the cell 8612 had occupied to get specific information about the escape plans, the superintendent went back to the Palo Alto Police Department to request transfer of our prisoners to the old city jail. His impassioned plea was only turned down at the last minute when the problem of insurance and city liability for our prisoners was raised by a city official. Angered at this lack of cooperation, the staff formulated another plan. Our jail was dismantled, the prisoners, chained and blindfolded, were carted off to a remote storage room. When the conspirators arrived, they would be told the study was over, their friends had been sent home, there was nothing left to liberate. After they left, we would redouble the security features of our prison making any future escape attempts futile. We even planned to lure ex-prisoner 8612 back on some pretext and imprison him again, because he had been released on false pretenses. The rumor turned out to be just that—a full day had passed in which we collected little or no data, worked incredibly hard to tear down and then rebuild our prison. Our reaction, however, was as much one of relief and joy as of exhaustion and frustration.

When a former prison chaplain was invited to talk with the prisoners (the grievance committee had requested church services), he puzzled everyone by disparaging each inmate for not having taken any constructive action in order to get released. "Don't you know you must have a lawyer in order to get bail, or to appeal the charges against you?" Several of them accepted his invitation to contact their parents in order to secure the services of an attorney. The next night one of the parents stopped at the superintendent's office before visiting time and handed him the name and phone number of her cousin who was a public defender. She said that a priest had called her and suggested the need for a lawyer's services. We called the lawyer. He came, interviewed the prisoners, discussed sources of bail money and promised to return again after the weekend.

But perhaps the most telling account of the insidious development of this new reality, of the gradual Kafkaesque metamorphosis of good into evil, appears in excerpts from the diary of one of the guards, Guard A:

Prior to start of experiment: "As I am a pacifist and non-aggressive individual I cannot see a time when I might guard and/or maltreat other living things.

After an orientation meeting: "Buying uniforms at the end of the meeting confirms the gamelike atmosphere of this thing. I doubt whether many of us share the expectations of 'seriousness' that the experimenters seem to have."

First Day: "Feel sure that the prisoners will make fun of my appearance and I evolve my first basic strategy—mainly not to smile at anything they say or do which would be admitting it's all only a game . . . At cell 3 I stop and setting my voice hard and low say to 5486, 'What are you smiling at?' 'Nothing, Mr. Correctional Officer.' 'Well, see that you don't.' (As I walk off I feel stupid.)"

Second Day: "5704 asked for a cigarette and I ignored him—because I am a non-smoker and could not empathize . . . Meanwhile since I was feeling empathetic towards 1037, I determined not to talk with him . . . after we had count and lights out [Guard D] and I held a loud conversation about going home to our girlfriends and what we were going to do to them."

Third Day (preparing for the first visitors' night): "After warning the prisoners not to make any complaints unless they wanted the visit terminated fast, we finally brought in the first parents. I made sure I was one of the guards on the yard, because this was my first chance for the type of manipulative power that I really like—being a very noticed figure with almost complete control over what is said or not. While the parents and prisoners sat in chairs, I sat on the end of the table dangling my feet and contradicting anything I felt like. This was the first part of the experiment I was really enjoying . . . 817 is being obnoxious and bears watching."

Fourth Day: ". . . The psychologist rebukes me for handcuffing and blindfolding a prisoner before leaving the [counseling] office, and I resentfully reply that it is both necessary security and my business anyway."

Fifth Day: "I harass 'Sarge' who continues to stubbornly overrespond to all commands. I have singled him out for special abuse both because he begs for it and because I simply don't like him. The real trouble starts at dinner. The new prisoner (416) refuses to eat his sausage . . . we throw him into the Hole ordering him to hold sausages in each hand. We have a crisis of authority; this rebellious conduct potentially undermines the complete control we have over the others. We decide to play upon prisoner solidarity and tell the new one that all the others will be deprived of visitors if he does not eat his dinner . . . I walk by and slam my stick in the Hole door . . . I am very angry at this prisoner for causing discomfort and trouble for the others. I decided to force-feed him, but he wouldn't eat. I let the food slide down his face. I didn't believe it was me doing it. I hated myself for making him eat but I hated him more for not eating."

Sixth Day: "The experiment is over. I feel elated but am shocked to find some other guards disappointed somewhat because of the loss of money and some because they are enjoying themselves."

We were no longer dealing with an intellectual exercise in which a hypothesis was being evaluated in the dispassionate manner dictated by the canons of the scientific method. We were caught up in the passion of the present, the suffering, the need to control people, not variables, the escalation of power and all of the unexpected things that were erupting around and within us. We had to end this experiment. So our planned two-week simulation was aborted after only six (was it only six?) days and nights.

We've traveled too far, and our momentum has taken over; we move idly towards eternity, without possibility of reprieve or hope of explanation.

—Tom Stoppard, *Rosencrantz and Guildenstern Are Dead*

Was it worth all the suffering just to prove what everyone knows—that some people are sadistic, others weak and prisons are not beds of roses? If that is all we demonstrated in this research then it was certainly not worth the anguish. We believe there are many significant implications to be derived from this experience, only a few of which can be suggested here.

The potential social value of this study derives precisely from the fact that normal, healthy, educated young men could be so radically transformed under the institutional pressures of a "prison environment." If this could happen in so short a time, without the excesses that are possible in real prisons, and if it could happen to the "cream-of-the-crop of American youth," then one can only shudder to imagine what society is doing both to the actual guards and prisoners who are at this very moment participating in that unnatural "social experiment."

The pathology observed in this study cannot be reasonably attributed to pre-existing personality differences of the subjects, that option being eliminated by our selection procedures and random assignment. Rather, the subjects' abnormal social and personal reactions are best seen as a product of their transaction with an environment that supported the behavior that would be pathological in other settings, but was "appropriate" in this prison. Had we observed comparable reactions in a real prison, the psychiatrist undoubtedly would have been able to attribute any prisoner's behavior to character defects or personality maladjustments, while critics of the prison system would have been quick to label the guards as "psychopathic." This tendency to locate the source of behavior disorders inside a particular person or group underestimates the power of situational forces.

Our colleague, David Rosenhan, has very convincingly shown that once a sane person (pretending to be insane) gets labeled as insane and committed to a mental hospital, it is the label that is the reality which is treated and not the person. This dehumanizing tendency to respond to other people according to socially determined labels and often arbitrarily assigned roles is also apparent in a recent "mock hospital" study designed by Norma Jean Orlando to extend the ideas in our research.

Personnel from the staff of Elgin State Hospital in Illinois role-played either mental patients or staff in a weekend simulation on a ward in the hospital. The mock mental patients soon displayed behavior indistinguishable from that we usually associate with the chronic pathological syndromes of actual mental patients: incessant pacing, uncontrollable weeping, depression, hostility, fights, stealing from each other, complaining. Many of the "mock staff' took advantage of their power to act in ways comparable to our mock guards by dehumanizing their powerless victims.

During a series of encounter debriefing sessions immediately after our experiment, we all had an opportunity to vent our strong feelings and to reflect upon the moral and ethical issues each of us faced, and we considered how we might react more morally in future "real-life" analogues to this situation. Year-long follow-ups with our subjects via questionnaires, personal interviews and group reunions indicate that their mental anguish was transient and situationally specific, but the self-knowledge gained has persisted.

By far the most disturbing implication of our research comes from the parallels between what occurred in that basement mock prison and daily experiences in our own lives—and we presume yours. The physical institution of prison is but a concrete and steel metaphor for the existence of more pervasive, albeit less obvious, prisons of the mind that all of us daily create, populate and perpetuate. We speak here of the prisons of racism, sexism, despair, shyness, "neurotic hang-ups" and the like. The social convention of marriage, as one example, becomes for many couples a state of imprisonment in which one partner agrees to be prisoner or guard, forcing or allowing the other to play the reciprocal role—invariably without making the contract explicit.

To what extent do we allow ourselves to become imprisoned by docilely accepting the roles others assign us or, indeed, choose to remain prisoners because being passive and dependent frees us from the need to act and be responsible for our actions? The prison of fear constructed in the delusions of the paranoid is no less confining or less real than the cell that every shy person erects to limit his own freedom in anxious anticipation of being ridiculed and rejected by his guards—often guards of his own making.

This article is the result of a research project at Stanford University conducted by Philip G. Zimbardo, professor of psychology, and three graduate-student colleagues: W. Curtis Banks, Craig Haney and David Jaffe.

Resisting Mind Control

Susan M. Anderson and Philip Zimbardo

Effective mind control stems more from everyday social relations than from exotic technological gimmicks. Social control is part of everyday living. In personal relationships, in religious experience, and in encounters with advertising, influences tantamount to the alluring recruitment strategies of high-powered organizations and "cults" abound. Effective social pressures gain their potency by exploiting fundamental human needs.

Resisting social influences becomes important when they can appropriately be thought of as "mind control." When information is systematically hidden, withheld, or distorted, making unbiased decisions is virtually impossible.

What people need to know is how to reduce their susceptibility to undesirable, coercive controls, and to find a way to determine which influences to consider suspect.

In this article, pragmatic advice is interwoven with a conceptual analysis. The hope is that it may assist individuals to transform impulsive reactions to contrived communications into thoughtful, meaningful choices.

Exquisite torture devices, electroshock therapy, mind-altering drugs, hypnosis, and sensory deprivation have all been used to get targeted persons to do the bidding of various agents and agencies of control. Indeed, these methods carry enough wallop to distort and sometimes destroy the mind's normal functioning; but they are not adequate for the task of reliably directing behavior through specific scenarios as designated by would-be manipulators.

After a decade of intensive, costly research into the technology of mind control, the Central Intelligence Agency's MK- ULTRA program was deemed a failure. Covert operations could claim little more than being capable of turning unsuspecting victims into "vegetables."

Relying on technology was the mistake. Effective mind control exists in the most mundane aspects of human existence: the inner pressure to be bonded to other people, the power of group norms to influence behavior, and the force of social rewards such as smiles, praise, a gentle touch. It is people in convincing social situations, not gadgets or gimmicks, that control the minds of other people.

The more worried we are about being seen as ignorant, uncultured, untalented, or boring and the more ambiguous events are that are to be evaluated, the more likely we are to take on the beliefs of those around us to avoid being rejected by them.

Words like "hypnosis" and "brainwashing" mystify more than they clarify. Once ensconced in some social role, our behavioral freedom is compromised in subtle ways. Interviewees answer, but don't ask questions; guests don't demand better food; prisoners don't give commands; audiences listen; "true believers" believe; rescuers sacrifice; tough guys intimidate and others recoil.

These social expectations come to control us more completely than the most charismatic of persuaders. As a nation, we saw in the Watergate cover-up how the "best and the brightest" caved in to the pressures that required "team players" to win this one for the President. Unquestioned protocol persuaded them to betray their public offices.

Unquestioned protocol can also lead *us* to surrender our own better judgment. Most residents of Nevada in the 1950s had their own fears about atomic bomb testing near their homes. However, government officials refused to warn them about the risks of radiation fallout, so residents kept quiet and remained in the area. Similarly, the employees of the Kerr-McGee plutonium plant in Oklahoma were silent about flagrant safety violations for many years. When they aired their grievances among themselves and organized in protest, a court battle began. In 1979, Kerr-McGee was found guilty of misleading the public about the hazards of its operation.

It is a fact of social life that those "in power" define reality for the rest of us. By controlling the outflow of information, they conveniently restrict the range of options from which the rest of us seem to "freely" choose.

The "social programming" of childhood circumscribes our perception of these behavioral possibilities with a neat cleave. The "good child" learns his or her place in all social settings, stays put in his or her seat, is polite, speaks only when spoken to, is cooperative, does not make trouble, and never makes a scene. We are rewarded for going along with the group, not for insisting on getting our way. It is the wiser course of action to go with power; we are taught not to challenge it.

Developing a critical eye is vital for individuals to counteract compelling social pressures, to resist the lure of passivity. When people behave essentially as they are expected to, it becomes difficult for us to evaluate their actions critically or to be the one who deviates from what is expected in the situation.

We must learn to be vigilant in seeing discrepancies between the ideals people espouse and their concrete actions. Separating the preacher from the practice, the promise from the outcome, the perceived intention from the consequence is at the crux of resistance. It is too easy to mistake the label for the thing labeled, to deal in symbols and concepts instead of people and their behavior.

Many notable politicians, for example, gave their support to pastor Jim Jones without questioning why he was surrounded by a half-dozen guards, why his church had locked doors, and why newcomers were searched before being approved by the Welcoming Committee. People's Temple members admired "Dad" because he cared for them and because he said he cared most of all about his children. However, they failed to critically appraise or even acknowledge the reality that he punished them severely—at times with electric shock—and subjected them to public ridicule for minor transgressions. The result was the tragedy of Jonestown.

Effective manipulators often conceal their intent amid "normal" appearances. Information from rape prevention centers, for example, suggests that it is especially important for women to be aware of the effects of "normal appearances." Entering dangerous situations with potential rapists may seem "natural," tantamount to being polite and helpful, when you have been trained to be ladylike.

Answering all questions put to you with a friendly, gracious smile or always deferring to the protection and judgment of men, even when they are strangers, is not the best idea. Nor is being courteous and open with service personnel at the expense of requesting proper identification.

Resisting persuasion

Going passively along "on automatic" is often our worst enemy. When we habitually take simple assumptions for granted in a setting, we fail to check out the reality. The following are suggestions for awareness and resistance:

- Actively monitor social interactions. Practice thinking ahead, anticipating what will come next, checking discrepancies and noting how you feel about them.
- Be willing to disobey simple situational rules when you feel you should, to sound false alarms occasionally or cause a scene. Never do anything you don't believe just to appear normal or get someone off your back.
- At the very least, try to get more information so you can carefully consider the consequences of saying "no" to something that could turn out essentially "good" (could you return in a week or a year and say "yes"?), or of saying "yes" to something that could turn out essentially "bad" (could you lose your money, pride, or life?).

Millions of Americans are subjected to stress and intimidation in the presence of those whom society has termed "expert." Auto mechanics, for example, often make thousands of dollars each year for services and supplies they don't deliver. Last year, over 2,000,000 Americans underwent surgical operations that they did not need, at a cost of more than $4,000,000,000. Here, it is important to be assertive.

- Practice "seeing through" programmed responses to authority. Pay attention to the social roles you and others play, including such subtle indicators as clothing—the business suit, repairman's uniform, etc.
- Be aware of who is controlling whom in social situations, to what end and at what cost.
- To the extent that it seems possible, refuse to accept the initial premise that someone else is more powerful, more competent, more in control than you are.
- State your arguments with conviction if the other person does so.
- Learn to retain a sense of self-worth in the face of intimidating circumstances. Remember a time when some person or group of people thought you were the best thing to hit the planet; a violin if you are a virtuoso; a photograph, person, or place—anything that makes you feel exhilarated and alive, that you will not reveal to others, but will retain as an inner core that cannot be violated.

The best persuaders always appear to be just like us. They use our lingo and know the inside jokes in order to influence our attitudes. Attitude change is most effective when it goes unnoticed. Among some defenses, one should check for signs of ingratiation, for overemphasis on mutual interests, and for requests for just one small commitment now, with an open-ended contract for later. How deep do the stated similarities go? How well does the persuader really know the common friend you supposedly share?

Mind control typically involves coming to accept a new reality. We are often dissuaded from probing beyond surface illusions of meaningfulness by letting symbols substitute for reality, abstract maps for concrete territories.

Thus, the Watergate conspirators never referred explicitly to money, but spoke of "bites of the apple." At the extreme, it is easier to "waste an enemy" or engage in "revolutionary protest" than to murder other human beings. As some specific counterstrategies:

- Never accept vague generalities and inadequate explanations in response to your pleas, questions, or challenges.

- Learn to recognize when a message is actually confused or ambiguous, perhaps intentionally so, especially if someone suggests "you're just too stupid to understand" or "women get too emotional to think logically."
- Paraphrase other people's thoughts both aloud and to yourself to see if you're understanding clearly.
- Practice generating creative arguments and counterarguments as you listen to persuasive messages to avoid slipping into "automatic" processing.
- Always seek outside information and criticism before joining a group or making a commitment to invest time, energy, or money in some endeavor.
- Train yourself and your children to notice the "tricks" in deceptive packaging such as those used in TV commercials.

Associate Prof. Donald F. Roberts of the Stanford Institute of Communications Research has found that knowledge of make-believe constructions, of audiovisual distortion techniques, and of celebrities, experts, and overgeneralizations can build the kind of skepticism in children which is the front line of all resistance efforts.

Susceptibility to mind control becomes greater when individuals are forced to focus attention on themselves, making them feel deviant or silly. To combat this:

- Be sensitive to—and avoid—situations and people that put you on the spot, making you feel different, awkward, or inadequate.
- Try to focus on what you are doing, rather than on thoughts about yourself. Don't generate negative internal dialogs about yourself, and never accept a chronically negative view from someone else.
- Maintain some nonsocial interests that satisfy you while alone—painting, carpentry, working on cars, reading or writing, for example.
- Be willing to look foolish now and then, to accept being "different" as being "special," rather than inferior.

If you can develop a concrete sense of self-worth, a sense of who you are, what you are interested in, and where your competencies lie, quite apart from the values, interests, and judgments of others, you may feel better about yourself in their presence, as well as in their absence.

Many of the most powerfully persuasive appeals are based on making people afraid or anxious. The following are suggestions for reducing this influence:

- No matter what the relationship, avoid getting sucked into unwanted confessions that may later be used against you. Many cults and mind-control systems use public confessions, self-exposure "games," and the like to catalog the weaknesses of their followers for later exploitation.
- Avoid making decisions when under stress, particularly in the presence of the person who has triggered the emotional reaction. Tell them you'll decide *mañana*.
- As you feel yourself becoming uncomfortably aroused, begin taking slower, deeper breaths to help your body relax.

Gnawing feelings of guilt can also provide a powerful impetus for personal change. Patty Hearst's psychological transformation in the hands of the Symbionese Liberation Army came from exploiting the differences between her family's privileged position and the poverty of so many others. All conflicts were slowly relieved with each step she took in the direction of accepting her captors' definition of reality.

To counteract such tactics, learn to confront your frustrations and fears. Start by thinking about the least provoking aspects while in a state of total relaxation, then work up to the more difficult ones. Don't let people make you feel indebted to them. When you feel grateful, be prepared to acknowledge the sacrifices of others with sincere thanks, instead of the expected repayment in kind.

Once aware that their prey is bagged, the slickest operators then emphasize the victim's freedom of choice, after tactfully constraining the alternatives. The newly persuaded person chooses "freely" while the influencer bolsters his or her decision.

Alternatively, the persuader may deliberately provoke your reaction in the desired direction. A salesperson thus might declare: "Excuse me for saying so, but this is quite an exclusive line; you may not be able to afford it." Some helpful hints:

- Be wary of people who overemphasize how free you are to choose among the options they have prescribed. Electing Anacin over Bayer is not the same as deciding whether you want an aspirin.
- Test the limits of your options by selecting "none of the above" or by proposing unexpected alternatives, at least tentatively, especially when you create them yourself and think they are better.
- Test others' intentions by giving them the impression you'll comply with their demands and then observing their reaction. ("You're right, that merchandise is too expensive.") If they start pushing in the opposite direction or simply look befuddled, you may have uncovered a hidden agenda.

Resisting systems

Large-scale systems of social persuasion depend on controls which impart a sense of belonging to a broad movement. Tightly structured situations are dangerous when we lose sight of who we are, when we forget that we have feelings and histories other than those programmed by the immediate social setting and the roles we are led to play in it. Some suggestions:

- Test for the presence of stated or unstated rules that unnecessarily restrict freedom of speech, action, and association. By subtly violating some of the rules and roles, you may discover how much latitude is allowed for eccentric or creative self-expression.
- Resist the lure of uniforms and other disguises that make you look like one of the bunch.
- Develop a sense of humor about yourself to retain a creative view of your situation and deal with any apparent personal weakness without undue anxiety.
- Listen to criticisms of your most cherished beliefs and institutions. Know them, but don't accept them uncritically.
- Retain your sense of individual integrity in the system by calling others by name and referring to yourself by name. If people are typically referred to by title, try adding their first or last name to the conventional address, abbreviating it casually, or somehow reformulating the typical approach.
- Disclose personal observations about your surroundings and about experiences you've had elsewhere to those you feel might share your views. Elicit feelings and ideas from them so that, together, you can disengage the "scripts" that specify the basic, unquestioned rules of the present setting.
- Remember that ignoring social rules is not easy and is sometimes met with censure.

When groups become preoccupied with seeking and maintaining unanimity of thought, they tend to isolate themselves from outside sources of information, and their decision-making processes deteriorate.

Persuaders bring us to their place of power, separate the good or aware "us" from the evil, ignorant "them," and then proceed to limit our access to ideas that they find heretical, traitorous, or not in their best interests.

When we are isolated from outside information, it is impossible to make unbiased decisions. Police interrogators question suspects at the station, not at their homes. Synanon rehabilitates alcoholics and drug addicts—and keeps its other members in line—by removing them from their usual haunts and restricting their liberty.

When we come to believe so thoroughly in our favorite concepts that we begin to hate those who don't share our views, to develop rehearsed, programmatic responses to discrediting arguments, and to acknowledge only ideas stated within our terminology, it may be time to make our belief systems a little more permeable. Some suggested tactics:

- Try to establish whether you can actually have an impact upon decision-making processes or whether you are simply part of the clean-up crew for decisions that have already been made.
- Refuse to accept a we-they dichotomy that cuts you off from outsiders and suggests you should think of them in terms of dehumanizing labels like animals, sinners, queers, rednecks, women's libbers, the teeming masses, etc.
- Suspect appeals that encourage you to detach your feelings from the rest of your being; assert the harmony of mind and body, intellect and emotion, past and present.
- Try to encourage independent thinking among group members.
- Remember that the minority may at times have the only accurate view of the issues. Any worthwhile group should tolerate dissent or be abandoned.
- Question commitments if they are no longer appropriate for you. Consistency in the face of contrary evidence is usually not a virtue, but a sign of rigidity, delusion, or prejudice.
- Maintain outside interests and sources of social support. Reject the appeal that devotion to the cause requires severing these ties. Battered wives, religious converts, undercover agents, Mafia informants, and inmates of prisons and mental hospitals all suffer from impoverished connections to outside systems.
- Family and friends should leave the path back home open. Your unconditional accessibility to those who have strayed, no matter what they've done or said, may be their only hope.

Disowning children, friends, or relatives when you disapprove of their decisions is much less effective in the long run than a gentle hand and some warm words. "Love bombing" is the favorite tactic of most cults because it works best among the love-deprived—those to whom we have not given love.

Challenging the system

The tighter a system is, the more likely that minor challenges will be met with retaliation. In prisons, mental hospitals, religious or political cults, military establishments, concentration camps, and so on, people have virtually total control over the existence of others. Threats to that power are intolerable. Even systems that appear less authoritarian may wield comparable punishments onto dissidents. For this reason, it's often more practical to challenge systems from outside, especially by forming other systems. Some final suggestions:

- Don't let your silence pass for agreement with the system. While talking with others, subtly imply your discontent in areas where you think they might agree.

- Once you establish a group of allies and decide that you cannot escape the system or that you are committed to change it, band together in opposition. A consistent minority, firm in its conviction, can often undo a majority.
- Begin by assessing the power of those who hold the reins. By determining what contributions you make to the system that are important to its functioning, you can collect a significant repository of such resources to withhold from the system when bargaining time arrives. Citizens' action, organized labor, the women's movement, and others follow this strategy.
- Appeal to the same human needs that the power-holders in the system manipulate in others. Collective resistance by a group that states its problems concisely and specifies clear and concrete goals, resources, and strategies is infinitely more likely to be successful than are disorganized revolts and spit-and-run tactics.
- Exit those situations in which disobedience is likely to be futile and punishable, if you can. Escape plans must be carefully thought through in concrete terms, not wished about vaguely. Above all, try to take others with you, rather than going alone.

It takes a firm sense of social commitment to escape a system of mind control and to then persist in challenging it from without. However, it is because we can exercise our ability to critically evaluate ideas, institutions, and our own behavior that we can perceive options beyond those provided by convenient dogma and ostensibly inescapable circumstances. In this way, we are "free" to make meaningful choices and to not be controlled. Even so, buyers do well to beware. "Every exit is an entry somewhere else."*

---

*Tom Stoppard, *Rosencrantz and Guildenstern Are Dead* (New York: Grove Press, 1967).

The authors are, respectively, a doctoral candidate in psychology and professor of psychology, Stanford (Calif.) University. Their views are based on a survey of pertinent social and psychological research, as well as interviews and personal experience with con men, cultists, supersalesmen, and other perpetrators of mind control.

The Perils of Higher Education

Steven Kotler

We go to college to learn, to soak up a dazzling array of information intended to prepare us for adult life. But college is not simply a data dump; it is also the end of parental supervision. For many students, that translates into four years of late nights, pizza banquets and boozy weekends that start on Wednesday. And while we know that bad habits are detrimental to cognition in general—think drunk driving—new studies show that the undergrad urges to eat, drink and be merry have devastating effects on learning and memory. It turns out that the exact place we go to get an education may in fact be one of the worst possible environments in which to retain anything we've learned.

Dude, I Haven't Slept in Three Days!

Normal human beings spend one-third of their lives asleep, but today's college students aren't normal. A recent survey of undergraduates and medical students at Stanford University found 80 percent of them qualified as sleep-deprived, and a poll taken by the National Sleep Foundation found that most young adults get only 6.8 hours a night.

All-night cramfests may seem to be the only option when the end of the semester looms, but in fact getting sleep—and a full dose of it—might be a better way to ace exams. Sleep is crucial to declarative memory, the hard, factual kind that helps us remember which year World War I began, or what room the French Lit class is in. It's also essential for procedural memory, the "know-how" memory we use when learning to drive a car or write a five-paragraph essay. "Practice makes perfect," says Harvard Medical School psychologist Matt Walker, "but having a night's rest after practicing might make you even better."

Walker taught 100 people to bang out a series of nonsense sentences on a keyboard—a standard procedural memory task. When asked to replay the sequence 12 hours later, they hadn't improved. But when one group of subjects was allowed to sleep overnight before being retested, their speed and accuracy improved by 20 to 30 percent. "It was bizarre," says Walker. "We were seeing people's skills improve just by sleeping."

For procedural memory, the deep slow-wave stages of sleep were the most important for improvement—particularly during the last two hours of the night. Declarative memory, by contrast, gets processed during the slow-wave stages that come in the first two hours of sleep. "This means that memory requires a full eight hours of sleep," says Walker. He also found that if someone goes without sleep for 24 hours after acquiring a new skill, a week later they will have lost it completely. So college students who pull all-nighters during exam week might do fine on their tests but may not remember any of the material by next semester.

Walker believes that the common practice of back-loading semesters with a blizzard of papers and exams needs a rethink. "Educators are just encouraging sleeplessness," says Walker. "This is just not an effective way to force information into the brain."

Who's Up for Pizza?

Walk into any college cafeteria and you'll find a smorgasbord of French fries, greasy pizza, burgers, potato chips and the like. On top of that, McDonald's, Burger King, Wendy's and other fast-food chains have been gobbling up campus real estate in recent years. With hectic schedules and skinny budgets, students find fast food an easy alternative. A recent Tufts University survey found that 50 percent of students eat too much fat, and 70 to 80 percent eat too much saturated fat.

But students who fuel their studies with fast food have something more serious than the "freshman 15" to worry about: They may literally be eating themselves stupid. Researchers have known since the late 1980s that bad eating habits contribute to the kind of cognitive decline found in diseases like Alzheimer's. Since then, they've been trying to find out exactly how a bad diet might be hard on the brain. Ann-Charlotte Granholm, director of the Center for Aging at the Medical University of South Carolina, has recently focused on trans fat, widely used in fast-food cooking because it extends the shelf life of foods. Trans fat is made by bubbling hydrogen through unsaturated fat, with copper or zinc added to speed the chemical reaction along. These metals are frequently found in the brains of people with Alzheimer's, which sparked Granholm's concern.

To investigate, she fed one group of rats a diet high in trans fat and compared them with another group fed a diet that was just as greasy but low in trans fat. Six weeks later, she tested the animals in a water maze, the rodent equivalent of a final exam in organic chemistry. "The trans-fat group made many more errors," says Granholm, especially when she used more difficult mazes.

When she examined the rats' brains, she found that trans-fat eaters had fewer proteins critical to healthy neurological function. She also saw inflammation in and around the hippocampus, the part of the brain responsible for learning and memory. "It was alarming," says Granholm. "These are the exact types of changes we normally see at the onset of Alzheimer's, but we saw them after six weeks," even though the rats were still young.

Her work corresponds to a broader inquiry conducted by Veerendra Kumar Madala Halagaapa and Mark Mattson of the National Institute on Aging. The researchers fed four groups of mice different diets—normal, high-fat, high-sugar and high-fat/high-sugar. Each diet had the same caloric value, so that one group of mice wouldn't end up heavier. Four months later, the mice on the high-fat diets performed significantly worse than the other groups on a water maze test.

The researchers then exposed the animals to a neurotoxin that targets the hippocampus, to assess whether a high-fat diet made the mice less able to cope with brain damage. Back in the maze, all the animals performed worse than before, but the mice who had eaten the high-fat diets were most seriously compromised. "Based on our work," says Mattson, "we'd predict that people who eat high-fat diets and high-fat/high-sugar diets are not only damaging their ability to learn and remember new information, but also putting themselves at much greater risk for all sorts of neurodegenerative disorders like Alzheimer's."

Welcome to Margaritaville State University

It's widely recognized that heavy drinking doesn't exactly boost your intellect. But most people figure that their booze-induced foolishness wears off once the hangover is gone. Instead, it turns out that even limited stints of overindulgence may have long-term effects.

Less than 20 years ago, researchers began to realize that the adult brain wasn't just a static lump of cells. They found that stem cells in the brain are constantly churning out new neurons, particularly in the hippocampus. Alcoholism researchers, in turn, began to wonder if chronic alcoholics' memory problems had something to do with nerve cell birth and growth.

In 2000, Kimberly Nixon and Fulton Crews at the University of North Carolina's Bowles Center for Alcohol Studies subjected lab rats to four days of heavy alcohol intoxication. They gave the rats a week to shake off their hangovers, then tested them on and off during the next month in a water maze. "We didn't find anything at first," says Nixon. But on the 19th day, the rats who had been on the binge performed much worse. In 19 days, the cells born during the binge had grown to maturity—and clearly, the neurons born during the boozy period didn't work properly once they reached maturity. "[The timing] was almost too perfect," says Nixon.

While normal rats generated about 2,500 new brain cells in three weeks, the drinking rats produced only 1,400. A month later, the sober rats had lost about half of those new cells through normal die-off. But all of the new cells died in the brains of the binge drinkers. "This was startling," says Nixon. "It was the first time anyone had found that alcohol not only inhibits the birth of new cells but also inhibits the ones that survive." In further study, they found that a week's abstinence produced a twofold burst of neurogenesis, and a month off the sauce brought cognitive function back to normal.

What does this have to do with a weekend keg party? A number of recent studies show that college students consume far more alcohol than anyone previously suspected. Forty-four percent of today's collegiates drink enough to be classified as binge drinkers, according to the survey of 10,000 students Harvard University. The amount of alcohol consumed by Nixon's binging rats far exceeded intake at a typical keg party—but other research shows that the effects of alcohol work on a sliding scale. Students who follow a weekend of heavy drinking with a week of heavy studying might not forget everything they learn. They just may struggle come test time.

Can I Bum a Smoke?

If this ledger of campus menaces worries you, here's something you really won't like: Smoking cigarettes may actually have some cognitive benefits, thanks to the power of nicotine. The chemical improves mental focus, as scientists have known since the 1950s. Nicotine also aids concentration in people who have ADHD and may protect against Alzheimer's disease. Back in 2000, a nicotinelike drug under development by the pharmaceutical company Astra Arcus USA was shown to restore the ability to learn and remember in rats with brain lesions similar to those found in Alzheimer's patients. More recently Granholm, the scientist investigating trans fats and memory, found that nicotine enhances spatial memory in healthy rats. Other researchers have found that nicotine also boosts both emotional memory (the kind that helps its not put our hands back in the fire after we've been burned) and auditory memory.

There's a catch: Other studies show that nicotine encourages state-dependent learning. The idea is that if, for example, you study in blue sweats, it helps to take the exam in blue sweats. In other words, what you learn while smoking is best recalled while smoking. Since lighting up in an exam room might cause problems, cigarettes probably aren't the key to getting on the dean's list.

Nonetheless, while the number of cigarette smokers continues to drop nationwide, college students are still lighting up: As many as 30 percent smoke during their years of higher education. The smoking rate for young adults between the ages of 18 and 24 has actually risen in the past decade.

All this news makes you wonder how anyone's ever managed to get an education. Or what would happen to GPAs at a vegetarian university with a 10 p.m. curfew. But you might not need to go to such extremes. While Granholm agrees that the excesses of college can be "a perfect example of what you shouldn't do to yourself if you are trying to learn," she doesn't recommend abstinence. "Moderation," she counsels, "just like in everything else. Moderation is the key to collegiate success."

Steven Kotler, based in Los Angeles, has written for *The New York Times Magazine, National Geographic, Details, Wired* and *Outside*.

Candid Camera

Stanley Milgram and John Sabini

Since 1947 millions of television viewers have watched the program *Candid Camera,* created by Allen Funt. The program consists of filmed records of people spontaneously responding to unusual and sometimes bizarre situations set up by the producer. In a representative episode, a naive person approaches a mailbox in order to deposit a letter, and is startled to find a voice from within the mailbox addressing him. The camera focuses on the responses of the person to this anomaly, and typically the reactions of a sequence of individuals confronting this situation are shown. Each episode ends by informing the person that the experience he has undergone is part of a *Candid Camera* episode. In the course of a single program, four or five different situations are shown.

The *Candid Camera* program merits examination for several reasons. First, the very fact of a program built on the exposure of spontaneous human behavior is itself symptomatic of broader cultural currents which we need to examine. Second, the *Candid Camera* episodes constitute a repository of documented behavior of potential interest to social scientists. We are not the first to recognize this value. James Maas and his associates at Cornell University have classified and annotated more than 1,500 such episodes. But we need to assess both the utility and the limits of such an archive. The value of such material will depend in part on their methods of collection. Here we note an interesting feature of the *Candid Camera* program: it participates, at least fractionally, in the methodology of the social sciences.

For social science, *Candid Camera* possesses a number of attractive features. First, each episode begins with a question about human behavior, for which we do not fully know the answer. The question is examined in concrete circumstances somewhat the way an experimental social psychologist might proceed in his laboratory. An illustrative question might be: "How would a customer in a clothing store react if the salesman took out a tongue depressor and started to examine the customer with it?" One senses that a question such as this touches on a larger sociological issue centering on role theory. We might tend to think that in the case of the above episode, because the clothing salesman's act is so bizarre, none of the clients will go along with it. The filmed records show, however, that at least some clients do cooperate with the salesman, thus, the procedures seem capable of yielding surprises, perhaps even making discoveries.

At least one group of social scientists, experimental social psychologists, shares with *Candid Camera* the idea that one ought to create synthetic situations as a means of revealing human behavior. For social psychologists, the synthesized situation is called the experiment. For *Candid Camera,* it is a typical program episode. Both experimentalists and Funt construct situations into which the participants are brought, but which are unfinished, the completion of the scene being accomplished by the performance of the person. The exact character of the performance is seldom entirely known by those who set up the situation.

Indeed, behavior which deviates from what is expected, that is, surprises, are particularly valued by those who organize such occasions.

An obvious merit of *Candid Camera* is that it presents us with behavior, not just hearsay. Through the visual and auditory document, we are able to see how certain situations are set up and exactly how people respond to them. It is not merely a statement of how people think they *would* act or feel they *ought* to act in a given situation; it is a record of how they do in fact act. We are presented with a richly textured, though unanalyzed, record which is precise at the level of the individual case. Such firsthand data would seem to be of considerable value in any science of human behavior.

Because the behavior has been recorded on film, it can continually be reexamined by social scientists, a task now facilitated by the availability of an annotated archives of *Candid Camera* episodes. Generally, in social science, we must be content with an account of an event provided by the investigator. But this account, whether in quantitative or verbal descriptive form, is an abstraction taken from a more complex behavioral situation which is no longer accessible to us. While experiments, and often sociological observations, are in principle replicable, there are many practical limitations to such replication. How much more satisfactory it is to have access to the actual behavior, or at least filmed records of such behavior. We may find in such iconic material features which would never be mentioned in a skeletal verbal account, and we are better informed of the exact tone or expressive character of the event.

Moreover, the events depicted in *Candid Camera* are embedded in the stream of everyday life. Funt creates his episodes in a variety of familiar environments: hotel rooms, banks, on the street, in parks, in bars and canteens, in zoos, elevators, bowling alleys, and numerous other settings that individuals encounter in their daily rounds. Those who serve as confederates play a variety of real life roles: bartenders, salesmen, bank clerks, etc. Insofar as sociological theory has as its goal the explanation of real life behavior, Funt's ecological imagination would seem to be a considerable advance over the more sterile methods which remove subjects from the natural contexts of life.

Candid Camera shares another feature with certain social science strategies. It gives us a new vision through the disruption of the habitual. It frequently makes evident what we take for granted by altering some of the normal assumptions of daily life. Thus, when a client enters a clothing store, and the salesman begins to examine the client with a tongue depressor, the audience laughs because of the discrepancy between normal expectancies as to the appropriate behavior of the salesman, and the behavior actually engaged in. It has often been observed that harmoniously functioning systems may be more difficult to analyze than those that show some degree of dysfunction. Freud believed that by using neurosis as a point of departure, he could better understand how the normal processes of personality work. Enthnomethodologists such as Harold Garfinkel attain an understanding of the normal rules of everyday life by deliberately violating them. Funt frequently relies on a similar disruption of the usual in order to generate insights.

A further merit of *Candid Camera's* materials is embodied in the very name of the enterprise: the behavior is observed without the awareness of the participant. Ethically, this aspect of *Candid Camera* is problematical; scientifically it is indispensable to a full understanding of human behavior. The essence of a social situation is not merely that there are two people present, but that each of the parties has a representation of the other in his field of awareness. When a person is aware that he is being photographed or filmed or merely observed, he reflexively calls into play a range of self-presentational mechanisms. These include both censorship mechanisms (he suppresses certain behaviors, such as picking his nose) and positive acts (he smiles, straightens his shoulders). When a person is not aware that he is being photographed or observed, he has no chance to make the adjustments needed for a social encounter. Thus *Candid Camera* presents us with behavior uncontaminated with the reactivity of an observer. (Sometimes, however, Funt will use a confederate to create a needed social scene, or to provoke the behavior of the target.)

Funt states that *Candid Camera* catches the person "in the act of being himself." More precisely, the camera catches the person acting under the belief that he is unobserved, or at least that his behavior is not being recorded for the later scrutiny of others.

A final point which social scientists may admire in *Candid Camera* is the sheer creativity evidenced over the years in the construction of *Candid Camera* episodes: taxis that split in half; drivers that land their automobiles in trees; waitresses in an ordinary diner who break into a Broadway chorus as they serve apple pie; bystanders who suddenly find themselves on stage in the midst of a theatrical performance, walls that vanish, mailboxes that talk, etc. The sheer variety and inventiveness of the incidents is undeniable. Funt is not interested in sociological theory per se, but his incidents are informed by a keen, though unarticulated, intuition about the forces that shape behavior in a social context.

But *Candid Camera* is not social science, nor are its materials free of problems for use by scientists. Before examining such deficiencies, let us start by pointing to the most obvious difference between *Candid Camera* and scientific research. This concerns the institutional framework within which each is conducted. Above all, *Candid Camera* is a commercial activity. The overriding goal of the producer is to create materials that can be sold to a network or a sponsor. Such materials are saleable insofar as they are able to attract and hold a large television audience. Thus, within this framework the entertainment value of an episode is the ultimate test of its worth. Funt treats his incursions into the study of human behavior as a marketable commodity, and each episode has a dollar and cents value. The scientific deficiencies of the *Candid Camera* material stem from its origin as commercial entertainment.

The most obvious scientific deficiency of *Candid Camera* is the lack of adequate sampling. There is no guarantee that the behavior depicted is typical behavior. Indeed, we have every reason to feel that the selections actually used in *Candid Camera* are chosen for their maximum value as entertainment. Funt indicates that he often shoots at a film ratio of 100/1; thus, even when a sequence of respondents is shown, we cannot assume the persons depicted represent anything other than a highly uncharacteristic set of responses.

Consider the situation in which a delivery boy finds Funt bound and gagged, asks whether the victim ordered a hamburger, then leaves nonchalantly when Funt indicates no. Clearly, the laughter promoted by this response indicates that it is entertaining. But is the behavior typical? We are not told how many delivery boys needed to be filmed before this particular boy left the incident. It seems that the more appropriate response of untying the victim, and offering him assistance, would be less amusing to an audience and thus less likely to appear in the *Candid Camera* archives. We have no systematic record of the range and centrality of responses to any given situation. We are thus presented with behavior which is shown to be possible (and of no small value for this reason) but with no idea of its probability.

Moreover, we are only shown those segments of the subject's behavior which produce a maximally humorous impact. We are not shown sequelae which may be critical to establishing the meaning of the behavior as experienced by the subject. In the episode cited above, we are not informed whether this particular delivery boy left the scene of his victim permanently, or whether, upon leaving what he perceived to be a dangerous situation, he immediately called the police. This latter possibility would give an entirely different interpretation to the delivery boy's behavior.

Candid Camera differs from scientific experiments in another important way. Experiments take account of and proceed beyond work that has already been done. Thus an experiment can be evaluated by the degree to which it contributes to the cumulative growth of a discipline. Funt does not evaluate his episodes by this criterion. All that is required is that each episode differs in some way from what has gone before, and that it be entertaining. Thus, while the *Candid Camera* episodes grow in number, they do not accumulate in any specifiable direction. *Candid Camera* is thus an enterprise that offers novelty, but not progress.

Candid Camera shares with experimental social psychology the observation of behavior within constructed situations, but social psychologists make use of experimental variation, in which one systematically alters the situation to find the causes of behavior. Moreover, an experiment must have a certain degree of precision and control. Each subject must confront the same stimulus; there must be a specifiable and metrical aspect to both the stimulus and the response. Some would argue that the quantification of experimental social psychology has led to an impoverished picture of human behavior. But merely to record behavior, for all its surface vitality, gives us no clue as to its significance in some larger framework of understanding. We are left with raw material which may amuse us, but which in itself explains nothing.

In sum, the *Candid Camera* record is probably more important in raising than answering questions, since it is a haphazard rather than a disciplined approach to the study of human behavior. The questions the *Candid Camera* sequences ask are often of the "what would happen if . . ." variety, selected to produce interesting and amusing effects rather than to elaborate a system of causal explanations. This lack of conceptual discipline at the outset of its inquiries finds its parallel in a lack of rigor in the documentation of results, the responses to the situations one sees may not be representative, since entertainment value rather than adequate sampling is the criterion for selection. Further, the film record falls short as a report of empirical results since it does not select, from all that a subject does, the scientifically interesting component. Since the sequences do not flow from some larger body of conceptual issues, there are no criteria for selecting important questions from less-significant possibilities or from abstracting the most important response dimensions. These scientific criticisms are quite irrelevant, of course, to the producer of *Candid Camera,* since his aim is to entertain rather than to inform.

Let us consider further how *Candid Camera* entertains. One important determinant of the viewer's response is his relative superiority to the subject on the screen. The audience is in on the joke; acting from this privileged perspective of full information, viewers laugh at the target's confusion or dilemma rather than share in it.

Instructions in how to respond begin with the show's opening moments, which create an unserious tone. As the show progresses, the viewer is instructed by the narrator about exactly what to look for; his comments reinforce the notion that what we are about to see will be funny. Studio laughter accompanies each episode as a way of continually defining the actions as funny, prompting the home viewer to experience the scene as amusing, rather than feeling sympathy or compassion for the victim's plight, or searching to understand it.

The audience is also offered an opportunity to see things to which it usually has little access. The situations involve circumstances which might not occur without intervention in a lifetime of observation. Although these situations may be somewhat bizarre, they are not beyond the audience's understanding. In order to understand the subject's response, the audience must be given some inkling of the perception of the situation from the subject's point of view. The *Candid Camera* technique invites the viewer to put themselves in place of the subject, they know what he is thinking; they laugh because they can see that his mode of thought will lead to ineffectual or inappropriate behavior. The behavior is funny rather than inexplicable or weird, precisely because the viewer can enter the phenomenology of the subject and understand that it is the unreasonableness of the circumstances rather than irrationality on the part of the subject which produces the maladaptive behavior.

The ability of *Candid Camera*-like techniques to expose the usually covert processes of an actor's phenomenology has made them an attractive tool for theorists of a phenomenological bent. It is apparent that the Garfinkel-type demonstrations, so intimately linked to ethnomethodology, are precisely in the mold of *Candid Camera* episodes. Like *Candid Camera* writers, enthnomethodologists deal with human action from the standpoint of the actor's perception of the situation, the likelihood of his constructing meaning out of novel and even bizarre circumstances, and the belief that he *will* respond to situations in terms of the meanings he can impute to them. Indeed, we may speculate that *Candid Camera,* a cultural phenomenon of 30 years standing, has exerted an intellectual influence in stimulating ethnomethodological thought. In *Candid Camera,* we see repeated demonstrations of the ethnomethodological arguments that people continuously construct meanings out of the flux of daily life, even out of incongruity. We laugh at the person's struggle to extract meaning out of a situation so constructed as to frustrate this effort.

Much of the impact of *Candid Camera* results from the impression that people have been trapped into showing themselves as they "really are." The target's self-presentational mechanisms are thwarted by his incomplete understanding of the real situation. The audience sees him vainly attempting to maintain his proper self in the absence of proper understanding. The attempt to maintain an adequate self fails for a variety of reasons. One aspect of an adequate self presentation is giving an appropriate response to one's environment, but what is an adequate response to a talking mailbox? In other cases, the subject attempts to conceal a deficiency he believes is personal, while the audience knows that it is the environment which is impossible. (In one sequence, subjects conceal the fact that they cannot open a packet of sugar, while the audience knows that the packet cannot be opened.)

People may appear foolish if they unnecessarily lose their cool when the situation is quite normal, but they can be made to appear just as foolish when they attempt to maintain their cool in an abnormal situation. In stable, everyday experience, self-presentation can be maintained by enacting habituated patterns of behavior; in the extraordinary circumstances of the *Candid Camera* films, the audience sees people actively structuring a self out of the stacked oportunities the situation provides. *Candid Camera* repeatedly shows us that people operate with a certain amount of good faith and trust and that they have certain habitualized or routine ways of dealing with situations that may sometimes be misplaced in the face of bizarre circumstances.

There are several senses in which we may examine *Candid Camera* as a cultural phenomenon. First, we may ask in what way *Candid Camera* is an expression of the larger culture. What continuities does it have with other cultural forms? Is it a completely new form of activity or does it emerge from precedents?

The spirit of *Candid Camera* is largely the spirit of the prank or the practical joke. Consider the archetypic prank. A person walks along the street, sees a wallet lying on the pavement and attempts to pick it up. The wallet is attached to a string which is then pulled out of the reach of the person just as he stoops to pick it up. The person in initially startled, then realizes he has been the butt of a joke. If the prank is performed on April 1, its perpetrators will normally jog the person into a realization of its significance by announcing, "April Fool!" thus giving a cultural legitimacy to their activity and undercutting hostile reaction from the victim by admonishing him to be a "good sport."

Funt has extended April Fool's Day to a year-round activity. Moreover, the program has achieved a certain cultural penetration. Instead of announcing "April Fool," each episode typically ends when Funt says, "Smile, you're on *Candid Camera*." Upon hearing these words, subjects are almost always taken aback. Before responding to this interpretation, they search out the camera to confirm the interpretation. Indeed, pointing to the presence of a concealed camera to support the assertion that the person has been filmed, has become part of the ritual of *Candid Camera*. Suddenly, all of the confusing and even bizarre events that preceded these words fall into place. The subject is thus grateful that the strain placed on his coping with the environment was nothing but an extended practical joke. Confusion suddenly crystallizes into a meaningful interpretation. *Candid Camera* has acquired a genuine cultural standing insofar as the words, "Smile, you're on *Candid Camera*" give meaning and legitimacy to the events that preceded them.

At an aesthetic level, the *Candid Camera* program elevates the practical joke to the limits that a large budget, technological sophistication, and admirable ingenuity allow. Whatever else one may say about it, asking a cab driver to follow a car which splits in half is a masterful practical joke. *Candid Camera* is funny in part because it is an extension of a preexisting form of humor.

The practical joke is not the only cultural precedent for *Candid Camera*. Western society offers many other instances of creating an entertainment out of the manner in which people spontaneously respond to unusual and unforseen circumstances. Pitting people against others in gladiatorial combat, or more perversely, placing people in combat with carnivorous animals, drew a substantial audience to the Roman arena. Like the early Christians entering the arena, the participants in *Candid Camera* do not choose to be in the situation. Unlike the Roman arena, *Candid Camera* must create its entertainments within a fairly tightly circumscribed boundary of individual and legal rights. A *Candid Camera* participant may be confused, embarrassed, or made anxious by the situation in which he is placed, but these are transient emotions which are presumably limited to the situation in which they are generated, and the consequences are certainly less serious than, say, being devoured.

Unlike Funt, the Roman impresario was given free reign to create bold and gory entertainments. The critical difference was this: in Rome, audiences and actors were of juridically different statuses. Christians, captured warriors, etc., were presumed to be devoid of those rights which ordinary Romans enjoyed. But in both cases an audience is entertained by the sight of people forced to cope with circumstances that are out of the ordinary and not entirely predictable. *Candid Camera* perpetuates the spirit of the Roman arena, but as vitiated by the limits imposed by an egalitarian political culture, and without the punitive intent of the Colosseum. In *Candid Camera,* the presumed equality between spectator and participant serves an important dramaturgical effect, facilitating identification between the two.

There is another sense in which *Candid Camera* is closely tied to culture. Many episodes rely on a precise knowledge of the prevailing cultural practice, and derive their humor from a violation of cultural expectancies. Much *Candid Camera* humor, therefore, is effective only within the particular culture in which it was constructed. For example, in one episode, male workers enter a physician's office for a physical examination. The physician turns out to be an attractive woman. The workers feel awkward when they're asked to undress before her. The audience titters at this embarrassing situation. It is clear that such a response can occur only in a society in which women physicians do not typically examine men. Even within other parts of modern society, say in Scandinavia or the Soviet Union, the embarrassed and awkward response of the workers would be less likely. Some *Candid Camera* episodes which prove successful in America do not travel well.

In their willingness to tinker with social reality for the purpose of observing behavior, both social science and *Candid Camera* display a fundamental irreverence toward the existing social order, and thus—some would say—participate in the analytic, disintegrative tendencies of modern life. But for *Candid Camera,* at least, there are clear boundaries to irreverence. Funt carefully avoids incidents or the use of persons that would be regarded as offensive by segments of the population. "... we lean over backward not to use a weak or poor sample of a black person . . . if a guy looked as if he was too rough or too ignorant, or too Uncle Tom, I left him out of the picture." Moreover, while Funt does not regard the everyday operation of the social order as sacred, he treats certain social activities as immune from *Candid Camera's* intrusions. For example, *Candid Camera* does not create episodes intruding upon real funerals; nor does it carry out a prank on a person's wedding night, however rich the possibilities for humor. This would be considered too deep a violation of the couple's privileged moments. *Candid Camera* maps for us the domain of the sacred by leaving such activities alone. Like the prankster, it tweaks at the culture, without doing serious violence to it.

Finally, as its very name implies, *Candid Camera* is utterly dependent upon the technical culture of western society, and specifically on the availability of instruments for audiovisual recording. Thus, it was not possible to undertake an enterprise such as *Candid Camera* until the present century. At best, it was possible, through the use of actors, to recreate a scene that the participants thought was covert (as in Hamlet's recreation of the poisoning of his father). But this is a far cry from the detailed filmic documentation of behavior enacted under the illusion of being ephemeral and unobserved.

Readings Suggested by the Authors:

Cornell Candid Camera Collection/Catalog. Department of Psychology, Cornell University, Ithaca, New York.

Funt, Allen. "What Do You Say to a Naked Lady." In Alan Rosenthal, ed., *The New Documentary in Action: A Casebook in Film Making*. Berkeley: University of California Press, 1971: 251–53.

Garfinkel, Harold. "Studies of the Routine Grounds of Everyday Activities." *Social Problems* 11 (Winter 1964): 225–50.

Maas, James, and Toivanen, Kenneth. "Candid Camera and the Behavioral Sciences." *Teaching of Psychology* 5 (No. 4, 1978): 226–28.

Parapsychology—Andrew Weil's Search for the True Geller, Part II: The Letdown

Andrew Weil

Andrew Weil has described Uri Geller and his audiences during some typical performances. He bent keys, rings and silverware; he read the contents of hidden envelopes; he fixed long-broken wristwatches and made objects materialize; he also told stories of driving a car blindfolded through the streets of Berkeley, of causing a rosebud to bloom, and of making an airliner's movie projector spew film across the floor. His special powers, Geller explained, came "from another universe." All he needed to make things happen was an audience's sympathy and cooperation.

One evening Weil found himself alone with Geller at the psychic's apartment in New York. Martin Abend, a TV commentator who felt out of place reporting on the paranormal, had just left—gratefully—after witnessing a semisuccessful display of Geller's telepathic powers. Then Weil gave the exhausted Geller a penknife, a beltbuckle, a key, and at last, amid tremendous excitement, Geller bent the key while it lay clasped with the other objects in Weil's own hand.

"I was elated," Weil reports. ". . . I was a convert."

Later that night I watched the Channel Five news. There was Uri again, in a long segment, bending a key, receiving drawings, locating pieces of metal hidden in cans. The reporters presented him as unquestionably real—there was "no possibility" of deception.

Then came a round-table discussion between the reporters and a professional magician who wanted to discredit Uri. The magician came off badly. He didn't believe in psychic phenomena and said Geller had to be a phony. Martin Abend, the political commentator, defended Geller by recounting his own experience earlier that evening.

"I drew two intersecting circles," Abend told the magician, "and tried to send them to Geller. Now I think that's an unusual sort of figure. Geller first drew two circles tangent to one another. Then he drew two intersecting circles. It was an amazing thing."

I noted with interest that Abend had not reported this incident correctly. In fact, Uri had come closest with the tangent circles. Uri's second attempt to reproduce the hidden figure had been one circle *inside* another. Initially a skeptic, Abend had remembered what happened in a way that made Uri look even better than he was.

The Amazing Randi Nevertheless, I called several friends to tell them about my evening with Uri and about my new faith in him. By then, I was sorry I had made an appointment for the next day to see James (the Amazing) Randi, a professional magician who wanted to expose Geller as a trickster and who had once raised a few weak doubts in my own mind. After all, what could Randi possibly show me?

The Amazing Randi lives in New Jersey, in a house guarded by two beautiful macaws. On the door is a Peruvian mask, which sends forth martial music when you ring the bell. The door opens from the side opposite the doorknob. Inside are mummy cases, clocks that run backwards, and other strange and incongruous objects that advertise the inhabitant as a creator of illusions.

Randi turned out to be a delightful host, talkative and funny, with a twinkle in his eye and a roguish look that always let you know he might be up to some trick. I told Randi what I had seen Uri do. He listened attentively but made no comments. When I finished, he invited me over to a table covered with envelopes, paper, nails, nuts, bolts, and aluminum film canisters.

"What shall we try first?" he said. "Some telepathy?" He invited me to take a piece of paper and three envelopes. "Go to the other end of the room or out of the room," he instructed. "Draw any figure you like on the paper, fold it up, seal it in an envelope, seal that envelope in another envelope, and that in the third."

I followed his instructions and brought the sealed envelope back. Deep inside was a drawing of two intersecting circles.

"We'll put that aside now," Randi said, setting it down on the table. He handed me a carton of sturdy four-inch nails. "Pick any six that you think are perfectly straight." I did. I also looked to make sure they were all real nails. "Now put a rubber band around that bunch and set them aside." I did so.

Emanations from Metal "Meanwhile, let's try one of Mr. Geller's favorite tricks." He picked 10 film canisters and told me to stuff one of them full of nuts and bolts—"so tightly that it won't rattle if moved." He went out of the room while I did what he told me. "Now mix them all up," he shouted from the kitchen. When I had done so, Randi came back and sat down at the table.

He studied the canisters and moved his hand over them without touching them. "I'm going to eliminate the empty ones," he told me. "When I point to one and say it's empty, you remove it. And set it down quietly, so I can't tell anything from the sound." He made passes over the canisters, just as I had seen Uri Geller do on television. "That one's empty," he said confidently, pointing to a canister in the middle. I removed it and set it aside. "Don't tell me if I'm wrong," he said. "That one's empty." He pointed to another. Randi had a great sense of drama; I felt involved in his performance. He eliminated another canister, and another. Finally, there were just two left. He passed his hand over each one as if feeling for emanations from the metal inside. "That's empty," he said at last, indicating the one on the left. I removed it. It was empty. The remaining can was full of nuts and bolts. He had neither touched the canisters nor jarred the table. I was amazed.

"Now," Randi told me, "that was a trick. And I'm going to show you how to do it. But I want you to promise you won't reveal the method, because we magicians aren't supposed to reveal secrets. This is a special case."

I gave my promise and Randi taught me how he did it. It was simple—so simple a child could master it. In fact, Randi said he had taught the trick to several children. It is based on a subtle but easily perceptible difference between the full can and the empty ones, a difference that can be seen by anybody who knows what to look for.

"What if the canister is filled with water?" I asked.

"It's the same idea—you just look for different things. Do you remember when Mr. Geller tried to do that on 'The Tonight Show'?" Randi asked. I thought I did. "Let's look at it," he said.

Studying the Tapes Randi had a video-tape machine in his house, together with recordings of most of Geller's television appearances. "I learned how he does most of his tricks by studying these tapes," he explained.

We relived the famous "Tonight Show," where Uri had failed, according to Randi, because Randi and Carson (a former magician himself) had safeguarded the props. There was Johnny Carson telling Uri to go ahead and do something. Uri stalled. There were the film canisters, one full of water. "Carson and I handled those cans in a way that eliminated the difference," Randi said. Uri was moving his hand over the canisters. "No, I'm not getting it," he said, and gave up. So ended one of Uri's most famous disasters.

"Now look at this," Randi said. He turned on a videotape of the "Merv Griffin Show," where Uri had appeared a few nights later. I heard Griffin tell his audience that Uri's failures with Johnny Carson had convinced him Uri was real, since a trickster would never have failed. The high point of the show was the bending of a nail.

"Like Woggily-Woggilies" "All right, back to the table," Randi said. He picked up the bunch of six nails. "Let's find one that's absolutely straight." He rolled each one back and forth on the table, keeping up a constant patter while eliminating any nails that had "little woggily-woggilies," as Randi called them—slight irregularities which kept them from rolling smoothly. He ended up with one nail he liked, holding it between thumb and forefinger, midway along the shaft. "Now, keep your eye on it," he said, "I'm going to try to bend it." He moved it back and forth slowly and gently between his thumb and forefinger. I hardly knew what to expect.

Suddenly the nail began to bend before my eyes. "Look at that," Randi chuckled. Sure enough, it was bent about 30 degrees, and by a stage magician.

I shook my head in astonishment. "Not bad, huh?" Randi asked. I allowed that it wasn't bad at all. "That's incredible!" I said. I took the nail. It wasn't warm or unusual in any other way. Just bent.

Then, before my eyes, Randi showed me in slow motion how he had substituted a bent nail for one of the straight ones, how he had concealed the bend from me until the proper moment and how he had then revealed it while rubbing the nail between his fingers. But I had *seen* it bend. Suddenly, I experienced a sense of how strongly the mind can impose its own interpretation on perceptions: how it can see what it expects to see, but not see the unexpected.

"Now, let's watch that tape of the "Merv Griffin Show" and see how Uri does it," Randi suggested. Sure enough, there was Uri Geller manipulating three nails just as Randi had. And under Randi's tutelage, I could see that one nail was never really shown in its entirety to the close-up camera, even though Uri was claiming to hold up each nail, one at a time, to prove its straightness.

Secrets of the Envelope "Ready for the telepathy?" Randi asked. "Let's try that sealed envelope." He went back to the table, sat down, took pad and pen, and held the envelope to his forehead. "You concentrate on the figure," he told me.

He started making marks on the paper, attempting to reproduce the secrets of the envelope. First he drew an equals sign; he seemed to be way off. "Now don't tell me how I'm doing," he said, "Just let me work on it." Slowly he extended the lines, then made them cross into a flat "X." He muttered to himself while working. Then the lines began to curve. "Oh, I see it now," he said happily. And there on the pad appeared the two intersecting circles, exactly as I had drawn them. Obviously, Randi had known what was in the envelope. I opened the envelopes, one by one, took out the folded paper, and showed it to Randi. "Well, well," he said, pleased with himself. "Look at that."

Randi showed me how he did that one, too. There is only one way to know what is inside an envelope without using paranormal powers: you have to get your hands on the envelope for a while and use your eyes.

"People come back from seeing Uri Geller," Randi told me, "and they say, 'He never touched the envelope.' But if you question them carefully, what they really mean is: he never touched it in ways that *they* think would have let him know what was inside. That's the basis of stage magic. You take advantage of little opportunities to do the dirty work, when you're certain people aren't going to notice you. Geller is a master opportunist."

"Have you ever seen him doing the dirty work?" I asked.

A Glance at the Blackboard "I sure have. I was at Town Hall the other night. The thing that really irks me is how much people let him get away with—things they wouldn't let a magician get away with. He asked a woman to write a foreign capital on the blackboard, and she wrote "Denver"? The whole audience was annoyed at her for not following instructions. At one point, you could just see every head in the audience turn to glare at her, and right then old Uri just shot a glance at the blackboard. It's that simple. And when he broke a zodiac ring at the end, he said, 'Let's try two rings at once.' What he did was click off his microphone for an instant, wedge one ring into the other, and give a hard squeeze so that the zodiac ring broke where the setting was joined."

"And you saw that?"

"I saw it. Everybody looks for complicated explanations, and the explanations are always simple. That's why you don't see them. And the people who are easiest to take in with that sort of thing are intelligent people, especially scientists. The people who are hard to fool are children, because they look at what they're not supposed to look at. Scientists are pushovers."

"Has the Stanford Research Institute ever had a professional magician act as a consultant in their studies of Geller?" I asked.

"Never! Isn't that unbelievable? They get insulted if you suggest it, or they say that a magician would put out 'bad vibes' that would interfere with Uri's abilities."

"All right," I said. "I'm impressed with everything you've shown me and told me. But last night Uri Geller bent one of my keys for me. Can you do the same?"

"Got a key?" Randi asked. I brought out the brass key that Uri had failed to bend. "Give it to me." Randi took the key and played with it for a while. "Yes, I think that will work," he said. He sat down across from me and held the key under my nose, rubbing between his thumb and forefinger.

"Look at that," he said, "I think it's going." The key was bending. In a trice it was bent to about 30 degrees, looking for all the world like a Geller production.

"No!" I protested. My faith in Uri Geller lay in pieces on the floor.

"All I needed was a moment in which your attention was distracted to bend the key by jamming it against my chair; I made the bend appear just as I did with the nail." Again I had seen not just a bend, but actual bending.

"Have you ever tried to bend a key with your hands?" Randi asked.

"I've assumed I couldn't."

A Very Good Magician Randi showed me how he could bend a key with his hands, and I was able to do the same, although with difficulty. I saw clearly that with practice one could get very good at bending metal objects quickly and surreptitiously, without recourse to lasers concealed in the belt or any other complicated devices.

Randi also made a fork bend for me, although he couldn't simulate the fork I had seen melt over Uri's hand. He astounded me with other tricks; and even when I knew what to look for I couldn't see him doing the dirty work.

"Do you think," I asked Randi, "knowing what I do now, that I could see Geller doing it?"

"I doubt it," Randi replied. "He's very good. He can take advantage of any situation. And people want to believe in him."

I remembered how Martin Abend had misremembered Uri's telepathic performance, and how I had embellished some of what I'd seen when telling others about it.

"What about the time I saw Uri make a ring sag into an oval shape without touching it?" I asked.

"Look, I can't explain all of what he does, especially if I haven't seen it. I repeat, he's good. And he probably has many different techniques available. But if an accomplished professional has a chance to watch him closely, it can all be figured out. That's why Uri won't come near me or any other magician."

"How did you get a chance to watch him up close?"

"First by masquerading as a reporter when he was interviewed at *Time*. And then by studying the videotapes."

"Do you want to expose him?"

"I'd love to, but I don't think that will be easy. The fact that I can duplicate his feats by magic tricks proves nothing. The only way would be to catch him substituting a bent nail, or jamming a key against a chair leg; that will be difficult."

I thanked the Amazing Randi for his time and went on my way, suitably amazed. I had never before had the experience of going from such total belief to such total disbelief in so short a time. Nor had I ever doubted my perceptions so thoroughly. Uri's unwillingness to perform in the presence of magicians seemed especially damning.

Irate Physicists Since then I have thought a lot about Uri Geller and have talked with others about him. One person I spoke to was Ray Hyman, a professor of psychology at the University of Oregon in Eugene, who teaches a course called "The Pseudopsychologies." It deals with astrology and various psychic and occult phenomena. Hyman describes himself as a "openminded skeptic who has never seen a genuine psychic phenomenon." He doesn't know what kind of evidence it would take to change his mind. Hyman was once a magician, and he spent a day at the Stanford Research Institute watching Uri Geller last December. He decided that Uri was "a very good magician but that he could replicate most of what Uri did by simple tricks."

"What I find most interesting about Uri Geller are the reactions to him," Hyman told me. "For instance, the physicists at Stanford were irate at the suggestion that Geller might be tricking them. They were physicists—real scientists—and I was only a psychologist. I was astounded that they had never bothered to check up on Uri's background in Israel."

Hyman showed me correspondence from a professor of psychology at the Hebrew University of Jerusalem, who described Uri's early work as a stage magician. The professor had also enclosed clippings from Israeli papers denouncing Geller as a fraud. At one point, an Israeli court ordered him to refund money to a man who contended that he had simply performed tricks of magic rather than the psychic phenomena advertised.

The Unanswerable "The question of whether he's real or not," Hyman went on, "is less interesting to me than what he's showing us about the nature of evidence and the way belief shapes perception. Uri Geller is an important person; we can learn a lot from him."

What is there to conclude from this maddeningly contradictory mass of data? I think the question of whether Uri Geller is real or not is essentially unanswerable. As deeply as I have pursued the answer, the data comes back reading: maybe yes and maybe no.

I can't say with certainty that Uri Geller doesn't have the powers he claims. I have an intuitive conviction that such powers exist. I also have a strong feeling that Uri is, among other thing, a brilliantly artistic stage magician, whose ability to create belief is great. But I am not sure that stage magic can explain completely everything I saw him do. And that is just about as far as I can go without getting very confused.

It must mean, as Ray Hyman says, that the question of whether Uri Geller is real is the wrong one to ask. A better question might be: How are Uri Geller and James Randi the same? I find them the same in that they both boosted my mood when I was around them, and both, in their ways, improved my powers of discrimination. They showed me very clearly that my sense impressions of reality aren't necessarily the same as reality, and I value that experience. But Uri believes in psychic phenomena while the Amazing Randi denies them. They balance each other nicely. Uri's excesses of belief (his preoccupation with intelligences outside the universe, for example) and Randi's excesses of skepticism ("psychic healing is a bunch of nonsense") form complementary pictures of reality.

Selective Perception People who believe in things like telepathy and psychokinesis are sometimes accused of thinking wishfully. I have always thought that people who *denied* the existence of such things were also thinking wishfully, for they, too, ignore certain types of evidence while paying attention to others. Leon Jaroff, the editor who did *Time* magazine's first negative story about Uri Geller, once said: "There has never been a single adequately documented 'psychic phenomenon.' Many people believe in things like this because they need to." That view discounts completely the evidence of direct experience. It, too, is based on a need to see things a certain way.

Selective perception of evidence is the basic method by which we construct our models of reality. Many systems of thought urge us to distinguish between reality and our models of it. For example, one of the important themes in Don Juan's philosophy, as transmitted by Carlos Castaneda, is that what we call "objective" reality is nothing more than a consistent model—one of many possible models—constructed out of learned and habitual ways of selecting evidence and interpreting perceptions.

As a student of psychology and of drugs, I have always been interested in the concept of set, the body of expectation that determines experience. When I conducted research on marijuana I found that people who were unfamiliar with the drug, in the absence of any encouragement to get high, felt nothing at all even after receiving large doses. On the other hand, subjects who are ready to get high can get high on a placebo. In other words, our unconscious needs and expectations can lead us to experience things that other people rarely notice, while at the same time they lead us *not* to notice some things that other people see perfectly well.

It might be possible to take more conscious control over the process by which reality is shaped and made to seem objective. "Wishful thinking," though it has a negative connotation, is an appropriate term to describe this process. We all engage in it, often unconsciously, to bring things into reality according to our needs, and to make them leave reality according to our needs.

That is why certain questions like, "Is Uri Geller a fraud?" or "Do psychic phenomena exist?" are unanswerable. The answer is always yes and no, depending on who is looking and from what point of view. Each of us has the power to make such phenomena real or unreal. The first step toward making them real is to believe that evidence exists. As for Uri Geller, I wish him good fortune and the wisdom to use his abilities well. From knowing him I have learned an enormous amount about the way I see things and the need for care in evaluating evidence—especially the kind of evidence which seems to prove things I want to believe.

Andrew Weil is a 31-year-old M.D. who has spent the past two-and-a-half years studying unfamiliar states of consciousness, mostly in Latin America and Africa. Weil is a fellow of the Institute of Current World Affairs in New York, and a research associate in ethnopharmacology at Harvard's botanical museum.

Two Ballgames

Douglas A. Kleiber and Edward C. Devereux

Film Synopsis

"Two Ball Games" is a documentary film focusing on a comparison between spontaneous child-directed games and sports organized for children by adults. With very few exceptions the action in the film is factual and uncontrived. Every attempt was made to present the reality of each situation objectively, as it naturally occurred.

The overall intent of the film is to create the comparison between two game settings for the purpose of evaluating each as an influence in child development and socialization. As the film proceeds it cuts back and forth from a small city park where preadolescent children organize and direct their own action, to a playoff little league baseball game where a large number of adults are in attendance and several are directly involved in the action. The audience is invited to consider the experience of the children in each setting.

Background

The tremendous growth and expansion of organized sports for children in this country continues unimpeded. While traditional sports like baseball and football are the forerunners of this movement, youth programs in hockey, basketball, soccer and other sports are rapidly emerging. Estimates of the number of children involved are in the range of 20 million. With practice and games included, the investment of time in "child-hours" in these activities is incalculable.

At the same time, there appears to be a noticeable decline in participation in traditional child-organized games, so much a part of the neighborhood experience of children in the past. It may be with the more sophisticated children of today, game playing is not the charming simulation of social reality that it has been for children in the past. If games do not relate to reality in some symbolic way, then children may be needing other kinds of activities to prepare them for the future. It is also likely that the increase in television watching among children, and the large amount of time taken up by participation in organized sports, contribute to this trend.

Whatever the explanation for the increase in adult-organized sports for children and the decrease in child-directed games, a significant question remains as to the effects of these trends. What, if any, are the advantages and disadvantages with respect to development and socialization? What do little league baseball players learn about life which those lacking the experience do not? There are strong arguments on both sides of this issue and what is needed is further investigation, discussion, and subsequent understanding. The film *Two Ball Games* is an attempt to document the issue and promote this process.

The Issue

There is no inherent antagonism between the organized sports movement and the life of neighborhood games. Co-existence would seem entirely possible even with the same children participating in both kinds of activities. But as it happens, supporters of one position are most often detractors of the other. Some of the arguments for and against each position follow.

Proponents of organized sports for children say:

. . . Ours is a competitive society. Children must learn to compete—to strive to win. Organized sport is a preparation for the "game of life."

. . . Organized sports emphasize "fair" competition, within the framework of rules impartially enforced. Children must learn to live within rules, accept authority, etc.

. . . Children must learn to accept defeat gracefully, resolving to try harder next time.

. . . Team sports require and teach cooperation, teamwork, working together for a higher goal.

. . . Adult-coached and supervised sports teach the relevant skills and discipline necessary for future excellence in athletics.

. . . Adult supervision and tested professional equipment assure physical safety of participants.

. . . Kids really enjoy tight competition, if it is fair.

. . . The excitement of high tension sports leads in many cases to a growth producing experience.

. . . Kids enjoy mastery of physical skills and striving for excellence. Organized sports provides a character-building discipline for them.

. . . Kids enjoy the esteem of peers and adults when they perform well. Children who perform indifferently at school may gain success experience and needed self-esteem through achievement in sports.

. . . Organized, adult-controlled sports provide a setting in which parents and children share in one activity which both enjoy, and in which the parent can help teach the child something he/she really wants to learn.

. . . Children enjoy learning to do something which will make their parents proud of them.

. . . Such organized activities bring families together.

Critics of highly organized children's sports make the following points:

. . . In spite of good intentions and training programs, most adult coaches are not really good. They may let kids get into bad habits and teach the wrong "fundamentals."

. . . Little League games are organized more for the benefit and pleasure of parents and coaches than for children.

. . . Adults care more about winning and competing than the kids. Hence, they may:

- put much more pressure on the children than they can really handle.
- keep such a tight control on the kids that the fun is eliminated.
- employ excessive and abusive sanctions against kids who make errors, thus diminishing their self-esteem.
- be tempted to cheat a little in the interest of winning—e.g., by leaving weaker players on the bench, attempting to stack the batting order, allowing some stronger players to remain in the game to the point of exhaustion and possible physical injury.

. . . Adults are more concerned about what is happening to the ball than about what is happening to the kids on their team especially those on the bench, those who have made costly errors, etc.

. . . Players in organized sports in fact learn little about rules, because this is left entirely in the hands of the adults.

. . . While winning is fun, losing or making serious errors which damage the team, are not. In spite of best intentions, coaches, parents in stands and other kids address wounding comments to players who make mistakes, destroying their self-confidence and producing humiliation and anxiety.

. . . Since the decisions are made almost entirely by adults, kids get little experience in leadership or decision making.

. . . The regimentation and overspecialization of roles leads to inhibition of spontaneity, creativity and experimentation in the game.

. . . Coached to imitate professionals, children run serious risks of injury and physical damage (e.g., Little League elbow).

. . . Highly structured, competitive sports preclude most of the fun and incidental learning. Adult-organized games resemble "work" more than "play."

. . . Despite rhetoric about "cooperation," little effort is made to recognize and reward the cooperative aspects of the game.

. . . Adults who promote organized sports often know very little about children, child development, etc. and hence make wholly unreasonable demands upon players, forgetting that they are still little children.

. . . Rigidity of schedule, (e.g., full six-inning games, scheduled throughout the season, with frequent practice sessions in between) involves a major commitment from kids, keeping them from alternative activities, demanding that they continue, even if they are bored or having an unsuccessful, 'no-fun' season.

Proponents of child-directed games argue that:

. . . The fun of the activity is in the process of playing rather than the product of winning.

. . . They provide an opportunity for children to experiment with new roles without fear of lasting consequences or critical evaluation.

. . . When children direct their own games they learn the value of cooperation and agreement in the interest of making the games work.

. . . Child-directed games allow children to make their own decisions and arbitrate their own problems.

. . . Children set their own pace for the activities, thereby controlling the intensity to suit their own needs.

. . . In such situations children see the direct effects of their initiative in contrast to other contexts where adults direct or intervene.

. . . Children learn to accommodate their differences in the interest of satisfaction for all. Thus, younger, smaller, more inexperienced or handicapped children are not taken advantage of as they are in highly competitive activities.

. . . In their own games children frequently modify rules to fit their purpose and they experiment creatively with the performance of different roles.

Opponents of child-organized games point out that:

. . . Unsupervised activities may lead to physical injury.

. . . Without adult supervision older and bigger children are likely to bully others.

. . . Unstructured activities are inefficient by comparison to those structured by parents, teachers, and coaches; children spend most of the time arguing.

. . . Children's conflicts are more fairly and effectively settled by an impartial adult.

. . . In child-directed games children are likely to form bad habits that interfere with subsequent performance in organized sports.

What to Look for in the Film

The film begins by providing a view of the way in which each setting is organized. The "choose up" and laying out the bases in the sandlot situation are contrasted with coaches drawing up lineups and the work of a "ground crew" in the organized setting. As the games get underway disputes arise in each and the resolution of conflict by the children in the sandlot setting can be compared with the involvement of umpires, coaches and irate parents in the organized setting. The management of peripheral problems, such as the retrieval of foul balls, is also examined. The expressions of the participants, both nonverbal and verbal, and the interchanges between children on the same and opposing teams provide more information for the comparison process. The reactions to the culminations of the contests produce the clearest contrast of all.

Do Black Shirts Make Bad Guys?

Jack C. Horn

Ask pro football fans to name the roughest, toughest, dirtiest team in the National Football League (NFL) and the Los Angeles Raiders will get most of the votes. Ask the same question of National Hockey League (NHL) fans and you're likely to hear nasty things about the Philadelphia Flyers, sometimes known as the Broad Street Bullies.

Both these teams wear uniforms that are predominantly black. Is this a coincidence, or does it reflect a color bias that affects what players do or how referees judge their actions? Unfortunately, as black activists point out, black has been unfairly linked to evil doings and evildoers for centuries. Even in the movies, you could tell the bad cowboys from the heroes by the color of their hats.

Psychologist Thomas Gilovich of Cornell University wondered whether there was any real connection between team reputations, playing style and the color of their uniforms. Working with Mark G. Frank, then a doctoral student at the university, he used statistics and psychological experiments to examine two questions: Do pro football and hockey teams that wear black get more penalties? If so, why?

The first question was easier to answer. Gilovich and Frank looked at league records for every season from 1970 through 1986 and compared the total penalties piled up by teams that wore black with those that didn't. For the NFL, they computed the total number of yards penalized, for the NHL, they added up the total minutes team members spent in the penalty box.

The black-clad teams in the NFL, in addition to the Raiders, were the New Orleans Saints, Pittsburgh Steelers, Cincinnati Bengals and Chicago Bears. (The Bears actually wear navy blue uniforms, but fans think of them as black.) In the NHL, the Flyers, the Boston Bruins and the Chicago Black Hawks wore black during all the years studied, and two other teams switched to black during this time: the Vancouver Canucks at the start of the 1978–79 season and the Pittsburgh Penguins during the 1979–80 season.

Gilovich and Frank found that the five black-uniformed teams in the NFL were penalized more yards than the leaguewide average in all but one of the 17 seasons. And, averaging penalties assessed against each team over all 17 years, these same teams ranked 1st, 3rd, 7th, 8th and 12th among the 26 teams in the NFL. So all five were in the top half of the league in penalties, with the Raiders well in front.

The hockey results were even more striking. Players for black-clad NHL teams spent more time than average in the penalty box every year, and when the researchers averaged penalty minutes for all the years, the 1st, 2nd, 3rd, 6th and 10th (among 23 teams) were those with black uniforms. The Flyers lived up to their thuggish reputation: they led the penalty parade by a wide margin.

One explanation could be that certain teams deliberately recruit especially aggressive players and dress them in black to intimidate other teams. But the drastic change in the Penguins from the first 44 games of the 1979–80 season, when they wore blue uniforms, to the last 35 games, when they wore black, belies this explanation. With the same players, same ownership and same coach, the Penguins averaged 12 minutes per game in penalties after the switch, compared to 8 minutes before, a 50 percent increase.

The link between black-clad teams and penalties held firm even when they wore their other uniforms. Football and hockey teams actually have two uniforms, a colored one that is dominated by the team's primary color and a basically white one that is trimmed with the color. The colored uniform is always worn by visiting teams in the NHL and usually worn by home teams in the NFL.

Using data from two recent seasons, Gilovich and Frank found that the 10 teams with black uniforms were penalized more than the others no matter what they wore. Apparently, the effect a team's primary color has on its players or on the referees persists. This didn't surprise the researchers. As they point out, teams and fans "identify themselves by their primary color. . . . One frequently hears comments like 'C'mon, blue' and 'let's go, red' . . . never 'hang in there, white.'"

Having established that these teams were actually penalized more, the researchers moved on to the question of why was it what they did, or did the referees look at them with color-coded eyes?

Since there was no way to test these alternatives directly in the leagues themselves, Gilovich and Frank set up a series of more general experiments to examine how wearing black affects both social and self perceptions. They taped a brief scrimmage in which teams ran two plays twice each, once with the defensive team wearing white and once wearing black. The offensive team always wore red, and the plays were staged carefully to make the two versions of each play as identical as possible in action and aggression. The researchers choreographed the action so that the defense played, to use the researchers' words, "in borderline compliance with the rules of the game. The first play depicted two members of the defensive team grabbing the ball carrier, driving him back several yards and throwing him to the ground with considerable force; the second play showed a ball carrier trying to leap over a tackler and being violently hit in mid-air. . . ."

Forty football fans and 20 college and high school referees were split into two groups so each could watch a different version of the tape. The people who saw the defensive team wearing black were much tougher. They called more penalties on the defense, rated it as more aggressive and said that if they had to referee a game involving that team, they would "call a tight game" to make sure "aggression does not get out of hand."

In this case, social perception—what the people expected to see—clearly played a part in the black-clad team's penalty problems. But in the case of the NFL and NHL teams, self-perception could also have been a factor. Perhaps wearing black, the color of evil and death, leads men to play dirty.

To test this possibility, Gilovich and Frank set up three-person teams of students, telling each that they would be competing against another team in five different games they would pick from a list of 12. (The researchers had selected the games to offer a wide spectrum of aggressiveness, ranging from a dartgame duel at one extreme to stacking blocks and shooting baskets on the other.) The students selected the games they wanted to play twice, first voting dressed in whatever clothes they happened to be wearing and again as a team, wearing either white or black jerseys "to build team cohesion."

In the first round of choices, there was no difference between the average aggressiveness of the games picked by students who eventually ended up on the two teams. But when they chose as members of a team, the black-clad students picked more aggressive games, on average, than the white-clad players. Their tastes ran to tug-of-war and hitting a punching bag rather than basketball shooting or log rolling.

So it seems that both social and self perception can contribute to the penalty-provoking effect of black uniforms. This doesn't mean, of course, that donning black always produces more aggression. As Gilovich and Frank point out, "The black garments worn by Catholic clergymen and Hassidic Jews [don't] make them any more aggressive than their secular peers." Rather, the link between the color black and aggressiveness is strongest in areas "that already possess overtones of competition, confrontation and physical aggressiveness. . . ." In many sports, "various forms of aggression [are] not only tolerated but actively encouraged."

Who Likes Whom and Why

Elliot Aronson

Mr. and Mrs. Doting, who have been married for 10 years, are preparing to leave their house for a cocktail party. He compliments her—"Gee, honey, you look great." She yawns. She already knows that her husband thinks she is attractive.

Mr. and Mrs. Doting arrive at the cocktail party. A male stranger begins to talk to Mrs. Doting and after a while he says, with great sincerity, that he finds her very attractive. She does not yawn. The compliment increases her liking of the stranger.

This little episode is an example of what some of my students have called Aronson's Law of Marital Infidelity. Once we have learned to expect love, favors and praise from a person close to us, that person may become less potent than a stranger as a source of reward.

The reason for this is that someone close is already operating near ceiling level as a source of rewards. It is not likely that he can provide much more. But the closer the person and the more he has been a constant source of reward, then the greater is his potential as a punisher. Withdrawal of his approval constitutes a loss of esteem. In effect, then, he has the power to hurt the one he loves, but very little power to reward him. In the words of the well-known ballad, you always hurt the one you love.

During the past several years, my students and I have been happily engaged in an investigation of what affects interpersonal attraction. Most persons act as if they like to be liked. They seek friendships, try to impress others with their abilities, they entertain, smile a lot, they are happy when told someone likes them, unhappy when someone ignores them or acts unkindly.

What are some of the conditions that lead us to like other persons? The research of psychologists has confirmed beyond doubt several important if obvious antecedents.

Propinquity—we like persons who are physically close to us more than people who are not near because it costs less in terms of time and effort to receive a given amount of benefit from those who are nearby.

Similar values and beliefs—we like those persons who agree with us more than those persons who disagree with us.

Similar personal traits—we like persons who are like us.

Complementary needs—we like persons who can satisfy our needs and whose needs are such that we can easily satisfy them.

High ability—we like able and competent persons more than incompetent ones, perhaps because we expect to gain more through association with highly competent persons.

Pleasant or agreeable behavior—we like persons who are nice or who do nice things.

Being liked—we like persons who like us, a reward in itself because most persons think rather highly of themselves.

All of these could be loosely summarized under a general reward-cost kind of theory. It may be that we like persons who bring us maximum gratification at minimum expense. But there are some phenomena that cannot be squeezed under the rubric of reward theory. For example, several researchers have shown that we like other persons for whom we have suffered. Reward in such instances is extremely difficult to define.

Moreover, certain behaviors that would seem to be highly rewarding at first glance do not always lead to a high degree of attraction. For example, though it does seem reasonable that we would like persons of extremely high ability more than we like those who are poorly endowed with ability, there is evidence that this is not always the case. It has been shown that persons who initiate most of the ideas and are acknowledged as the best idea men of a group are most often not the best-liked group members.

How can one account for these data? It may be the case that ability, in and of itself, might make a person seem to be too good, unapproachable, distant, nonhuman, and thus less attractive. If this is the case, then some manifestation of fallibility might actually increase the attractiveness of the gifted person.

We performed an experiment in order to test this proposition. We had individuals listen to a tape recording. They were told that they would be listening to a candidate for a television quiz show and that they were to rate him in terms of the impression he made and how much they liked him.

On one tape, the candidate was virtually perfect. He answered 92 per cent of the questions correctly. Moreover, in the interview he modestly admitted that in high school he had been an honor student, yearbook editor and a track-team member.

On another tape, using the same voice, the candidate answered only 30 per cent of the questions correctly and during the interview admitted that he had average grades and had been a proofreader on the yearbook, and that he failed to make the track team. On tape number three, we had the superior person again but this time he committed an embarrassing blunder. Near the end of the interview, he clumsily spilled a cup of coffee over himself. On the tape, this blunder was accompanied by a great deal of noise clatter and anguished talk.

The fourth tape was the candidate with the average ability and the coffee-spilling blunder.

The results were clear-cut: the most attractive candidate was the superior person who committed a blunder, while the least attractive was the person of average ability who committed a blunder. Thus, although a high degree of competence is probably rewarding and, therefore, attractive, some evidence of incompetence in high-ability persons leads to higher ratings of attractiveness.

Further tentative support of this notion is found in the case of John F. Kennedy. According to the Gallup Poll, Kennedy's personal popularity increased immediately after the Bay of Pigs fiasco. Here is a situation in which a President commits one of history's truly great blunders, and lo and behold, people like him more. The explanation? Perhaps President Kennedy was too perfect. He was young, handsome, bright, witty, a war hero, wealthy, charming, athletic, a voracious reader, a master political strategist, an uncomplaining endurer of physical pain. He has a perfect wife, two cute kids and a talented, powerful, close-knit family. Some evidence of fallibility, like the Bay of Pigs fiasco, could have served to make him appear more human, hence more likeable.

In order to obtain a more precise matrix of predictions, it may be necessary to abandon the attempt to apply a loose global theory and instead construct limited, small-scale "mini-theories."

In recent years, a mini-theory I have been working on is the gain-loss theory: *increasing rewards and punishments from a person have more impact on his attractiveness than constant, invariant rewards and punishments.*

As Spinoza wrote 300 years ago in Proposition 44 of *The Ethics:*

> Hatred which is completely vanquished by love passes into love, and love is thereupon greater than if hatred had not preceded it. For he who begins to love a thing which he was wont to hate or regard with pain, from the very fact of loving, feels pleasure. To this pleasure involved in love is added the pleasure arising from aid given to the endeavor to remove the pain involved in hatred accompanied by the idea of the former object of hatred as cause.

Thus, a person whose liking for us increases over time will be better liked by us than a friend who has always liked us. Also, a person whose liking for us decreases over time will be disliked more than one who has always disliked us.

Imagine that you are back at the cocktail party with the Dotings. You have a conversation with a person whom you have never met before. After several minutes he excuses himself and drifts into another group. Later that evening, while standing behind a potted palm, you overhear him talking about you. Now suppose you run into this person at several consecutive parties, talk to him at each, and chance to overhear his comments about you each time.

There are four possibilities that I find interesting: 1) you overhear the person saying only positive things about you, 2) you overhear him saying only negative things about you, 3) he begins with negative comments but gradually they become increasingly positive, 4) he begins with positive comments but gradually they become increasingly negative. Our theory, if correct, should be able to predict the circumstances in which you would find this stranger most attractive to you.

To test this theory I set up an experimental analogue of the cocktail situation in collaboration with Darwyn Linder. In our experiment college students interacted during seven sessions with a student who was actually a paid confederate. After each session the subject was surreptitiously allowed to overhear the confederate evaluate her to the experimenter.

The results confirmed the predictions of our gain-loss theory. A person who began with negative comments about the subject and gradually became more positive was liked more by the subject than persons who made only positive comments. Also, a person who began with positive comments that gradually became negative was liked less than a person who made only negative comments about the subject.

Why does a gain or loss of liking have more effect than either constant positive liking or constant disliking? When a person expresses negative feelings toward us, we probably experience anxiety. If the person gradually becomes more positive in his feelings toward us, this is reward in itself and it also reduces the prior anxiety he has aroused. Thus the attractiveness of an individual who has first created and then reduced anxiety is increased.

The same reasoning applies to the loss part of the theory. When negative feelings follow positive ones, they not only punish but they wipe out the reward of the earlier positive behavior.

The anxiety-reduction explanation is further supported by another finding in my experiment with Darwyn Linder. When the overheard comments were first neutral and then increasingly positive, the eavesdropper liked the talker almost precisely the same as she liked the talker who made only positive comments. Thus a negative evaluation seems essential to maximize the effect.

Next, in collaboration with Harold Sigall I did an experiment to further ascertain the importance of prior anxiety on attraction. We reasoned that if a person is aware that he is about to be evaluated, he will experience anxiety. All other things being equal, the more attractive the evaluator the greater the anxiety—because it is more important to receive a high evaluation from an attractive person.

Thus, according to our theory, if a beautiful woman were to evaluate a male favorably, she would be liked more than a homely woman who evaluated him favorably. If a beautiful woman were to give a negative evaluation, she would be disliked more than a homely woman who had evaluated him unfavorably, because the beautiful woman would leave the male with more anxiety.

Sigall and I took a naturally attractive young woman and, in one set of experiments, made her look homely by dressing her in loose, ill-fitting clothes, providing her with a rather ugly wig, and giving her complexion a rather oily, unappetizing look. Thus, we showed that while only God may make a woman truly beautiful, all it takes is a couple of diabolical experimenters to make a beautiful woman look ugly.

In the experiment, our confederate posed as either a "beautiful" or an "ugly" graduate student in clinical psychology who was interviewing and testing a number of men. She then gave each man her personal clinical judgment, which was either favorable or unfavorable. The results confirmed our predictions: the beautiful-positive woman was best liked; the beautiful-negative woman was least liked. The males did not seem to care much about the impressions they made on the ugly woman.

We also had an unexpected finding. Despite the fact that they said they disliked the beautiful woman who evaluated them negatively, many of the males expressed great desire to return and be in another experiment with the woman. Our interpretation is that the males wanted to see the beautiful woman again because they hoped to be able to change her impression of them from unfavorable to favorable.

This experiment demonstrated that anxiety is an important component of the gain-loss phenomenon. But it may not be the only component. There may be another reason for our liking a person whose attitude toward us begins by being negative and gradually becomes positive. It may be that we like him because, by inducing him to change his opinion of us, we enable him to give us a feeling of competence or effectiveness. Since this is a good feeling, it increases our liking for the person who provided it. In his Ph.D. thesis, Harold Sigall investigated this possibility in what we have called the conversion effect. The question is: does a missionary feel more kindly disposed toward someone he has converted to the faith than toward someone who has always been a loyal member of the flock? On the basis of our theory, we would predict that the missionary would like the convert more because there is a greater gain involved.

Sigall speculated that the degree of effectiveness in shifting opinion and the extent of the missionary's ego involvement would both affect attractiveness. Suppose you felt that marijuana should be made available to everyone, all the time, and you were presenting your argument to a person who believed that all marijuana and marijuana seeds should be destroyed. After hearing your argument, this person comes to believe that marijuana could be used on Saturday nights under supervised conditions by persons over 35. On a scale from –10 to +10, his position has moved from say –10 to –2. He still disagrees with you, but you have shifted his position and have every right to feel proud and effective.

In his experiment, Sigall manipulated both the degree of opinion shift and the involvement. In the low-involvement condition, the missionary-type was given a prepared speech to read without dramatics. In the high-involvement condition, he had to organize the argument himself and present it as effectively as possible.

When there was low involvement, subjects liked best the persons who agreed with them and had no opinion shift. They liked least the persons who disagreed even though they shifted their opinions slightly. When there was high involvement, the findings were just the opposite. Thus persons like similar persons better than converts unless they are ego-involved in converting them. Then they like the converts better.

It is difficult for me to summarize the major thrust of my results without becoming depressed—for my data do suggest a rather dismal picture of the human condition. Like Mrs. Doting, we seem to be forever seeking compliments from strangers and being hurt by those we love.

Before we become too pessimistic about the human condition, however, let us look at a different dimension—namely, what action does a person take when he is hurt by another person? On this score the evidence suggests that the more important the relationship, the more likely a person will try to maintain it—in spite of the hurt. Some support for this contention can be gleaned from the experiment we reported on beautiful and homely women. Recall that our subjects expressed greatest dislike for the beautiful woman who treated them badly—but, at the same time, it was these very subjects who expressed the greatest desire to return to that situation—perhaps to try to make a better impression on her. This phenomenon receives still stronger support from an experiment by one of my students, Joanne Floyd. Floyd placed two young children in a room together—either close friends or strangers. She assigned one a task for which he was allowed to earn several trinkets. The child was instructed to share the trinkets with his partner (the subject). The experiment was rigged so that the subjects would get different impressions of the generosity of their partners. Some subjects were led to believe that the friend (or stranger) was treating them in a stingy manner, others were led to believe that he was treating them in a generous manner. Floyd then allowed the subject to earn several trinkets of his own and instructed him to share them with his partner. She found, as predicted, that subjects showed the most generosity in both the gain and the loss conditions—i.e., they were most generous toward either a generous stranger or a stingy friend. In short, they were relatively stingy to the stingy stranger (why not?—the stranger had behaved as they might have expected) and to the generous friend ("Ho-hum, so my friend likes me—what else is new?"). But when it looked as though they might be *gaining* a friend (the generous stranger), they reacted with generosity—and likewise, when it looked as though they might be *losing* a friend (the stingy friend), they responded once again with generosity.

Personally, I find this last datum a touching aspect of the human condition. While it appears to be true, as the line goes, that "you always hurt the one you love," the hurt person appears to be inspired to react kindly rather than in kind in an attempt to reestablish the intensity of the relationship. This suggests the comforting possibility that individuals have some motivation toward the maintenance of stability in their relationships. To return to Mr. and Mrs. Doting for a moment, while Mr. Doting has great power to hurt his wife (by telling her that he thinks she's ugly), if he does so, Mrs. Doting is apt to be very responsive to this criticism, striving to win back what she has lost by once more making herself attractive in the eyes of her husband. Carrying this speculation a step further, I would suggest that the more authentic a relationship is, the less the possibility of reaching the plateau that the Dotings appear to be stuck on. In short, if marriage partners do not dote on each other but remain honest and open, it may be the case that their relationship will stay close to the "gain" condition of our gain-loss experiment. My current research is aimed at testing this proposition.

The Pygmalion Effect Lives

Robert Rosenthal

Pygmalion created Galatea out of ivory and desire. In Ovid's account, Pygmalion fell in love with his own sculpture of the perfect woman, and Venus, who spent a lot of time granting requests in those days, gave life to Galatea. In George Bernard Shaw's version 19 centuries later, Henry Higgins turns a Cockney flower girl into an elegant lady, relying on language rather than love.

Most of us do not have Pygmalion's power to manufacture the ideal mate, nor do we all share Higgins' fondness for phonetics. But we may have an extraordinary influence, of which we are often oblivious, on others. Psychologists have not yet learned how to produce Galatea or her male equivalent in the laboratory, but they have demonstrated that the power of expectation alone can influence the behavior of others. The phenomenon has come to be called self-fulfilling prophecy: people sometimes become what we prophesy for them.

This point has long been argued on an intuitive basis. It is obvious, for example, that ghetto children, whose academic performance worsens the longer they remain in school, tend to have teachers who are convinced that the children cannot learn. However, one could argue that teachers expected little because the students behaved poorly, rather than the other way around. To see which comes first, the expectation or the performance, we turned to the laboratory.

In the first study of this problem, over a decade ago, Kermit Fode and I asked 10 students to be "experimenters." We gave each experimenter, in turn, about 20 subjects. The experimenter showed each of his subjects a series of faces, which the subject rated on "degree of success or failure" from +10 to –10. We had previously selected photos that most people consider quite neutral.

We gave our experimenters identical instructions on how to administer the test, with one exception. We told half of them that the "well-established" finding was that the subjects would rate the photos positively; we told the rest that subjects would probably rate the photos negatively.

Expectant Voices

In spite of the fact that all experimenters read the same instructions to their subjects, we found that they still managed to convey their expectations. Experimenters who anticipated positive photo ratings got them, while those who expected negative ratings got them too. How did the experimenters silently let their subjects know what they wanted? John Adair and Joyce Epstein repeated this experiment and tape-recorded the experimenters reading the instructions. They got the same results we did, and then repeated their experiment, this time using only the tape recordings of their experimenters to instruct their new sample of subjects. They found that subjects exposed only to these tape recordings were just as much influenced by their experimenter's expectations as were those subjects who had experienced "live" experimenters. Apparently, tone of voice alone did the trick.

Such results generated a spate of studies. Larry Larrabee and L. Dennis Kleinsasser found that experimenters could raise the IQ scores of children, especially on the verbal and information subtests, merely by expecting them to do well. Samuel Marwit found that patients will interpret Rorschach inkblots as animals or human beings, depending on what the examiner has been led to expect. And Ronald Johnson, in an ingenious and carefully controlled study, found that experimenters could improve their subjects' performance on a task requiring subjects to drop as many marbles as possible through one of several holes in the table top by expecting them to do well.

Self-fulfilling prophecies even work for animals. Bertrand Russell, who had something to say about nearly everything, noticed that rats display the "national characteristics of the observer. Animals studied by Americans rush about frantically, with an incredible display of hustle and pep, and at last achieve the desired result by chance. Animals observed by Germans sit still and think, and at last evolve the solution out of their inner consciousness."

Fondling Smart Rats

Russell was not far off. Fode and I told a class of 12 students that one could produce a strain of intelligent rats by inbreeding them to increase their ability to run mazes quickly. To demonstrate, we gave each student five rats, which had to learn to run to the darker of two arms of a T-maze. We told half of our student-experimenters that they had the "maze-bright," intelligent rats; we told the rest that they had the stupid rats. Naturally, there was no real difference among any of the animals.

But they certainly differed in their performance. The rats believed to be bright improved daily in running the maze—they ran faster and more accurately—while the supposedly dull animals did poorly. The "dumb" rats refused to budge from the starting point 29 percent of the time, while the "smart" rats were recalcitrant only 11 percent of the time.

Then we asked our students to rate the rats and to describe their own attitudes toward them. Those who believed they were working with intelligent animals *liked* them better and found them more pleasant. Such students said they felt more relaxed with the animals; they treated them more gently and were more enthusiastic about the experiment than students who thought they had dull rats to work with. Curiously, the students with "bright" rats said that they handled them more but talked to them less. One wonders what students with "dull" rats were saying to those poor creatures.

If rats act smarter because their experimenters think they are smarter, we reasoned, perhaps the same phenomenon was at work in the classroom. So in the mid-1960s Lenore Jacobson and I launched what was to become a most controversial study.

Intellectual Bloomers

We selected an elementary school in a lower-class neighborhood and gave all the children a nonverbal IQ test at the beginning of the school year. We disguised the test as one that would predict "intellectual blooming." There were 18 classrooms in the school, three at each of the six grade levels. The three rooms for each grade consisted of children with above-average ability, average ability, and below-average ability.

After the test, we randomly chose 20 percent of the children in each room, and labeled them "intellectual bloomers." We then gave each teacher the names of these children, who, we explained, could be expected to show remarkable gains during the coming year on the basis of their test scores. In fact, the difference between these experimental children and the control group was solely in the teacher's mind.

Our IQ measure required no speaking, reading, or writing. One part of it, a picture vocabulary, did require a greater comprehension of English, so we call it the verbal subtest. The second part required less ability to understand language but more ability to reason abstractly, so we call it the reasoning subtest.

We retested all the children eight months later. For the school as a whole, we found that the experimental children, those whose teachers had been led to expect "blooming," showed an excess in overall IQ gain of four points over the IQ gain of the control children. Their excess in gain was smaller in verbal ability, two points only, but substantially greater in reasoning, where they gained seven points more than the controls. Moreover, it made no difference whether the child was in a high-ability or low-ability classroom. The teachers' expectations benefited children at all levels. The supposed bloomers blossomed, at least modestly.

This experiment, and the book we wrote based on it, met with vigorous criticism. Professor Arthur Jensen of UC, Berkeley, for example, offered three basic arguments.

First, said Jensen we should have compared classrooms rather than individual children, and this would have produced only negligible IQ changes. But Jensen ignored the fact that we had done that analysis, and that it led to even larger effects than the per-child comparisons.

Second, Jensen objected to the fact that we used the same IQ test twice. The children were familiar with the test when they took it again, he said, so their scores might have improved for that reason. However, Jensen must then explain why the experimental children showed more of these "practice effects" than the control children, who also took the test twice.

Finally, Jensen did not think that the teachers themselves should have given the tests. However, we had already accounted for this problem by having people who knew nothing of the experiment retest the children. The effects of the teachers' expectations actually increased.

R. L. Thorndike added another objection, namely that our IQ test was an unreliable measure, especially for the youngest children, and that any inference based on such a test would be invalid. I do not think that our test was as worthless as Thorndike implies, but even if it was seriously unreliable we are still left with the basic question. Why did the experimental children improve significantly? An unreliable measure would make it *harder* to find differences between the two groups, not easier.

The most ambitious critique of our Pygmalion in the classroom work was a book by Janet Elashoff and Richard Snow, who completely reanalyzed our original data. They could not disprove the fact that the experimental children did gain more IQ points than control children, even though they transformed our original IQ measure into eight different forms, some of which were biased statistically to minimize any effects of teachers' expectations.

The debate continued, and so did the research. Others sought to discover the Pygmalion effect, and not everyone was successful, which contributed to the controversy. By now 242 studies have been done, with all sorts of subjects and situations. Of these, 84 found that prophecies, i.e., the experimenters' or teachers' expectations, made a significant difference.

But we must not reject the theory because "only" 84 studies support it; on the contrary. According to the rules of statistical significance, we could expect five percent of those

242 studies (about 12) to have come out as predicted just by chance. The fact that we have 84, seven times more than chance would dictate, means that the Pygmalion effect does exist in certain circumstances. Moreover, it is not limited to young children and rats; adolescents and adults are affected too.

And the Pygmalion effect is as likely to occur in the real world as in the experimenter's tower. Of the 242 studies that have been done to date, 57 took place outside the laboratory—in a classroom, a factory, an office, and the like. The proportion of significant results is about the same for experiments conducted in the field as in the laboratory, some 37 percent for the field and 34 percent for the laboratory.

For example, Randy Burnham and Donald Hartsough found Pygmalion in the swimming pool. Their subjects were boys and girls, ages seven to 14, who were learning to swim at a summer camp. Half of the instructors were led to think that they were dealing with a "high-potential" group, and their students became better swimmers, by the end of their two-week camping period, than the regular group. And another team of researchers found that it took only two weeks for teen-age girls, who were institutionalized for various offenses, to show a marked improvement in their classroom behavior when they had been labeled "potential bloomers."

Even the United States Air Force Academy Preparatory School succumbed. W.R. Schrank randomly assigned 100 enlisted airmen to one of five math classes, and he told the teachers that each class contained students selected for different levels of ability. The boys in the supposed high-ability classes improved their math scores substantially.

J. Michael Palardy tested the popular assumption that boys have a tougher time learning to read than girls. First- grade teachers are well aware of this folk belief, and thus have clear expectations when they give reading lessons. Palardy surveyed 63 teachers and found five who believed that boys could learn to read as well as girls in the first grade. He matched these five on a number of factors—background, teaching methods, etc.—with five who believed in the stereotype. Indeed, teachers who expected to discover sex differences in reading ability found them. But the boys did just as well as the girls when their teachers thought they would. (As a footnote to this study, the "well-known" sex difference in learning to read also tends to disappear when the children learn from teaching machines rather than from teachers.)

Albert King moved the Pygmalion paradigm into the work world with an ingenious set of five experiments. King was interested in the effects of supervisor expectations on the job performance of disadvantaged workers (unemployed or underemployed, mostly black and members of other minorities). In three of his studies the workers were women in training to become nurses' aides, presser-machine operators, or assemblers of electronic equipment. In the other two studies, the workers were men who were learning to become auto mechanics or welders.

In each experiment, King randomly picked the names of some of the trainees, and told the supervisors that these workers showed a special potential for their particular job. King collected several measures of the workers' performances: objective tests, peer ratings, absences and so on. (King ignored the supervisors' ratings of trainees, since these might reflect only their perception and not actual changes in their performance.) The Pygmalion effect worked in four of the five experiments—for every group of trainees but the nurses' aides. Trainees whose supervisors had expected high job performance of them did much better than the control groups. However, the effect was especially marked among male workers, the welders and mechanics, and less so among female workers, the pressers and assemblers. Perhaps the supervisors found it harder to accept the idea that women could have "special potential" for their work.

TABLE 1

Average Performance Ranks (Lower Ranks Indicate Superior Performance):

study	experimental group	control group
1 welders	9.9	3.6
2 mechanics	10.7	4.3
3 pressers	9.2	5.3
4 assemblers	11.3	7.8
5 nurses' aides	9.2	8.3

All of this research supported our feeling that self-fulfilling prophecy is a real phenomenon, that it occurs both in and out of the classroom and the laboratory. The next step was to figure out what subtle forces are going on in the exchange between teacher and learner. What makes average kids increase their IQ, neophytes swim better, and trainees learn faster? How does A *communicate* his or her expectations to B, especially when both A and B probably are unaware of the process?

Explaining the Pygmalion Effect

The current evidence leads me to propose a four-factor "theory" of the influences that produce the Pygmalion effect. People who have been led to expect good things from their students, children, clients, or what-have-you appear to:

—create a warmer social-emotional mood around their "special" students (*climate*);

—give more feedback to these students about their performance (*feedback*);

—teach more material and more difficult material to their special students (*input*); and

—give their special students more opportunities to respond and question (*output*).

There is nothing magical or definitive about the choice of these four, and in fact, none of them is independent of the others. My criterion for including each as a factor is that there be at least five studies that support it and that no more than 20 percent of the studies bearing on each factor contradict it.

The Climate Factor

"Climate" apparently has to do with warmth, attention, and emotional support. Fourteen studies have investigated this factor, 12 of which came out as predicted. Not all of them dealt with the teacher-student relationship; some took place in industrial and clinical contexts as well.

For example, Geri Alpert told a group of psychiatrists that some of their patients had been specially selected for them on the basis of "therapeutic compatibility." She gave them no expectations about the rest of their patients. Later Alpert asked the patients to describe their therapists and their sessions together. From a patient's-eye view, psychiatrists behave more warmly toward people with whom they expect to be compatible and who are likely to get well.

Alan Chaikin, Edward Sigler, and Valerian Derlega asked male and female college undergraduates to teach a short unit on home and family safety to a 12-year-old boy. One third of the "teachers" thought that the boy had an IQ of 130 and did very well in school; one third thought that the child had an IQ of 85 and did poorly in school; and the last third had no information about the boy's IQ. Then the experimenters videotaped the exchange between teachers and student to see what nonverbal cues were going on.

Teachers who thought they were dealing with a bright student were more likely to smile at the boy, nod their heads approvingly, lean toward the boy, and look him in the eye for longer periods. A variety of analogous studies have found that "special-potential" subjects report their teachers or counselors as being more positive, accepting, perceptive, friendly, fond of them and supportive.

The Feedback Factor

The difference between this factor and the previous one (for both involve warmth and attention) is that feedback depends on a response from the student. A teacher can be generally warm, but still react critically or indifferently to a child's answers or comments. Feedback refers specifically to how much active teaching occurs: often the teacher rewards a desired response, corrects a wrong answer, asks for the student's further thoughts, and so on. Ten studies explored this factor, of which eight supported it.

Jere Brophy and Tom Good asked first-grade teachers to name their high and low achievers. The researchers then watched the teachers work with the children. The teachers ignored only three percent of the high achievers' answers but they ignored 15 percent of the low achievers' answers. The good students, then, get more feedback, whether their responses are right or wrong.

Teachers give more feedback to apt undergraduates as well as to apt first-graders. John Lanzetta and T.E. Hannah offered college students the chance to play teacher, and gave them the choice of five kinds of feedback for use in teaching a concept task: a strong electric shock, a mild shock, a neutral light, a small amount of money, and a larger amount of money. The "learner," who was a confederate of the experimenters, gave 36 correct and 84 incorrect answers in all cases.

When the student teachers thought the learner had a "high potential," they rewarded him with a larger sum of money when he was right, and shocked him more severely when he was wrong. When they thought that the learner had a "low learning potential," however, they gave him the lesser reward or punishment. In other words teachers send clearer, stronger evaluations to students for whom they have greater expectations.

But another experiment found that children believed to be bright got more praise, but not more criticism; criticism was reserved for children believed to be dull. Yet a third study found that supposedly "gifted" children get more praise from their teachers, but found no difference between 11 gifted" and "regular" children in the criticism they got. The matter is complicated. Perhaps criticism for a wrong answer needs to be accompanied by enough praise and support on other occasions; otherwise the student may see the teacher as overly critical and cold. We can say with modest certainty that praise is a factor in achieving the Pygmalion effect, but the role of criticism is less clear.

The Input Factor

There are only five studies that directly deal with this factor, but all five find that teachers literally teach more to children of whom they expect more.

The most dramatic case in point is W. Victor Beez's work with 60 preschoolers and 60 teachers in a Headstart program. Beez told half of the teachers that they could expect poor performance from their supposedly "below-average" children; the rest expected exceptional performance from their "bright" children. Observers, who had not been told what the teachers' expectations were, noted the exchanges between teacher and child. The teachers worked much harder when they believed they had a bright child. In a unit on word learning for example, 87 percent of the teachers of "bright" children taught eight or more words; but only 13 percent of the teachers of the "dull" children tried to teach them that many. Not surprisingly, 77 percent of the "bright" children learned five or more words, but only 13 percent of the "dull" children learned that many.

Such results tell us that a teacher's expectations about a student's performance are not simply transmitted in subtle voice nuances and a casual facial expression. The expectations may be translated into explicit, overt alterations in teaching style and substance.

Number of words taught:	Teachers' expectation:	
	dull children	bright children
11 or more	0	14
9 or 10	1	10
7 or 8	7	3
5 or 6	15	1
4 or less	7	2
	30	30

The Output Factor

Eleven studies out of 12 support this factor, indicating that teachers encourage greater responsiveness from students of whom they expect more. They call on such students more often, ask them harder questions, give them more time to answer, and prompt them toward the correct answer. Output is therefore closely related to feedback.

Mary Budd Rowe gives us a good example. She was interested in how long teachers wait for an answer to their question before going on to the next child. She found that many experienced teachers wait only one *second* before they ask the question again, often of someone else. However, Rowe found that teachers wait longer for the students whom they believe to be bright. When Rowe pointed this out to the teachers involved, they reacted with surprise and insight. "I guess we don't expect an answer [of the poor students]," said one, "so we go on to someone else." When these same teachers then deliberately increased their waiting time for their "slower" students, they got increased responsiveness.

Jeffrey Hersh's work illustrates another facet of the output factor. He asked graduate students to administer the Stanford-Binet IQ Test to children in a Headstart program. Examiners who had been told the children had high intellectual ability immediately began with more difficult questions. They demanded more of the children, and got more.

An Unexpected Galatea

We knew from our original Pygmalion experiment in the classroom that favorable expectations could have a beneficial effect. At the end of the year the teachers had all sorts of good things to say about the "intellectual bloomers": they had a better chance of being successful in the future, said the teachers; they were more appealing, better adjusted, more affectionate and autonomous. So the teachers perceived them, in any case.

We thought that perhaps it was because the experimental children gained more in IQ that the teachers rated their behavior and aptitudes more highly. So we looked at the control-group children who had also gained in IQ that year, to see whether the teachers liked them as much as the bloomers. Such was not the case. To our astonishment, the more the control students increased in IQ, the *less* well adjusted, interesting and affectionate the teachers thought them.

It seems, then, that when a child who is not expected to do well does so, his teacher looks upon his behavior and personality as undesirable. This was especially true, we discovered, for children in low-ability classrooms. Teachers may have a difficult time thinking that a child who has a low-ability label can show an intellectual spurt. They may interpret this change as "maladjustment" or "troublemaking." Perhaps the child doesn't know his place. Several subsequent experiments confirmed this finding, so the hazards of unpredicted success are likely to be real rather than a freak of one study. Alfred Shore, for example, asked teachers to predict their students' intellectual achievement and to describe their students' classroom behavior. A month later, Shore gave the teachers the students' real IQ scores and asked for a reappraisal. Again, teachers downgraded those students in personality and adjustment who had done "too well"—i.e., contrary to their expectations.

Eleanor Leacock studied four schools in four neighborhoods, two poor and two middle-income. Within each income level one school was essentially all black and the other essentially white. Leacock interviewed the fifth-grade teachers about their feelings for the children, and scored their comments for positive, neutral, or negative feelings and attitudes.

Double Handicap

Leacock found that the teachers were much less favorable to the lower-class children than they were to the middle- class children; 40 percent of their comments about the poorer children were negative, compared to 20 percent of their comments about the middle-class children. And the teachers were even more likely to talk negatively about black children than white children, 43 percent to 17 percent.

Leacock then went on to relate the children's IQ scores to the teachers' feelings toward them. IQ scores of the middle-income children, both black and white, were clearly related to the positive attitudes of their teachers. This relationship did *not* hold for the low-income children; in fact, it was reversed. That is, lower-income children who had *higher* IQs tended to have teachers who viewed them *negatively* and this was especially true for lower income children who were black. The children who surpassed their teachers' expectations got resentment and complaints for their pains.

Thus children who are both black and lower-income have a double handicap. And this result cannot be attributed to white teachers' bias; both of the teachers of the black children were themselves black. The prejudice of stunted expectations knows no race barrier.

We still do not know exactly how the Pygmalion effect works. But we know that often it does work, and that it has powers that can hinder as well as help the development of others. Field and experimental studies are beginning to isolate the factors that will give some insight into the process. Such awareness may help some to create their Galateas, but it will also give the Galateas a chance to fight back.

The Trouble with Hypnosis

Keith Harary

Imagine yourself lying on an operating table in a humid hospital tent near a battle front during the Vietnam War. Writhing in agony, you plead with the medics to give you something to relieve the pain in your leg. But the supply lines were interrupted hours ago and there is no more anesthetic. What's more, the leg can't be saved. If they don't operate immediately, you hear someone saying in the background, you're going to bleed to death.

The nurse seems unexpectedly centered as she sits beside you, leans over, and looks into your eyes. "It's going to be all right," she says, and you can't help noticing the smell of the soap she uses and the tiny lines around the corners of her mouth. "I know you're a little nervous," she slowly continues, "but you're in excellent hands. You're just going to feel a little pressure while we fix you up." She is so reassuring that you find yourself wanting to believe her. You also find yourself going along with the suggestion that you're only a little nervous, and even feeling relieved to know you're in excellent hands.

As the surgeon attends to your leg, the nurse continues talking to you as though nothing unusual is happening. "You just feel a little more pressure," she says calmingly, and you find yourself imagining that none of the pain you've been experiencing all along is really all that bad. The operation is completed in what seems like no time at all.

It never occurs to you that you are under the influence of hypnosis, but that is what they tell you when you later ask what happened. You are thankful for the relief you experienced while the surgeon sawed off your leg. You are testimony to the popular belief that hypnosis is a special state of consciousness in which many mental feats become possible—such as enduring surgery sans anesthesia.

Ever since Franz Anton Mesmer proposed his theory of animal magnetism more than 200 years ago, hypnosis has fought an uphill battle for scientific credibility. The establishment relegated it to the domain of stage performers and quacks for most of that time. But in the past few decades the phenomenon has enjoyed an increasing amount of scientific interest, as well as widespread clinical application for an array of medical and psychological purposes, from removing warts to retrieving memories long buried in the unconscious.

This sudden ascent to respectability began a little more than 30 years ago, when psychologist Ernest Hilgard, Ph.D., a former president of the American Psychological Association, set up the Laboratory of Hypnosis Research at Stanford University. At about the same time, psychiatrist Martin Orne, M.D., of Harvard and psychologist T. X. Barber, Ph.D., of the Medfield Foundation, pioneered hypnosis research at their respective organizations. Since then, dozens of research programs on hypnosis have sprung to life in universities and medical schools in the United States, Canada, Europe, and Australia.

The burgeoning hypnosis field also supports two independent professional organizations and two major journals devoted exclusively to the topic. The Society for Clinical and

Experimental Hypnosis, which publishes the *International Journal of Clinical and Experimental Hypnosis,* currently enrolls over 1,000 members. The American Society of Clinical Hypnosis, publisher of the *American Journal of Clinical Hypnosis,* boasts almost 4,000 members. Several smaller organizations flourishing in a number of foreign countries publish their own journals on the subject.

In clinical practice here and elsewhere, hypnosis has simply taken off. Inspired by the late psychotherapist Milton Erickson, M.D. (considered by many to be the father of modern medical hypnosis), thousands of self-proclaimed "Ericksonian" disciples regularly feature hypnosis therapy in their clinical repertoire. So do a large number of "classical" psychotherapists who don't remotely consider themselves Ericksonians. Then there are the thousands of practitioners, clinically unlicensed, who advertise their services as hypnotists.

Excitement is building over reports citing the effectiveness of the therapy for a growing number of medical and psychological applications. Here's a sampling:

- Hypnosis has been used in place of anesthesia to numb the pain of childbirth and major surgical procedures such as amputation, abdominal surgery, and the removal of testicular tumors, and such painful procedures as dental surgery and hemorrhoidectomies. The ability to tolerate such pain while under the influence of hypnosis is laid to an altered state that allows patients to dissociate from and become consciously unaware of it.
- Hypnosis is used in an effort to dislodge deeply buried memories relating to past events. Therapists employ "hypnotic regression"—mentally taking a subject back in time to reexperience the past. The thinking is that hypnosis affords direct access to unconscious memories without resistance or distortion, making it an exceptionally reliable tool for exploring long-forgotten details of early childhood and a powerful investigate tool for drawing out critical details of crimes.
- Numerous reports attest the effectiveness of hypnosis in the treatment of warts. In those who have been hypnotized, warts later disappeared entirely on their own, without medicine or surgery. Since warts are virally induced, this striking phenomenon has fueled belief that hypnosis somehow mobilizes immune response.
- Other reports allege the effectiveness of hypnosis for quitting smoking without withdrawal symptoms. This is done by allowing direct access to the unconscious, thereby overcoming any unconscious resistance to alleviating addiction.
- Hypnosis allegedly facilitates successful weight loss without the usual cravings of dieting by directly accessing and influencing the unconscious mind.
- Hypnosis is reported to alleviate longstanding phobias such as the fear of flying, overcoming the binge/purge cycle of bulimia, and resolving deep inner conflicts stemming from childhood sexual abuse, posttraumatic stress, and other serious psychological syndromes.

But what does it really mean to be under the influence of hypnosis? Many of those working most closely with it are surprisingly uncertain about exactly what hypnosis is. The absence of a standard definition is far more than a semantic quibble. It appears to signify a fatal flaw in the way we think about hypnosis—and in the way we think about ourselves. Decades of searching with sophisticated technology have not yet yielded a single shred of evidence that hypnosis is an altered state of consciousness. Indeed, it may not be a mysterious mental state at all. It may turn out to be a powerful confluence of much more accessible social and psychological processes rather than a single extraordinary phenomenon. In all likelihood, hypnosis is a metaphor for selling our own intrinsic mental capabilities short. Hypnosis may be the ultimate psychic sales spiel—a way for us to disown powers we already have and buy them back under a fancy label.

What Is Hypnotic Induction?

The ambiguity surrounding what it means to be under the influence of hypnosis starts right at the beginning, with no standard for hypnotic induction. Induction is supposed to be a ritualized set of procedures for bringing about the special hypnotic state. But it's not like a drug that's given in measured doses. There's no definition for what constitutes a dose of hypnotic induction. And here's the rub: In the absence of a standard, it is not possible to evaluate the effects of the induction process or even to state conclusively when a person is, or is not, undergoing hypnosis.

In the stereotypical image of hypnotic induction, there's an interaction in which one person temporarily assumes authority over another. The hypnotists gives the subject suggestions to relax and focus, to become compliant, to imagine situations such as an arm becoming heavy or a fly buzzing around the room, and then to follow suggestions meant to be therapeutic, such as letting go of pain and imagining another sensation replacing it.

In reality, however, almost any exchange imaginable has been defined as hypnotic induction, even an ordinary conversation. For some therapists induction is little more than another word for a typical psychotherapy session. For others the term implies helping a patient achieve an intensely focused and dissociated state of consciousness or the skillful use of suggestions such as, "You begin to notice the pain fading into the distance," or "You will be able to let go of the habit easily." And so-called self-hypnosis doesn't require two people.

A Trance Perchance?

Even if hypnotic induction withers in the light of scrutiny, surely there's some resulting state of mind all hypnosis subjects share regardless of the means used to achieve it? The Holy Grail of hypnosis research is a measurable trance state in which people somehow gain direct access to the deeper recesses of the unconscious, transcend pain, and stimulate their immune response. Such a state would reasonably be expected to show up as a signature pattern of brain waves or physiological correlates akin to the rapid eye movements of dream sleep.

Unfortunately, attempts to find brainwave patterns that distinguish hypnosis from ordinary waking consciousness have not panned out. The rare physiological sign of hypnosis spotted in the laboratory has failed to prove the existence of a hypnotic state. When Stanford psychiatrist David Spiegel, M.D., told hypnotized subjects to focus their attention elsewhere while receiving mild electric shocks, they showed a decreased physiological response to pain. But the same effect could be elicited from subjects not undergoing hypnotic induction—just by getting them to focus their attention elsewhere. "Every time we thought there was a physiological indicator it hasn't held up," concedes Thurman Mott, M.D., editor of the *American Journal of Clinical Hypnosis*.

The failure to sniff out objective evidence of a trance state has its effect. "It's nonsensical to argue that hypnosis involves some sort of special state when we can't find it no matter how long we look," says Robert Baker, Ph.D., author of *They Call It Hypnosis* and professor emeritus at the University of Kentucky. "Eventually you stop looking. It's like looking for ether." Baker has been practicing hypnosis for more than 20 years and has published original research in the field. "After doing all this work," he says, "it has become obvious to me, as it has to many people, that there is no such thing as an altered state of consciousness known as hypnosis."

It is entirely possible that hypnosis begets a state of mind that eludes current means of measurement. So, like the spotting tracks of Bigfoot, hypnosis proponents have tried to show that such a state exists by pointing to its alleged effects. Some seemingly miraculous bit of human behavior—say, calmly enduring a root canal without anesthesia—is seen as a sign that hypnosis was there.

But that doesn't hold up either. Even without hypnosis or any other known anesthetic, people sometimes simply do not respond to pain.

Terms of Endearment

Lacking objective criteria for defining the experience, some proponents of hypnosis invoke terms that are more poetic than scientific. For clinical psychologist Jeffrey K. Zeig, Ph.D., keeper of the Ericksonian flame as founder and director of the Milton Erickson Foundation in Phoenix, hypnosis is a lot like love: "Falling in love is an experience we all know that we have, but how do you define it objectively?" Being under the spell of hypnosis is more of a subjective state of mind than an objectively measurable altered state of consciousness, he contends.

So do many other clinicians. The upshot is there's no consistent and agreed-on set of procedures among practitioners. Any therapeutic incident can be considered hypnotherapy—as long as a therapist says it is. According to Nicholas Spanos, Ph.D., a leading Canadian hypnosis researcher and coeditor of the professional tome *Hypnosis: The Cognitive Behavioral Perspective,* therapists have designated as "hypnotherapy" such diverse procedures as psychoanalytic age regression, direct suggestion for symptom removal, systematic desensitization, and other behavioral therapies. The only thing really tying these together is the name "hypnosis," with its attendant aroma of altered states and unusual psychological mechanism—"mythology" in the words of Spanos.

Then there are those who insist that hypnosis is a psychotherapeutic method favored by the late Erickson himself: the strategy of immediately directing a patient toward solving a problem rather than stopping to analyze its causes. But this so-called strategic approach is also practiced by those who do not consider it hypnosis and is widely used by family therapists and crisis-intervention centers all over the country.

In the laboratory the guiding concept behind much research is the notion that hypnosis is not only a special state of consciousness but one that some people are better than others at entering.

Roughly 15 percent of the population is held to be highly hypnotizable. About 25 percent are though to be not hypnotizable at all. Researchers have expended a great deal of effort on attempts to identify highly hypnotizable people—they'd be proof positive of the existence of a special hypnotic state. Enter the hypnotic susceptibility scale. One of the most widely used scales was cocreated in 1959 by Stanford's Hilgard.

In the Stanford Hypnotic Susceptibility Scales, subjects who undergo hypnotic induction are given 12 suggestions—imagine a mosquito buzzing around, imagine weight in one hand—while the hypnotist watches for evidence of responsiveness such as shifting position to avoid the insect. On a scale of zero (not hypnotizable) to 12 (highly so), subjects are scored by the degree to which they appear to heed the 12 suggestions.

Recently 50 Stanford alumni were retested and received almost the identical susceptibility scores they got 25 years ago. That, to Hilgard, is evidence that hypnotizability is a stable—that is, innate—psychological trait. "That gives you a feeling you're measuring something," he says, and that those who rate high must be entering a special state of mind in order to perform.

But measuring external responses doesn't get at internal states, points out Charles Tart, Ph.D., the famed altered-states researcher at the University of California at Davis and the author of *States of Consciousness*. Some people just go along with the experiment and some really feel something unusual. "Those different types of involvement may or may not involve an altered state," says Tart.

A Talent for Compliance

Pursuing hypnosis as a single state of mind may make no more sense than viewing ordinary waking consciousness as a unified state. "A whole range of things commonly go under the name of hypnosis," says Tart. "People are lumping together a lot of different states, inner experience, and external phenomena. It's only in our ignorance that we treat everyone who undergoes hypnotic induction as if they're all having the same experience."

Hypnotic-susceptibility scores may reflect little more than a person's expectations and attitudes toward hypnosis and his or her willingness to comply with the test situation. Those who rate as high hypnotizables may not be faking outright, but they may be more inclined to suspend their disbelief and do what is asked of them—with or without entering a special state of consciousness.

Common laboratory attempts to validate distinctions between high and low hypnotizables may be similarly flawed, as they, too, rely on self-reports. In one such test, patients plunge a hand into icy water following hypnotic induction. Presumably only those very susceptible to hypnosis will report no pain. But critics see it differently.

If high hypnotizables are just those most willing to comply with the experimenter's wishes, then they are most likely to report having achieved the desired effect. "What they're really doing is selecting people who will be most responsive to manipulation," says Kentucky's Baker.

When the patients know whether they are hypnosis or nonhypnosis test subjects, the situation is even less like a scientific experiment than an exercise in placebo psychology. What's more, most clinical reports claiming success with hypnosis to cure medical and psychological ills are anecdotal—they lack control groups for comparing the effectiveness of treatments.

Calling the evidence anecdotal rather than experimental does not dismiss what happens when someone undergoes hypnotic induction and overcomes a longstanding fear of flying or a chronic case of warts. It just doesn't explain it. Nor does it easily account for such phenomena as calmly allowing a limb to be amputated without anesthesia.

A Dance, not a Trance

It may be possible to explain the effects attributed to hypnosis without invoking the existence of a unique altered state of consciousness. Whether or not hypnosis creates a single state of mind, it clearly involves a complex combination of other social and psychological factors. Chief among them are role-playing, imagination, motivation, and powerful responses to suggestion. In the emerging view of many researchers, understanding how these factors play together in the context of a social setting may provide the real key to understanding hypnosis.

No matter how hypnotherapy is defined or applied by its practitioners, the hypnotic interaction always involves a social process in which an individual takes on the role of an hypnotic subject. Simply enacting the role of a hypnotized subject begins with a certain element of role-playing and may even be a learnable ability.

But rather than being overpowered by the hypnotist, the hypnotic subject is a deliberately willing participant in the social process—whether or not he's aware he's being hypnotized. Assuming the role of hypnotic subject means striking a peculiar kind of bargain: temporarily agreeing to allow the hypnotist to assume a position of authority and to engage in a process of communication intensely focusing on a particular goal or problem.

Once a person agrees to enact the role of hypnotic subject, the bandwagon is rolling. "Some people get so deeply involved in role-playing that it feels as though they no longer have choice in the matter," observes Tart. Taking on the role hypnotic subject involves a kind of willing suspension of disbelief in one's own limitations.

Bringing out the Power

T. X. Barber, a hypnosis elder statesman, says he's known "from the very beginning" that people can bring out their own inner capabilities by direct requests to think, feel, and experience in a suggested way, without any need for hypnotic induction. "In my first study for my Ph.D., over 35 years ago," says the author of *Hypnosis: A Scientific Approach,* "the control-group subjects were simply told very seriously to feel one extended arm becoming very heavy, that they were becoming exceedingly thirsty, that they couldn't unclasp their hands, and so forth. They responded in this amazing way that showed people have unexercised capabilities to experience things that are typically associated with the word 'hypnosis.'"

Further experiments led Barber to conclude that "the secret of hypnosis has several components. One is some people are superb subjects who are able to fantasize in a hallucinatory way and provide the drama and excitement. Another is that the majority of the rest can respond to suggestions far more than hypnotists have realized if the suggestions are given firmly—and without the complexities of calling it hypnosis or administering a hypnotic-induction procedure."

"Hypnosis is the art of securing a patient's attention and then effectively communicating ideas that boost motivation and change perceptions" of what's going on, adds psychologist D. Corydon Hammond, author of the group's 600-plus-page bible, *Handbook of Hypnotic Suggestions and Metaphors.*

Metaphor is the basic language of hypnosis. So is suggestion. The hypnotist doesn't simply say to a patient who is afraid of flying, "You are no longer afraid of flying." Instead, the hypnotist might suggest that the patient imagine that riding in an airplane is like riding in a car. To a patient about to undergo a painful procedure the hypnotists does not say, "This won't hurt a bit." Instead, the hypnotist might suggest that the patient experience the pain as a feeling of warmth or pressure.

Because therapists do not know which ideas will be best received by any patient, they cast out an assortment of suggestions and metaphors. A person afraid of public speaking might be told, for example, to focus on all of the anxiety the situation engenders before getting up to speak and then let go of it, and to imagine the audience as a group of close personal friends.

The most effective hypnotherapists are therefore not those who exude some supernatural power of magnetism but those who are skilled at communicating with their patients in the language of metaphor and suggestion. Here is where the talent of Erickson is said to have revealed itself. His success as a hypnotherapist may have had more to do with language than with any supposed state of mind.

Power to the People

For every reportedly successful application of hypnosis, other possibilities than an altered state of mind readily suggest themselves. Critics offer these alternative explanations so we can know that the powers have really been ours all along.

- Those who seek out hypnotherapy to overthrow anxieties, phobias, or habits like smoking or overeating are, by definition, already highly motivated to change their behavior. They also have a certain amount of faith in the hypnotic process, by taking on the role of hypnotic subject and agreeing to listen to positive suggestions, they are demonstrating their commitment to overcoming personal problems. In itself, evidence suggests, this commitment may alter a person's innermost frame of reference and impact the subtle ecology of the unconscious, with no boost needed from hypnosis.

- Phobias and bulimia may be more severe disturbances, but that doesn't make them any less subjective in nature. Recent studies at Stanford and elsewhere show that people with such disorders also tend to score high on hypnotic susceptibility scales and to respond favorably to hypnotic intervention. The connection?

What is a phobia if not "a kind of environmentally suggested anxiety," says psychologist Joseph Barber, Ph.D., president-elect of the Society for Clinical and Experimental Hypnosis. "The very capacity that lends itself to developing the problem is the same that lends itself to developing that problem is the same that lends itself to solving it." Call it suggestibility. Phobias may be especially responsive to suggestions, whether or not the suggestions are wrapped in hypnosis.

- Phobias are one things; surgery is another. The truth is, though, that beyond the initial skin incision, much internal tissue is not pain-sensitive. In anecdotal reports of surgery conducted under hypnosis, it is not clear that those who are reportedly painfree are anything more than stoic or turning their attention away from it without entering a unique hypnotic state.
- As with surgery, warts respond to suggestions alone. In one set of studies, patients simply given the suggestion their warts would disappear did as well six weeks later as patients given the same suggestion under hypnosis, and both did better than a control group given no suggestion. "Now that's pretty amazing," says Canada's Spanos. "The hypnosis doesn't do anything. But what's amazing is that some psychological procedure is influencing a virally induced physiological process."
- And lastly, some claims for hypnosis are not what they seem. "You can find reputable clinicians who will tell you that hypnosis can be used or recover memories of past events in a totally reliable way," says Joseph Barber. "But there's very good evidence that's not the case. Some will tell you that age regression in hypnosis really regresses people back to some early life. That's also not true. Age regression is a metaphor. Nobody is really regressed to an early age. Even people who accurately remember things are not literally reliving that moment."

After examining the claims, the Council on Scientific Affairs of the American Medical Association recently found no evidence that hypnosis increases the accurate recollection of the past. In fact, it said, suggestions integral to the hypnotic process may even lead some people to fantasize freely and confuse suggested scenarios with authentic memory.

What, in the end, does it mean to be under hypnosis? Its influence resides more in a power transaction between hypnotist and subject than it does in some hypothetical paranormal state of consciousness. It's not that the claims made about hypnosis are wildly exaggerated. Many of the effects attributed to hypnosis really do occur, but packaging them under the label "hypnosis" conceals what is really going on. It doesn't even begin to suggest that they are our very own powers and there might be ways for us to get at them directly and entirely on our own.

Flights of Memory

Minouche Kandel and Eric Kandel

Jennifer H., a professional musician, was 23 when she sought help because she was having problems with sexual intimacy. While in therapy, she also began exploring the unexplained feelings of panic that had haunted her daily since early childhood. Gradually, she says, she traced her feelings of terror to their source, recalling memories she'd repressed since leaving home. She remembered her father first molesting her and then raping her from the time she was 4 until she moved out at 17. She recalled that he had throttled her, threatening to kill her if she told anyone. As these memories resurfaced, her panic attacks and other symptoms receded. But when she confronted her father, a mechanical engineer at a prominent northeastern university, he flatly denied abusing her.

Other family members remembered Jennifer's father grabbing her breasts. Jennifer herself had a memory—never forgotten—of his staring at her chest and making crude sexual remarks. Concerned that her father would abuse other children unless he acknowledged his problem, Jennifer turned to the courts, hoping a lawsuit might prod her father into treatment. The statute of limitations on filing criminal charges had expired, but in 1988 Jennifer brought a personal-injury suit against her father. In addition to her own testimony, the court heard her mother—by then divorced—testify to having seen Jennifer's father lying on top of Jennifer's 14-year-old sister; she also said he'd fondled a baby-sitter in her early teens. Jennifer's father's sister recalled his making sexual passes at young girls. In 1993 a Massachusetts jury ordered him to pay Jennifer $500,000 in damages. (Civil juries can't order people into treatment as part of a judgment.) Although Jennifer's father admitted to fondling the baby-sitter, he maintains to this day that he never abused his daughter.

Jennifer H.'s case is one of several recent cases at the heart of a fierce controversy over recovered memories—memories of sexual abuse that come back after a period of repression. It was only in the 1980s that adults who'd been molested as children began to press their claims in court, publicly confronting their abusers in the hope of forcing them to acknowledge their guilt. But as the number of cases has risen, a growing number of parents, researchers, and academics have begun to speak out about the dangers of false accusations. They question in particular whether it's psychologically possible to repress traumatic childhood memories and then recover them. And they suggest that some people, egged on by therapists or self-help books, are fabricating memories of incidents that never occurred. So far, people on both sides of the debate have relied on psychological, rather than biological, insights into how memory works to make their case.

Can biology in fact shed any light on whether and how memories might be repressed and recovered? Perhaps—but to appreciate the debate fully, we first need to put it in its sociological context.

Until the early 1970s the sexual abuse of children was largely ignored; their stories were doubted and minimized, or they were blamed for encouraging their molestation. But research within the past 15 years or so suggests that child molesting is far from rare. Depending on who is asked and how abuse is defined, studies find that between 9 and 38 percent of women say they were abused as children, while figures for men range from 3 to 16 percent. (The 38 percent figure is from a random survey in 1978 of 930 women in San Francisco that defined abuse as any unwanted sexual activity with a relative before age 18; fondling, rape, or attempted rape by a nonrelative of children under 14; and attempted or completed forcible rape by a nonrelative of children ages 14 to 17—descriptions consistent with criminal law definitions of child molestation.)

Many adults who were abused as children clearly remember the experience all too well. But studies by Harvard psychiatrist Judith Herman and others also suggest that temporarily repressing such memories may not be uncommon. In 1987 Herman found that of 53 women attending incest survivor groups, almost two-thirds reported partial or complete memory lapses at some point after the abuse occurred. These findings have since been echoed in a larger survey of men as well as women led by psychiatrist John Briere at the University of Southern California School of Medicine. The earlier the abuse occurred, and the more violent or persistent it was, the more likely victims were to block the memory for long periods—a finding that gels with the clinical studies of Lenore Terr, a psychiatrist at the University of California at San Francisco, who finds that children exposed to repeated traumas are more likely to repress them than children suffering a one-time traumatic event.

One of the most systematic efforts to track memory repression was recently conducted by Linda Meyer Williams, a sociologist at the University of New Hampshire. Williams interviewed 129 women who were treated for sexual abuse when they were young girls in the mid-1970s. More than one-third had no memory of, or chose not to report, the molestation documented in their medical records. Since over half of these women discussed other incidents of sexual abuse, selective amnesia is a more likely explanation for their response (or lack of it) than any unwillingness to discuss sex.

Most clinical psychologists believe that children can learn to block memories as a survival mechanism: if physical escape from their tormentors is impossible, psychological escape may become crucial. When children can't avoid abuse and know it's going to be repeated, some cope by tuning out—mentally dissociating themselves from the abuse while it's occurring—or by repressing the memory afterward.

But repression, according to this school of thought, may cease to be helpful in adult life. Away from the traumatic environment, adults may find their memories resurfacing, either gradually in fragments, or suddenly in vivid flashbacks. As in Jennifer H.'s case, these memories may return during therapy, but that's by no means always the case. Frank Fitzpatrick was 38, married, and securely employed as an insurance adjuster in Rhode Island when he spontaneously recalled being molested by Father James Porter 26 years earlier. Since being confronted by Fitzpatrick in 1990, the Roman Catholic priest has admitted to molesting dozens of boys and girls. When the news became public, 68 men and women said that they too had been assaulted by Father Porter. At least half a dozen recalled the abuse only after news reports triggered the return of their childhood memories.

But people accused of abuse don't often confess—and their accusers' stories can't easily be corroborated. That leaves memory as the basis of many criminal and civil cases and makes determining the accuracy of people's memories of paramount importance. Because child molestation is so abhorrent, the mere taint of suspicion can ruin lives. Those accused risk losing their families, careers, and reputations; they face high legal costs and potentially prison if criminal charges are pressed. According to the False Memory Syndrome Foundation, over 9,500 U.S. families now claim that their adult children have tarred them with abuses that never occurred. (The foundation was established in 1992 by Pamela and Peter Freyd after their daughter Jennifer, now a professor of psychology at the University of Oregon, confronted them with accusations of abuse by her father—an allegation they have energetically disputed.) Many of these families blame zealous therapists and popular self-help books for encouraging their children's "false memories."

Some researchers—among them psychologists Elizabeth Loftus of the University of Washington and Richard Ofshe of the University of California at Berkeley—have joined them in casting doubt on the believability of repressed memories. Publicity about child abuse, they argue, has fostered a climate in which it's all too tempting to believe that hidden abuse is the cause of many people's ill-defined symptoms of distress.

Loftus and Ofshe think that, consciously or carelessly, some therapists are seeding ideas into vulnerable patients' minds. Fictitious memories, they point out, can be implanted with hypnosis—or even without. Loftus cites a study in which five people were told a false story by an older relative about how they'd gotten lost in a mall or apartment complex as children. When they were later asked to recall further details, they related elaborate memories of the fictitious incident. Is it as easy to implant something as traumatic as being repeatedly raped by someone in your family? There may indeed be powerful disincentives to admitting to false memories. Nevertheless it's still striking how very few cases come to light.

As further evidence of the malleability of memory, Loftus and Ofshe cite the sensational case of Paul Ingram, a deputy sheriff in Washington State whose two daughters accused him of sexually abusing them as part of a Satanic cult. Ingram, a fundamentalist Christian, denied the charge. In jail, though, he was repeatedly questioned about the alleged incidents by the police and a minister, and was asked to visualize them by a psychologist—until he finally came up with lurid memories of the incidents. Ofshe was originally hired to interview Ingram by the prosecution, not the defense. To test Ingrain's suggestibility, Ofshe asked him about a scene—entirely invented—in which Ingram forced his son and daughter to have sex. At first Ingram recalled nothing. Then Ofshe encouraged Ingram to imagine the scene and to "pray on the image," as Ingram had done before. Ingram subsequently developed detailed memories about the invented scenario, casting doubt on all of his previous confessions.

The Ingram case suggests some conditions that might facilitate the creation of entirely false memories: institutionalization or religious pressure. Of ten "recanters" whose cases have come to light, one woman acquired her memories of abuse in the isolation unit of a private hospital. Another was hospitalized in a program run by a Christian organization. Two other recanters have accused their therapists of using powerful psychotropic drugs, which, like hypnosis, can increase susceptibility to suggestion. That false memories occur and that some people are unjustly accused can't be denied, but Ofshe and other skeptics seize on such cases to cast doubt on *all* repressed memories. In a 1993 article in *Society,* Ofshe concludes: "Only pre-therapy accounts of a person's history can be treated as a normal memory with only the ordinary component of error." In his view memory repression is no more than "unsubstantiated speculation."

What, then, can biology contribute to this difficult debate? Over the past 20 years neuroscientists have made considerable strides in understanding the workings of memory. Can science also explain the delayed recall of sexual trauma? The *rigorous* answer is no. There is, as yet, no proper understanding of what might happen in human brains when memories are repressed, or when they are recovered. However, biology *can* provide insights into how a memory is stored, how that storage is regulated, and whether this regulation is compatible with repression and with a later return of memory.

What are the cellular mechanisms that explain how memories are created? As far as we know, storing our experiences as memories involves altering the strength of connections—known as synapses—between nerve cells in the brain. In its initial phase, which lasts minutes and is commonly called short-term memory, the change is temporary; it doesn't alter the structure of the connections. One or more hours later, though, anatomical changes begin to convert the memory into a longer-lasting form. This consolidation period involves the growth of new connections between nerve cells, or in some cases, the retraction of existing connections.

We also know that both short-term and long-term memories consist of at least two distinct forms: implicit and explicit. Implicit memory deals with our unconscious knowledge of motor or perceptual skills, or "knowing how." Explicit memory deals with our knowledge of facts, people, and places, or "knowing that." Quite different brain systems participate in storing these two forms. Explicit memory is handled by the inside segments of the temporal lobes (the brain lobes located behind our ears) and an underlying region called the hippocampus. Implicit memory, in contrast, involves distinct motor or sensory pathways in the brain, the autonomic nervous system (which regulates involuntary actions such as breathing and heart rate), and two additional brain structures called the amygdala and the cerebellum.

The first evidence that the temporal lobes and hippocampus play a role in explicit memory came in the 1950s from studies of epileptic patients. Brenda Milner, a neuropsychologist at the Montreal Neurological Institute, described the now famous case of H. M., a 27-year-old assembly-line worker who suffered from uncontrollable temporal lobe seizures. To alleviate his seizures, a surgeon removed parts of his temporal lobe, including the hippocampus. This operation left H. M. with a devastating memory deficit: he could no longer form *new* long-term memories. Yet H. M. still had his store of previously acquired long-term memories. He remembered well events before his surgery, such as his job and his childhood experiences. From the study of H. M. and patients like him, it became apparent that the hippocampus is only an interim depository for long-term memory. The hippocampus processes the newly learned information for a period of weeks to months, then transfers the information up to the cerebral cortex for more permanent storage. Thus, although H. M. still had a perfectly intact short-term memory, he couldn't translate what he learned into long-term memory. He could converse normally with Milner every time he saw her, but he could not remember her from visit to visit.

At first it was thought that this shattering deficit applied to all forms of new learning. But Milner and others soon made a wonderful discovery that revolutionized thinking about memory. Patients with temporal lobe lesions *can* accomplish certain implicit types of learning tasks involving perceptual and motor skills—and they retain the memory of these tasks perfectly well. H. M., for example, could learn new motor skills, such as mirror drawing (drawing while looking at his hand in a mirror, rather than looking at the paper). Usually there's cross talk between the explicit and implicit memory systems, so that when you learn or experience something new, both systems come into play. In fact, some types of explicit memory can be transformed into implicit memory by constant repetition. Learning to hit a backhand in tennis at first involves deliberate, conscious thought, but hitting good ground strokes becomes almost reflexive with practice. You don't consciously recall what to do—you just know what hitting a backhand *feels* like.

This cross talk is particularly evident in memories of emotionally charged experiences such as sexual abuse, in which the emotion associated with the event, and the conscious recollection of the event are stored in separate systems. Much of what we know about "emotional memory" comes from work done by neuroscientists Joseph LeDoux at New York University and Michael Davis at Yale. These studies indicate that the conscious component of highly charged memories is initially stored in the hippocampus. But the unconscious, implicit component is probably stored through the amygdala, which links the brain's sensory and motor areas to the autonomic nervous system. In memories of very stressful events, the role of implicit memory may be particularly powerful.

Of course, like all memories, highly charged memories need a period of consolidation to become long-term, But Michela Gallagher at the University of North Carolina and others who study this process have found out something very interesting: the *strength* of long-term memory can be affected by the context in which the remembered event occurs. Some factors enhance memory consolidation, storage, and recall; others inhibit them.

Working with rats, Gallagher has found that implicit memories of fearful experiences are strengthened when noradrenaline—a neurotransmitter associated with alertness and stress—is released in the amygdala. In contrast, the release of naturally occurring opium-like substances, called endogenous opiates, weakens memory storage. Other researchers have since found that explicit aspects of fear can be similarly modulated. This finding suggests a fascinating possibility. If an incident is so distressing that the brain makes opiates to dull the pain, the opiates may interfere with the memory-storing process. Intriguingly, Gallagher finds that using a drug called nalaxone to block endogenous opiates at the time of consolidation *does* enhance memory recall in rats. Furthermore, some studies show that a weakly stored memory can be enhanced by injecting a stimulant drug like adrenaline.

Such studies give us a biological context for considering how traumatic memories might be suppressed in humans, but what about their retrieval? We can only speculate about how this might work.

Let's suppose that a memory is stored weakly in the explicit system because endogenous opiates interfered with its consolidation—so weakly that the person has no conscious memory of the original wrenching event. That same event, though, might also be captured by the implicit system through a characteristic physical sensation or gesture. Perhaps later the implicit system may provide clues—such as physical sensations—that help stir the recall of weak explicit memories.

In fact, people who say they were abused as children often *do* describe their memories returning first as bodily sensations: Jennifer H. was doing exercises to relieve the tension in her neck when she recalled her father's choking her. Sometimes, says Lenore Terr, a victim shows behavioral clues that reflect the traumatic event. Terr cites the case of Eileen Franklin, who said she saw her father rape her best friend and crush the girl's head with a rock. The father was also abusing Franklin, who was 8 at the time. From age 8 to 14, Franklin pulled out the hair from a particular part of her scalp until it bled, re-creating the wound she'd seen inflicted on her friend. Franklin repressed the memory until she was in her late twenties, when its resurgence resulted in her father's conviction.

Indeed, some survivors of abuse describe their recovered memories as qualitatively different from other memories: they feel as if they're actually reexperiencing the event, with all its textures, smells, and physical sensations. This parallels the intensity of flashbacks experienced by combat veterans. As we have seen, Gallagher found that implicit memory can be strengthened by stimulating noradrenaline in the amygdala. And studies at Yale have suggested that noradrenaline released in response to stress contributes to the powerful flashbacks of Vietnam veterans. Perhaps memories that sexual abuse survivors are normally unable to access are retrieved when their noradrenaline system is activated.

All this suggests that the activation of endogenous opiates and noradrenaline in the amygdala and hippocampus could begin to provide a biological framework for examining how memories are repressed and later retrieved. It may soon be feasible to examine these ideas directly. Animal studies have already shown that the signature of long-term memory, both implicit and explicit, is anatomical change—the growth or retraction of connections between nerve cells in the brain. Improvements in brain imaging (such as magnetic resonance imaging) may eventually let us examine even small structures in the human brain in a safe, noninvasive way. We may then be able to see whether sexual abuse leads to physical changes in the amygdala that reflect a person's memories of the event—and whether these changes can be modulated by the noradrenergic and opioid systems.

Indeed, existing imaging techniques—PET scans—have already let us glimpse why false memories might seem entirely real to those who experience them. Stephen Kosslyn at Harvard has found that the brain area involved in *perceiving* an image and storing it as a memory is also involved in *imagining* that image. For example, when you think about the face of a person you met yesterday, the medial temporal region—the very same region used to perceive that face in the first place—becomes active. Thus an imagined event might be mistaken for a perceived event since both use the same brain architecture. In fact, in many ways memory *is* like perception. Both are reconstructed events in the brain, creative elaborations that involve filling in details around a few solid visual landmarks. Much as the fine points of perception are fallible to illusion, the details of memory are fallible to suggestion.

Thus, viewed from a biological perspective, there's reason to believe that both sides of the repressed memory debate can be valid. Research in animals suggests that memory storage can be modulated and inhibited, and that once inhibited, memory can nevertheless return. At the same time, we also know that memory can be unreliable and we have an inkling of how fantasy might be mistaken for reality. How, then, to evaluate—right now—the data from any individual case? The answer is clear: ideally, one wants to see independent evidence to corroborate the putative victim's report—for instance, from family members, diaries, photographs, medical and police records. But in reality, given the private nature of child abuse and the threats made to children to prevent them from telling others, independent evidence often isn't available. (Failing independent corroboration, particularly compelling behavioral clues, like those displayed by Eileen Franklin, might sometimes help support a case.)

So the arguments continue. But what's disturbing about the current tone of the debate is the eagerness with which some media and academic critics are using the wedge of doubt to publicly discredit the very existence of delayed memories. Do the questions of the critics reflect a genuine effort to get at the truth, to defend the innocence of the wrongfully accused? Or are we sometimes witnessing a backlash against the struggle to bring child abuse out of the family closet? At an American Psychiatric Association meeting last year, Herman noted: "Until recently the sexual abuse of children was the perfect crime. The perpetrator was fairly guaranteed that he would never be caught or successfully prosecuted. Now women—and men—have begun to use the courts to hold them accountable for the first time, and we see the perpetrators fighting back."

Hidden Messages

University of California-Berkeley Wellness Letter

Subliminal tapes—the kind that whisper a message while you sleep or mask some exhortation ("you don't really want to smoke," "you will decide to lose weight") under the sound of music or rolling surf—have been around for years. At a recent meeting of the American Psychological Association (APA) in Boston, Anthony Pratkanis of the University of California at Santa Cruz noted that nearly 150 magazine articles on subliminal messages had appeared since 1955—the year a promoter in New Jersey claimed to have caused a run on a movie snack bar by flashing subliminal commands on the screen. Supporters of the subliminal theory, who have included such noted authors as Vance Packard and Norman Cousins, fail to mention the complete lack of any scientific evidence that such messages can alter human behavior. Nevertheless, one survey shows that 68% of the public believes in subliminal tapes, which are now a $50-million-a-year business.

There are tapes that claim to help you quit smoking, lose weight, enhance self-esteem or sexual performance, and improve work habits. There's even a hot new market in tapes that claim to help people overcome the effects of sexual abuse. Perhaps such tapes are harmless. All they cost is money and time. And yet, as reported at the recent APA meeting, double-blind tests have consistently shown that these products fail to produce their claimed effects. One research team noted a "nonspecific placebo effect," though tapes *without* subliminal messages produced a greater effect than those with them. A third of the 237 people tested "had the illusion of improvement," though nothing showed they had any real improvement. In the delicate area of human psychology, maybe illusions are good enough. Yet for a person trying to quit smoking or overeating, or recover from the effects of sexual abuse, illusions may not do much good. A subliminal tape might indeed do harm if a person needs professional help or a support group and fails to seek it.

Lately there have been claims that people are being controlled by secret, "powerful" messages hidden in rock lyrics, imprinted on crackers, buried in television commercials and movies, or planted wherever they may "play on our unconscious." One rock band, Judas Priest, was recently brought to trial—and acquitted, after much expense and publicity—for allegedly inciting two teenagers to suicide through subliminal messages in their recordings.

Pratkanis, who served as an expert witness for the defense in the trial, offered this comment on the "subliminal" myth. The death by suicide of two young men was, of course, a tragedy; the boys in question "lived troubled lives, lives of drug and alcohol abuse, run-ins with the law . . . family violence, and chronic unemployment. What issues did the trial and the subsequent mass media coverage emphasize? Certainly not the need for drug treatment centers; there was no evaluation of the pros and cons of America's juvenile justice system, no investigation of the schools, no inquiry into how to prevent family violence, no discussion of the effects of unemployment on a family. Instead our attention was mesmerized by an attempt to count the number of subliminal demons that can dance on the end of a record needle."

How to . . . uh . . . Remember!

Gordon H. Bower

I'll never forget dear old what's his name.

The fact that we forget things important to us is a source of embarrassment and irritation, to say nothing of inefficiency. Forgetting has also been a source of some irritation to psychologists, who are only slowly beginning to understand it.

Hermann Ebbinghaus completed the first studies of forgetting just before the end of the 19th century. Using himself as a subject. Ebbinghaus investigated how much we forget over a period of time. In order to slow down the learning and to avoid unwanted associations with familiar language, Ebbinghaus would learn a series of nonsense syllables (meaningless consonant-vowel-consonant combinations), and then try to recall them after varying periods of time. His famous forgetting curve showed large amounts of forgetting over the first few hours after learning, followed by progressively less loss over ensuing days and weeks.

Ebbinghaus' classic research demonstrated that forgetting occurred in a reliable, orderly fashion. A practical question was how to prevent forgetting, or at least slow it down. Ebbinghaus also had some suggestions there. His main prescription, supported by his evidence, was that forgetting could be reduced by overlearning the material originally, beyond the point of mastery; he also prescribed reviving and rehearsing the material every now and then before its final use. These prescriptions are clearly well taken and underlie most school study guides, which cite the need for periodic reviews for refreshing one's memory.

A second practical question is whether memorizing is a skill that can be improved by special means. Research suggests that the ability to remember is indeed a skill, one on which individuals differ reliably and consistently, and that there are a few clearly specifiable components or subskills to this overall ability. People can be taught some of these skills. As an elementary example, one component of the skill of learning people's names during introductions is that we must first explicitly attend to and register the name clearly as it is told to us. Most of us fail at this initial and most elementary step because we are preoccupied with the other tasks demanded by the occasion—shaking hands, smiling, planning the conversation ahead, or anticipating the next person to be met. In our preoccupation, the name fails to register clearly. So a first prescription would be that if you want to learn names, then you've got to reshuffle your "cognitive priorities" at the time of introduction and attend clearly to the name and repeat it aloud or to yourself. That at least is a beginning. A second component in remembering names, as in remembering many other types of information, is to embellish or elaborate the material to be learned into meaningful terms and then to associate items. Some features suggested by the name would be elaborated into a bizarre association with a distinctive feature of the face or person to the name. Mr. *Carpenter* can be visualized hammering that long spiked nose of his into the wall; *Miss Lockhart* can be visualized with a huge *padlock* going through her *heart* and wrapped around her chest; and so on.

From Olympus to Oculomotor. This second component, of elaboration and visualization to aid in associating materials to be learned, has been investigated recently under the title of "mnemonic strategies" or simply "mnemonics." Most of us already use elementary forms of mnemonics. Our principal is spelled "pal" because he was our pal, but some of us remembered him as the man without princi*ple*. Similarly we spell "conceive" that way because we learned the rule "i before e except after c."

One problem people have is remembering the right *order* of a set of familiar items. Specially coined phrases or coined words are helpful here. Biology students learn the ordering of the 12 cranial nerves by memorizing the lines "On old Olympus' towering top, a fat-assed German vaults and hops." The first letter of each word is also the first letter of one of the major cranial nerves. The "coined-word" procedure consists of taking the first letter of words to be remembered and making a new word from them. Thus the ordering of colors of the spectrum is suggested by the name ROY G. BIV for red, orange, yellow, etc. If we can remember the coined word or phrase, we can order the items correctly. These particular mnemonics fail in the long run because they do not maintain the actual items in memory. Biology students may recall the limerick long after they have forgotten the names of the cranial nerves. A better mnemonic would contain hints for remembering the items themselves as well as their order. For example, using key words that sound like the names of the nerve, they could remember the following story: "At the *oil factory* (olfactory nerve) the *optician* (optic) looked for the *occupant* (oculomotor) of the *truck* (trochlear). He was searching because *three gems* (trigeminal) had been *abducted* (abducents) by a man who was hiding his *face* (facial) and *ears* (acoustic). A *glossy photograph* (glossopharyngeal) had been taken of him, but it was too *vague* (vagus) to use. He appeared to be *spineless* (spinal accessory) and *hypocritical* (hypoglossal)."

One mnemonic technique is particularly useful whenever two or more things are to be associated. Examples include the principal products of a country, foreign-language vocabulary items, and definitions of new concepts. The method consists simply of searching for or elaborating some vivid connection between the two items. One way to establish a connection is to imagine the two elements interacting in some way. To remember the meaning of the word *porte,* one might picture a huge bottle of *port* wine dangling from a door. Thus the word's meaning—door—will be called forth by the image.

Consider learning 2 series of word pairs such as DOG-HAT, MAN-PENCIL, CLOCK-WOMAN, SOFA-FLOOR, and PIPE-CLOWN. People usually learn a list such as this by rapidly repeating each pair as often as possible in the allotted time. The method is reasonably satisfactory for short lists and over short retention intervals. But extend either the length of the list or the retention interval, and the rehearsal method falters seriously. People who have learned to use mental imagery to relate the items of a pair perform much better. They visualize—a dog wearing a hat, a man resting a large pencil on his shoulder like a rifle, a woman wearing a clock on a chain around her neck, a section of floor resting on a sofa, and a clown smoking a pipe. When provided with one word of each pair, they can call to mind the interactive image they had formed, and can name the other object in the image. This procedure can improve recall by as much as 100 to 150 percent.

Spinning Stories. The value of relating items to each other in a thematic way shows up clearly when one concocts narrative stories as an aid to serial learning. In one study of this "chaining method," Michal Clark and I instructed college students to make up a story around a list of 10 unrelated nouns which were to be remembered. It usually took a student about one or two minutes to construct his story. Each student studied 12 different lists of words in a period of 30 to 40 minutes. Our control subjects learned the lists using any method they chose; they were allowed to study for a time comparable to that taken by the students composing stories. Following presentation of the last list, we tested retention by giving the first word of each list and asking the student to recall the other items in that list in order. Students who had constructed stories recalled about seven times as many correct items as the control subjects did.

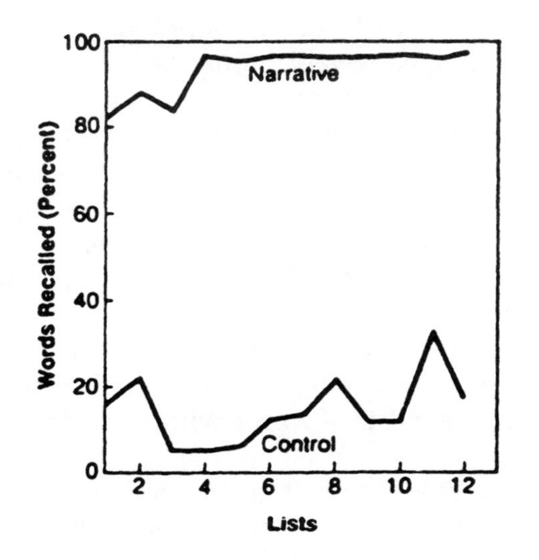

The narrative chaining method is a good mnemonic because the person provides an overall theme by which to organize the critical words. A second mnemonic for learning lists of items is the method of loci ("locations"): it works not by relating the items to be remembered to one another but rather by relating them to a standard list of known locations. One of the first references to this mnemonic system was made by Cicero, who tells the story of a man named Simonides. While attending a large banquet, Simonides was called outside and during his absence the roof of the hall collapsed, killing all of the revelers. The bodies of the victims were so mangled that they could not be identified by their relatives. Simonides, however, was able to identify each of the corpses by recalling where each person sat before the tragedy. He did this by visualizing the room and mentally walking about, "seeing" who had been seated in each chair. This feat so impressed him that he came to believe that all memory worked by placing objects or ideas into definite locations. The mnemonic is known as the method of loci because it depends on pigeon-holing items to be remembered into a series of "locations."

To use the method of loci, you must first establish a list of "memory snapshots" of locations taken from along a familiar route, such as a walk through your house. (A building, campus, or city would serve as well.) You must be able to see clearly and to recite the different distinctive locations on your list. To learn any new list of items you simply take a "mental walk" through your list of loci, placing successive items in your imagination at successive locations along your familiar route. You should connect the items to their locations by visualizing some vivid interaction between the item and the things at a given location. When you need to recall the items, you simply take another mental walk along your familiar route and see what items have been deposited there. For example, suppose that you need to buy many items at the grocery, including milk, bread, bananas and cigarettes as the first four. The first four snapshots of your pre-memorized list of locations might be your front hallway closet, the kitchen refrigerator, your favorite easy chair, and the living-room fireplace. To learn the first four items of your shopping list, you should visualize a vivid image of quarts of milk stacked up and bursting in your hallway closet, then a dagger-like loaf of bread piercing the refrigerator door, then large bunches of bananas piled up in your easy chair, and in the fireplace a large pack of cigarettes with several of them sticking out of the pack and smoking. A long list of items to be learned would require a long list of familiar locations in memory. As each object to be learned is studied, it is placed in imagination at the next location on your list of familiar loci. You should try to visualize a clear mental picture of the object "doing something interesting" at the location where it is placed. Later, in the grocery store, you can recall your shopping list by an imaginary walk through your house, pausing to "look at" what you've placed earlier at the standard locations in your route.

This system provides a series of memory hooks on which you can snag items and keep them from getting away. The number of loci can be expanded indefinitely according to one's needs. The system does more than just connect an item to something that is already known. It provides a series of permanent hooks or memory pegs to which you already have reliable access. Since the peg-list doesn't change, the pegs provide cues that can stimulate recall of the needed items.

A man who developed the method of loci to a fine art was the subject of Alexander R. Luria's book, The *Mind of a Mnemonist*. Known simply as *S*, this man performed remarkable feats of memory, recalling long lists of words without effort, and often retaining material many years.

There is also experimental evidence that the method of loci improves memory. Sometimes subjects who use this system are able to recall two to four times as much material as control subjects. In a study by John Ross and Kerry A. Lawrence, students studied a list of 40 nouns using the loci method. Immediately after each student studied the list, he tried to recall it in correct order. The next day the subject returned and again recalled the list before learning a new list of 40 items. Each student learned several lists this way. The average number of words recalled immediately after presentation of the list was 38 out of 40 in correct order. The average recall of words studied a day before was 34 out of 40 in correct order. This performance is vastly superior to that of students who use rote learning techniques.

Shopping with Mnemonics. In a direct comparison of the methods, David Winzenz and I had college students study five successive "shopping lists" of 20 unrelated words. They were allowed five seconds to study each word; they tried to recall each list immediately after studying it, and at the end of the session they tried to recall all five lists (100 items). Some subjects learned using the mnemonic or slight variations on it, while our control subjects were left to learn by their own devices (which typically consisted of rote rehearsal). The subjects using the mnemonic recalled the words far better than the controls on both the immediate test and the end-of-session test. At this end-of-session test, the mnemonic subjects remembered an average of 72 items out of 100, whereas the controls remembered only 28. Furthermore, the items recalled by subjects using the mnemonic were usually assigned to the right position on the right list, whereas the control subjects were very poor at remembering the position and list of the few scattered items they did recall.

A second mnemonic, called the "peg-word system," seems in most respects to be entirely equivalent to the method of loci. Where the method of loci uses mental snapshots of locations as memory pegs, the pegword system uses a familiar list of names of simple, concrete objects. A typical pegword list is one composed of rhymes of the first 20 or so integers. For instance, the pegwords for the first five integers might be 1-bun, 2-shoe, 3-tree, 4-door and 5-hive. The pegs should be names of concrete objects which you can visualize. This pegword list should be well learned so that it can be recited readily (the rhymes help at this stage) before it can be put to use in learning any new set of items.

To memorize a new set of items, you then use the pegwords during study much as you used the locations. You associate each item to be learned with a peg by imagining the two objects interacting in some way. For example, for our earlier grocery list, you would imagine pouring milk all over a soggy hamburger bun, then a shoe kicking and breaking a large stick of French bread, then bunches of bananas hanging from a tree, then a door puffing on a cigarette stuck in its keyhole. You can make up any bizarre image you like in order to link the pegword to the item to be learned. When recall is desired, you simply run through your familiar list of pegs and try to call to mind the image you formed earlier associated with each peg.

This system helps whenever the material to be learned is already familiar, but when the items are relatively unrelated, so that the problem is one of reminding yourself of all of them. Typical applications are to memorizing lists of errands, shopping items, geographical facts (e.g., the principal products of Brazil), unrelated sets of scientific laws, the sequence of points in a speech or sets of arguments you are to deliver, of main events in a play or history or novel you want to remember, and so on.

Since each pegword is attached to a number, you can recall a particular item without running through the entire list as you must do with the method of loci. If asked to recall the ninth item, you simply call to mind your pegword for number nine ("nine is wine") and this will cue recall of the ninth item. Going in the reverse direction, you can also identify the serial position of any item; from knowledge that an *orange* was last visualized drinking a bottle of *wine*, you know that *orange* was the ninth item on your list.

The numerical mnemonic is obviously very similar to the method of loci; the difference is that images of concrete objects rather than images of familiar locations are used as pegs, and that the pegs are numbered. Judith S. Reitman and I compared recall by students using the two mnemonics, and found them to be entirely equivalent so long as the student was asked only to recall the test items in the order he'd studied them. Both methods, of course, produced recall far superior to that of control subjects who were not using either mnemonic. The equivalence of the two methods is understandable if one notes that a "location" (such as my chair, my fireplace) is really nothing more than a coherent collection of "objects," like those prescribed for the numerical pegword system.

The same pegs or loci can be used over and over again to learn new lists of items. No particular difficulty is created by such multiple usages so long as you're interested only in remembering the most recent set of items you've stuck on your peg. Typically we can forget about arbitrary lists once we've used them: shopping lists are used but once, legal arguments before a jury are gone through but once, and a waitress has to remember only once that the current customer sitting on the left in the third booth gets the ham sandwich on rye. In such cases, the person has no need or desire to retain earlier lists.

Multiple Learning. But problems do crop up whenever the pegword system is used to learn many similar lists in succession, and the person needs to remember all of them later. One example might be learning on Sunday all of your hourly appointments for the coming week; another would be learning multiple shopping lists of things to buy at the grocery, the hardware store, the garden shop, and the drug store. In the experiment Reitman and I did, we simulated this kind of memorizing task by having some subjects use a pegword system and others a loci system to study five lists of 20 words presented once each. They were tested for ordered recall of each list immediately after they'd studied it. They were also tested unexpectedly for recall of all five lists at the end of the hour's session and again seven days later. We told some subjects to learn the items on each new list by calling to mind a separate, distinctly different version (and vision) of the pegword and to link that to the appropriate item. Thus, if the first pegword was 1-*bun,* they should visualize a small cloverleaf dinner roll for associating to the first item in the first list, a large hamburger roll for the first item on the second list, and so on. They were also told not to call to mind earlier images associated to the peg, but to study each list as a distinctly separate set. Other subjects received just the opposite instructions—to use exactly the same image for the pegword and to progressively elaborate grand imaginal scenes in which the peg was interacting in some way with all the prior objects to-be-remembered at that list position. Suppose, for example, that the second words in the first four lists were *dog, hat, bicycle,* and *cigar.* Then the peg 2-*shoe* would be elaborated successively over lists as follows: a *dog* wearing *shoes,* that *dog* wearing a *top hat* and those *shoes,* that *dog* riding a *bicycle* while wearing that *top hat* and those *shoes,* and finally that *dog* smoking a *cigar* while riding that *bicycle* and wearing that *top hat* and those *shoes.* Our college students had no difficulty concocting such progressive elaborations, even though they had no more time than those doing the "separate" imagery method.

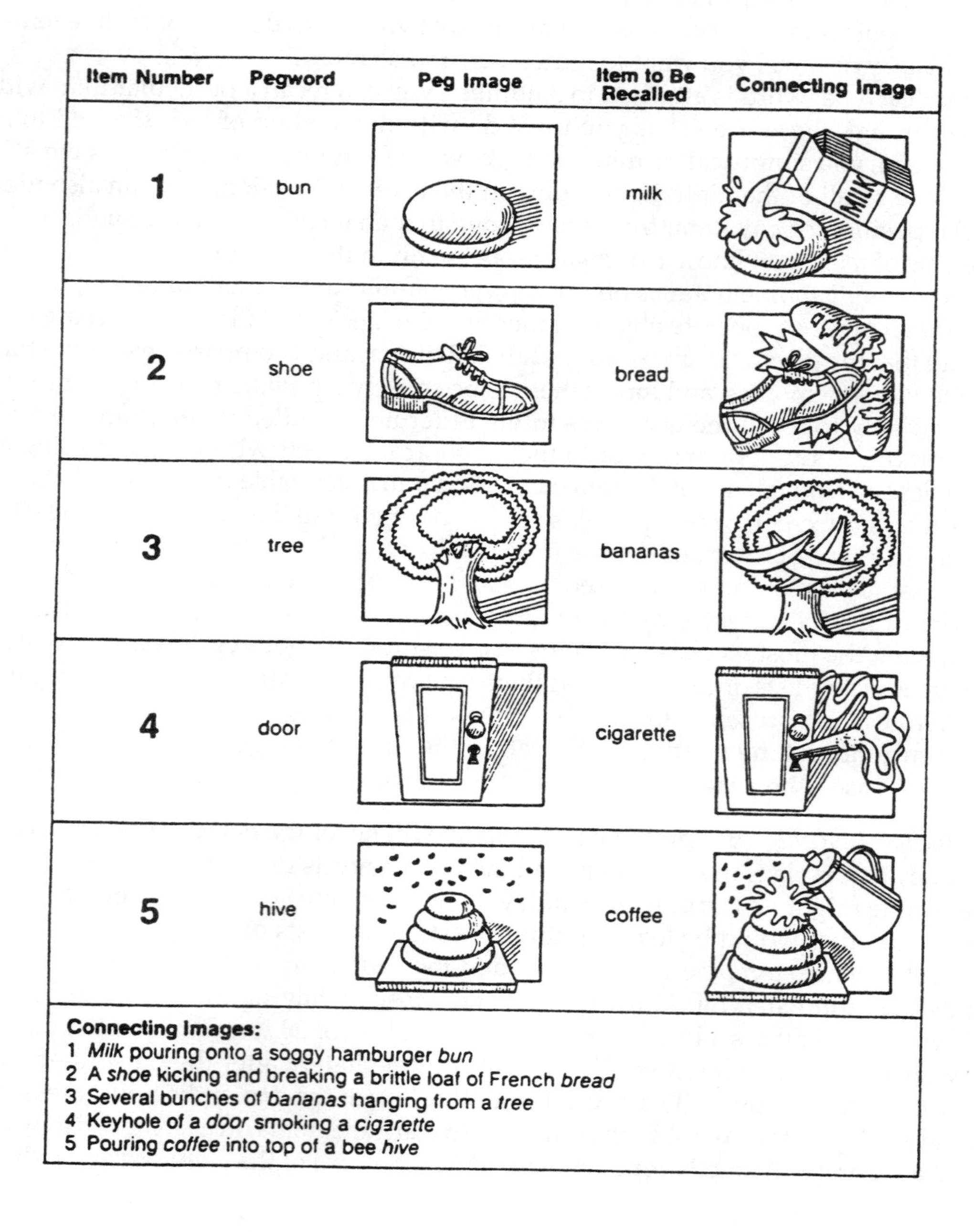

Connecting Images:
1 *Milk* pouring onto a soggy hamburger *bun*
2 A *shoe* kicking and breaking a brittle loaf of French *bread*
3 Several bunches of *bananas* hanging from a *tree*
4 Keyhole of a *door* smoking a *cigarette*
5 Pouring *coffee* into top of a bee *hive*

Although these two conditions gave the same high level of immediate recall after studying each list (86 percent vs. 87 percent), a huge advantage for the progressive-elaboration procedure appeared at the later tests. On the end-of-session test, the progressive elaborators recalled about 70 percent compared to 38 percent for the separate imagers. At the one-week test, the scores were 54 percent versus 12 percent, a fourfold difference.

The problem seemed to be that as the separate imagers learned each new peg-to-item association they tended to unlearn the prior associations from that peg. Consequently, on the end-of-session test, these subjects were good at recalling the last list they'd learned, but did progressively worse at recalling the earlier lists of the session. The progressive elaborators, on the other hand, learned each new item by first recalling and rehearsing their "peg scene" containing the prior items and then adding a new elaboration of that scene. By this means, later uses of a peg caused revival and strengthening rather than unlearning of earlier items attached to the peg. As a result, at the one-week test, these subjects did best on the first list they'd learned and worst on their final list.

Overloading the Pegs. The practical prescription is obvious: if many similar lists are to be retained simultaneously using the same pegword list, then you frequently have to revive and rehearse earlier lists as you learn new lists. There are two other obvious ways to avoid the interference and forgetting caused by learning multiple lists. One way is to use a very long list of pegs (say, 100) and segregate items so that List-1 items (e.g., Monday's appointments) go onto pegs 1–20, List-2 items (Tuesday's appointments) go onto pegs 21–40, and so on. A second way to learn multiple lists but still avoid overloading a peg is to have multiple pegword lists at your command. Along with your rhyming pegwords, you might have three lists of 20 loci corresponding to locations along a familiar route inside your house, down the street outside your house, and through the place where you work. Then you can use different peg lists to learn the several similar lists you have to keep in mind. With a little ingenuity, you can even work out a higher-order peg system to remember which class of items have been associated to which set of pegwords. Man's memory (or mind) seems quite at ease dealing with such superordinate hierarchies of units, since each hierarchy is built up according to a basic principle—namely, that a symbol can stand for an entire set of units but that symbol itself can enter into further associations.

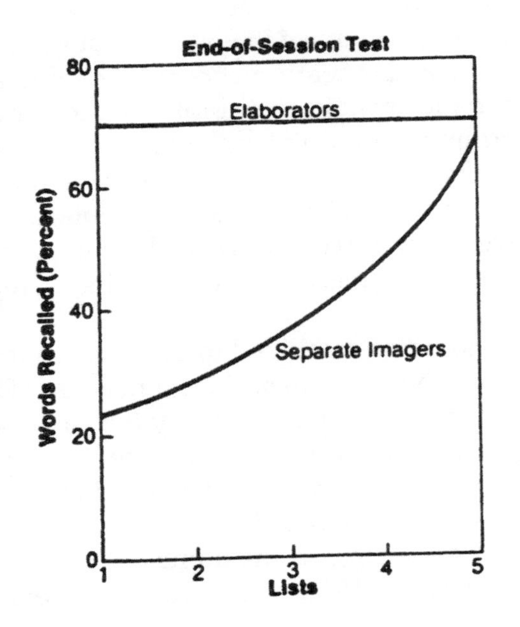

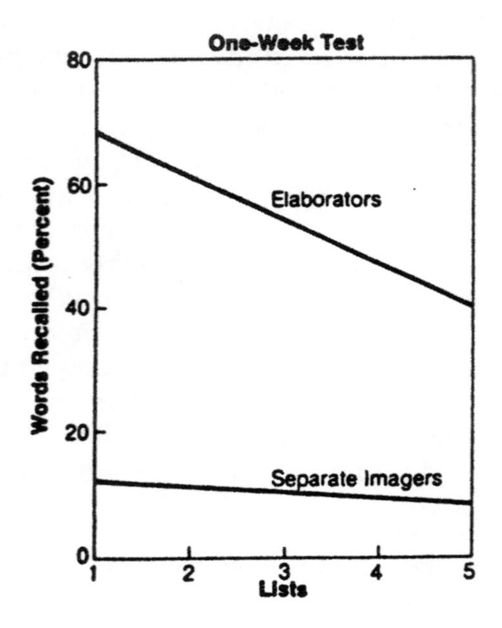

As effective as such pegword systems can be, they are of no value in learning meaningless materials like numbers, which cause one of the biggest memory nuisances. We would like to remember telephone numbers, social-security numbers, license plates, room or locker numbers; we need to recall birth dates, anniversaries, addresses and ages; students must remember historical dates and the populations of countries; businessmen need to know production figures and budget allotments. A mnemonic system that is particularly helpful with this kind of material is a number-to-sound coding system.

Meet in HAVOK. One first assigns consonant sounds to the numbers zero through nine. For example, the numbers zero through nine might be assigned the letters b, c, n, v, r, h, s, k, l, and t. (More elaborate codings can be used.) Once the code has been learned, then a number can be replaced by its assigned letters. Thus the number 537 becomes HVK. These letters can then be made into a word by adding vowels wherever they are needed, as in HAVOK. And so we recall that we are to meet in HAVOK—that is, in room 537.

Dates, appointment times, and other numbers can be coded and learned in the same fashion. Very long numbers typically have to be broken up into a series of words, to make a phrase. Of course, like learning to play a piano (which requires coding or "translation" from visual score to finger movements), the code needs to be practiced if it is to be effective. You have to become very proficient at rapidly replacing digits by code letters and these by words. However, once the code has been learned, it takes little effort to maintain, much less than the time we ordinarily spend in trying to remember—or look up—important numbers.

Two or more mnemonics can be combined to produce a spectacular performance. I once knew a 96-year-old man who could memorize a new list of 50 three-digit numbers shouted out to him by an audience one at a time every five or 10 seconds. Not only could he recall the list without error, but he could tell you what the 37th item was and that the number 259 was the 18th item. Since he was partly deaf, his main trouble wasn't in remembering the numbers, but in hearing them correctly in the first place. He achieved his mnemonic feat by combining the pegword system and the number coding system. He had concrete images as pegs for the first 50 numbers. He also had a coded conversion word with a concrete image for each of the first 1,000 numbers. When given a number, he converted it to its code word and formed an image to connect that code word to the pegword for the first item. For instance, if the third number to be learned was 546, he would convert that to its code word, say, for example, HORSE. If his pegword for the third item was tree, then all he had to do was form an image of a horse leaning up against a tree, or kicking a tree.

Teaching Memory Skills. Most of us feel no compelling urge to learn long lists of three-digit numbers. Such feats make for interesting conversation and may prove entertaining at parties, but are themselves useless. However, the methods underlying such feats can be put to many practical uses. Whether we like it or not, we all have a great many things to remember. We ought then to acquire those skills that would make memorization less painful and more efficient. Our schools should teach memory skills, just as they teach the skills of reading and writing. Although teachers typically describe educational goals in such lofty terms as teaching their students to be critical, insightful, curious, and deeply appreciative of the subject matter, these are usually only extra requirements beyond the learning of basic facts that is demanded as a minimum. Any geography student who thinks Istanbul is in France, or any art-history student who thinks Salvador Dali painted the Sistine Chapel, is going to flunk his exams if he pulls such boners often enough. The point is that we do demand that students learn a lot of facts just as we are constantly required to do in our daily life. You can get a feel for this if you try to carry on an intelligent conversation about some current event, say, the Nixon Administration's war on inflation, without having learned some facts about the topic. But the solution to the problem is probably at hand. By systematically applying the knowledge that we now have about learning, we should be able to improve our skills so that we spend less time memorizing facts. By the strategic use of mnemonics, we might free ourselves for those tasks we consider more important than memorization.

We ought to take advantage of what we know about memory, forgetting, and mnemonics, and we ought to do it soon. You are already beginning to forget the material you just read.

Memory Freaks I Have Known

In the popular mind, mnemonic devices are associated with magic, memory tricks, chess wizardry, lightning-fast calculations, and other Olympiad feats of mental gymnastics. Being a naive scientist, I vigorously disbelieved such popular dogma. I pictured instead lawyers, doctors and engineers using mnemonics to lighten the memory load of their jobs. To unmask the poppycock, I went to meet some professional mnemonists in the flesh at the first and only convention of a national mnemonics association in the Spring of 1968 in Hollywood, where else. To my chagrin, I discovered that the popular notion is true. The mnemonists I met were usually entertainers doing shows of magic and trickery. Some were simply zany characters who got their kicks from performing spectacular mental gyrations that leave the rest of us dumbfounded and awe-struck. Mnemonists love to entertain and dazzle one another even more than they do a naive audience. Like a reunion of comedians, each mnemonist loves to "top" the other one, with a new trick or new mental skill. They made a charming crowd for a convention: slightly pixilated, wild, madcap, and surprising in their unexpected mental skills.

Arriving at the convention, I saw some 30 people scattered in small conversation groups. My first surprise came when I registered and received a name tag. The small conversation groups turned out to be mnemonists comparing notes on how best to do some memory trick. One group was discussing several variants of the "perpetual-calendar" system, which enables the user to calculate rapidly, in his head, the day of the week on which any date fell. The system will tell you that February 12, 1809 was a Sunday and July 15, 1922 was a Saturday. Other groups were discussing schemes for fast memorization of the Morse code, or the order of cards in a shuffled deck, or ways to fool an audience into believing you'd memorized a thousand eight-digit numbers or the entire Los Angeles telephone directory. It was amazing guile but trickery nonetheless.

The convention program consisted principally of performances by these talented people. There was a 96-year-old man who memorized 50 three-digit numbers shouted out to him by the audience. Another participant had memorized the powers of 2 up to 2^{100}, which is a very large number indeed. He did it by recalling a key sentence associated with pegword N, the sentence composed of words which were a phonetically coded translation of successive digits in 2. These coding techniques are explained in my article. The two most spectacular performances were turned in by John Stone, and Willis N. Dysart, whose stage name was Willie the Wizard.

At age 66, Stone had taught himself several complex skills allowing him to carry out nearly simultaneously several activities which, for most people, would interfere with one another. In one of these performances, he would begin with four six-letter words shouted out at random by the audience, from which he proceeded to write rapidly and upside-down a complexly transformed word salad. For instance, given the words GEORGE, STOLEN, MARKER, and ARMPIT, Stone would quickly write a sequence such as:

G N W T E Ǝ ∀ I O ⅂ R Ԁ R O K M G ⊥ E Я E S ꓤ A

The pattern of the sequence can be shown by selective erasure or by rearranging letters vertically as follows:

G E O R G E
N Ǝ ⅂ O ⊥ S
W ∀ ꓤ K E ꓤ
T I Ԁ M Я A

The four words appear on each line, either properly ordered, reversed, upside-down (turn page), or a combination.

The amazing feature was the rapidity with which Stone could reel off these letters, writing them upside-down, all the while reciting "The Shooting of Dan McGrew." He was like a one-man band of mental instruments, a walking counterexample to the "limited channel capacity" hypothesis of cognitive psychologists. Seeking to unlock the secrets of the cognitive universe, I asked Stone what went on in his mind as he did this trick. His answer was totally unrevealing: "I practiced it so long that my hand just automatically knows what to do as my eye looks at successive letters of the key words." Such answers, to the dismay of cognitive psychologists, are also about what we get if we ask a pianist or one-man band to explain how he does his "trick." It's like asking the common man how he can understand rapid speech. He doesn't know; he just can do it.

Willie the Wizard was a lightning-fast mental calculator who could multiply and divide very long numbers at a startling speed. He was led through his paces by his manager, a sort of carnival barker who would announce Willie's next feats, solicit problems from the audience, keep track of problems on a blackboard, and call for applause. The general class of problems Willie liked to work on were freaks of the following form: "If a flea jumps two feet, three inches every hop, how many hops must it take to go around the world, the circumference being 25,020 miles? Also, how long would it require for the journey if the flea takes one hop per second?" Almost before such questions were finished, Willie would have started rattling-off the answer, "It would take 58,713,600 hops, requiring one year, 314 days, 13 hours, and 20 minutes." Like most mental calculators, Willie had memorized a vast array of arithmetic facts (e.g., products of all three-digit numbers); he also used many shortcuts which speed up mental calculations. Such skills are poorly understood. As a person, Willie was shy, with few interests beside arithmetic; higher math like calculus held no interest for him. He was somewhat of an innocent pixie regarding human relations. His business manager helped shield him from people who would exploit that innocence.

The evening following the conference a banquet was held in a private club for magicians, with haunted-house decor straight out of the Addams family. Throughout dinner we were entertained by conferees doing card tricks and memory tricks. I recall one stunt in which the mnemonist looked briefly through a shuffled deck of cards, then recited from memory the order of the 52 cards. As another trick, after shuffling and dealing you one or more cards, he could inspect the remaining deck and tell you which cards you'd taken. For these stunts, he used a prememorized code word (and image) for each of the 52 cards in conjunction with the pegword system explained in my article.

Such tricks kept us entertained throughout the evening. The only memory failures I noticed in the crowd were some late arrivals who had mistaken the time and place of the banquet and two conferees who forgot where they'd parked their cars. As the evening ended, one stage mnemonist shook my hand with that direct, sincere look and said, "It's been a pleasure meeting you, Dr. Flowers."

Extraordinary People

Darold Treffert

Leslie has never had any formal musical training. Yet upon hearing Tchaikovsky's Piano Concerto no. 1 for the first time when he was a teenager, he played it back on the piano flawlessly and without hesitation. He can do the same with any other piece of music, no matter how long or complex. Yet he cannot hold a utensil to eat and can only repeat in monotone that which is spoken to him. Leslie is blind, is severely mentally handicapped, and has cerebral palsy.

George and his identical twin brother, Charles, can rattle off all the years in which your birthday fell on a Thursday. They can also tell you, within a span of forty thousand years backward or forward, the day of the week on which any date you choose fell, or will fall. In their spare time George and Charles swap twenty-digit prime numbers for amusement. Yet they cannot add simple figures or even tell you what a formula is, let alone write one out.

Kenneth is thirty-eight years old but has a mental age of eleven. His entire conversational vocabulary consists of fifty-eight words. Yet he can give the population of every city and town in the United States that has a population of over five thousand, the names, number of rooms, and locations of two thousand leading hotels in America; the distance from each city and town to the largest city in its state; statistics concerning three thousand mountains and rivers; and the dates and essential facts of over two thousand leading inventions and discoveries.

All of these people are examples of the fascinating phenomenon called the *idiot savant,* a term coined by J. Langdon Down of London some one hundred years ago, when the word *idiot* did not have the negative, comical implication it now carries. At that time, *idiot* was an accepted medical and psychological term referring to a specific level of intellectual functioning—an IQ level of less than twenty-five. The word *savant* was derived from a French word meaning "to know" or "man of learning." The observation that persons with severe mental handicap displayed advanced levels of learning, albeit in very narrow ranges, led to the once descriptive, still colorful juxtaposition of the two words.

Understandably, some people object to the term *idiot savant* because the word *idiot* now gives the condition a connotation that is neither deserved nor fair. Therefore, the terms *savant* and *Savant Syndrome* will be used hereafter in referring to these remarkable people and the astonishing phenomenon they represent.

Savant syndrome is a condition in which persons with major mental illness or major intellectual handicap have spectacular islands of ability and brilliance that stand in stark, startling contrast to their handicaps. In some savants—those I call *talented savants*—the skills are remarkable simply in contrast to the handicap, but in other, more rare savants—those I call *prodigious*—the abilities and skills would be remarkable even if seen in normal people.

Until now, the scientific articles and media presentations describing the several hundred savants discovered during this past century have been isolated, anecdotal accounts of single individuals and their extraordinary stories. But there is much more to Savant Syndrome than interesting stories. Among these remarkable people, diverse as they may at first appear, is a commonality that deserves study, for in the future it may provide a key to better understanding not only how *they*—handicapped but with uncommon talent—function, but also how *we*—without handicap but with common talent—function as well. Of particular promise is what Savant Syndrome might tell us about memory (and thus conditions such as Alzheimer's disease), the nature of creativity, and the elusive relationship between memory and emotion.

At present, the significance of Savant Syndrome lies in our inability to explain it. The savants stand as a clear reminder of our ignorance about ourselves, for no model of brain function—particularly memory—could be complete unless it included and accounted for this remarkable condition.

When confronted by Savant Syndrome, so many questions leap up: How can extremely handicapped persons possess these islands of genius? What do they have in common? Why, with all the skills in the human repertoire, do the skills of the savant always fall in such narrow ranges and include such rare talents as calendar calculating?

Why is phenomenal memory seen in all the savants, no matter what exceptional individual skills they exhibit? Is the savant's memory qualitatively different from normal memory? Is their genius a direct result of their deficiencies, or do the two factors coexist coincidentally?

What can we learn about this spectacular dysfunction of mind and memory that might provide clues to normal mind and memory? Might the existence of these geniuses among us suggest that some such genius lies within each of us, waiting to be tapped?

The time has come to take the savants out of the "Gee Whiz" category and learn what we can about them, and from them—not just about memory and brain function, but about human potential as well.

I met my first savant on July 1, 1959. I was twenty-six years old and had just completed a residency in psychiatry at University Hospital in Madison, Wisconsin.

My first professional assignment was to develop and direct a thirty-bed Children's Unit at Winnebago State Hospital near Oshkosh, Wisconsin. As I walked onto the unit that first day, I noticed David. He stood there with a device he had fashioned out of cardboard and pencils that held a rolled-up paper scroll on which perhaps a hundred names were neatly written. As David turned the pencil on which the scroll had been wound, each name came into view, one at a time, through an opening in the cardboard that had been placed over the scroll. The device looked just like the window on the front of a bus where the destinations are listed and changed as the bus route changes. And that's just what it was. The names on David's homemade scroll were the names of streets—Capitol Drive, State Street, Lincoln Avenue. David had memorized the bus system of Milwaukee. If you gave him the number of a bus and the time of day, he could tell you at which corner the bus was then stopping.

David was a very disturbed boy. His violent temper and his severe behavioral problems necessitated continuous hospitalization. His overall functioning was at a very low level—except for this one peculiar area of exceptional ability. He would have made a great cab dispatcher.

There were other savants on this unit. Billy could make free throws. Could he ever make free throws! He was like a baseball pitching machine, except he used a basketball. He always stood in exactly the same place at the free-throw line, with his feet in exactly the same position and his body in the same stance. For every shot his arm motions were identical, as were the arcs of the ball. He never missed. He showed no emotion, no overcorrection or undercorrection. There was nothing to correct. He was a basketball robot. Unfortunately, he had the same robot-like approach to everything. His mutism and his inability to communicate were evidence of his profound emotional and behavioral disturbance, which required his hospitalization on a long-term basis.

Then there was Tony. Unlike Billy, Tony did use language and, in fact, was a voracious reader. But he, too, had a serious behavioral condition that caused him to make vicious attacks against himself, and sometimes toward others. Tony knew history. He delighted each day in approaching visitors or staff—including new young doctors like me—asking them the significance of that particular date in history. Usually he elicited no answer, or just a few wild guesses, and so Tony would begin spouting off a long list of events that occurred throughout history on that day, much like the radio announcer on the morning show that I listened to on my way to work. Except that the announcer read his information from an almanac. Tony, it seemed, *was* an almanac.

There were other cases on the unit similar to those of David, Billy, and Tony. I was struck by the islands of intelligence, even genius, that existed in what otherwise was a sea of severe handicap and disability. I soon became fascinated by this paradox of ability and disability, and began my research studying its appearance in patients with Early Infantile Autism, a form of childhood schizophrenia marked by withdrawal. My work eventually put me in touch with researchers throughout the world who were working in related fields. But it also left me with some lingering questions regarding Savant Syndrome—questions that remained unanswered for years.

After two years developments in my career forced me to put aside my work with Savant Syndrome until 1979, when I left Winnebago to begin a private practice and run a 150-bed community mental health center in the nearby community of Fond du Lac. Though I had mentally filed away the data on the autistic children I had seen fifteen years earlier on the Children's Unit—and on the savant skills present in some of them—the phenomenon continued to intrigue me.

I didn't see many autistic children in my Fond du Lac practice. What I did see, though, were a number of adult patients on whom I was conducting sodium amytal (truth serum) interviews as a means of enhancing their recall of buried memories and hidden traumas. In those interviews, patients remembered—in extraordinarily minute detail—a whole variety of experiences they thought they had forgotten. It was a demonstration of memory powers that, like Savant Syndrome, seemed to redefine human potential.

In some instances an entire journey down a particular street on a particular night would be recalled with exquisite attention to particulars—changing traffic lights, street signs, and passing cars. Both the patients and I were often startled by the voluminous amount of material that was in storage but unavailable in an everyday waking state. It was as if some sort of tape recorder were running all the time, recording all of our experiences. The memories were there. What was missing was access and recall.

Simultaneously, reports were cropping up in scientific literature about neurosurgical studies of brain mapping, especially concerning the use of tiny electrical probes to determine epileptogenic foci—the seizure trigger—in the exposed cortex of patients who suffered certain kinds of seizures. The brain itself has no pain fibers within it; the pain fibers are in the surrounding capsule of the brain, the dura mater. Once the dura is numbed with a local anesthetic, the patient can remain awake while the surgeon uses a tiny electrical probe to find the site where certain kinds of seizures are triggered. This site then can be surgically removed and some seizure disorders corrected. In the random search for these foci, the probe hits a variety of spots on the cortex, and when it does, memories flood the patient's consciousness.

These memories, long forgotten by our conscious minds, are the kind of "random" recollections we often experience in our dreams: the fifth birthday party, including all the guests present; a day in class twenty years earlier; a walk on a particular path on a particular day, complete with the accompanying aromas and sound. If we were to remember such dream memories upon awakening, we would dismiss them, wondering, Where did that come from? But we know their origin in these instances: The probe had activated a circuit or pathway not ordinarily available to us.

I filed away these accounts, too, along with my observations of the savants I had known, as I continued to be busy with many other things.

Then, in June 1980, I met Leslie Lemke.

The department of social services had invited May Lemke and her remarkable foster son, Leslie—then twenty-eight—to give a concert honoring the foster parents of the county. I did not attend, but a short time afterward, in the wake of the publicity that followed, I became intrigued and decided to visit Leslie and his foster parents at their small cottage on Lake Pewaukee.

When I arrived, Leslie was sitting in a chair in his music room, a converted porch. He sat motionless and silent, but he seemed contented and at ease. He echoed my name when May told him who I was. Then he sat motionless and mute once again. May could hardly wait for him to play for me. She was so proud. Despite his blindness he walked unaided, feeling his way, from the chair to the piano.

Then he played. I don't recall what the song was, but I do recall what I felt—astonishment, fascination, and inspiration. I still have the same reaction, many years and many tunes later, whenever I see and hear Leslie play. Here was someone with a triple handicap—blindness, retardation, and cerebral palsy—playing for his audience of three, a concert worthy of an audience of a thousand. Though he had had no formal training, piece after piece poured forth: hymns, concertos, arias, popular songs, and imitations of singers. Some pieces he sang; some he just played. Some of the lyrics were in English, some in German, and some in Greek.

Leslie is the most remarkable savant I have ever met, read about, or studied. He was born prematurely in Milwaukee on January 31, 1952, and his mother immediately gave him up for adoption. He spent the first months of his life at Milwaukee County Children's Home. There it was noticed that the baby did not open his eyes, which were swollen and hard and had cloudy corneas. The doctors diagnosed his condition as retrolental fibroplasia, a disorder often seen in premature infants in which the retina proliferates wildly and sometimes, as in this case, blocks drainage in the eye, creating childhood glaucoma or a condition called *buphthalmos*. When Leslie was four months old, his left eye had to be removed. Six weeks later his right eye also was removed because of the glaucoma and because his doctors feared that the eye would burst. That was the source of Leslie's blindness.

Soon thereafter, at age six months, this frail and pathetic baby was given to the care of a remarkable woman. May Lemke was then fifty-two. She had been a nurse/governess and had developed a reputation for the extraordinary skill and love she showed in caring for children, handicapped or well. May received a call from the Social Services Department of Milwaukee County and, without a moment's hesitation, took on the role of foster mother, tutor, therapist, mentor, model, cheerleader, and inspiration to this blind, palsied, and intellectually handicapped little boy.

When Leslie was seven years old, May bought him a piano. She would play and sing for her foster son, running his fingers up and down the keyboard so he could identify the notes. By age eight Leslie could play the piano as well as a number of other instruments, including bongo drums, ukulele, concertina, xylophone, and accordion. By nine Leslie had learned to play the chord organ. Medical notes indicate that, at age ten, Leslie still was not conversant, with the exception of repetition and imitation. He required help in dressing himself. He could not feed himself anything that required the use of utensils.

One evening, when Leslie was about fourteen, he watched a movie on television called *Sincerely Yours,* starring Dorothy Malone and Basil Rathbone. May and her husband, Joe, watched it, too, but then went to bed. At about three o'clock in the morning, May awoke, thinking that Joe had left the television on. She went to the living room to check. There sat Leslie. He had crawled over to the piano and was playing Tchaikovsky's Piano Concerto no. 1—the theme song to *Sincerely Yours*—vigorously and flawlessly. Leslie had heard it one time. That was sufficient. He played it through from beginning to end.

To this day, if you ask Leslie to play that piece, you get not only the song, but the entire television introduction, mimicked exactly as he heard it in true echolalic fashion: "Tonight's movie is *Sincerely Yours,* starring Dorothy Malone and Basil Rathbone. As he falls in love with the beautiful black-haired woman . . . [In the background are heard the beautiful strains of Tchaikovsky's Piano Concerto no. 1.] And now, The *Sunday Night Movie* is proud to present. . . ." Usually, there is no stopping Leslie once he begins. He's like a jukebox: You put in your quarter and you hear the whole song. Until recently, the *Sincerely Yours* recitation and lengthy piece were virtually unstoppable. (That was a real hazard during Leslie's live television appearances, where time was so very limited.) Leslie now can be persuaded to stop, or at least to bring the piece to an end more quickly, with a gentle tap on the shoulder from Mary Parker, May's daughter, who acts as Leslie's guardian and caretaker now that May is frail.

Leslie was twenty-two years old when, in 1974, he gave his first public concert, at the Waukesha County Fair, a few miles from his home. He played and sang his hymns and did his Louis Armstrong and Tiny Tim imitations. He was a smash hit. He was "incredible," the newspaper said. As would happen at all of his concerts to follow, the audience members at the Waukesha County Fair shook their heads in astonishment and wiped tears from their eyes as he closed the concert with "Everything Is Beautiful."

Leslie recently completed a tour that included twenty-six cities in Japan. His repertoire now features thousands of pieces and is continually expanding. He is gradually becoming more polished in his presentations, more spontaneous in his conversations, and more sociable in his interaction. He appears to love what he is doing, is remarkably good at it, and seems to enjoy the appreciation and applause of his audiences, whether large or small, prestigious or ordinary, young or old. He has not yet reached his limits.

My personal familiarity with Leslie and his remarkable family made me a popular interview subject whenever the media turned to the topic of savants. These exposures put me in touch with a wide variety of researchers and scientists around the world who shared an interest in this condition. They in turn brought many new cases to my attention, cases I never would have known about were it not for this sudden attention to and curiosity about the puzzling paradox of being backward and brilliant at the same time.

The overriding question for any researcher in this field is all too obvious: How do they do it? How does someone like Leslie Lemke, a person of clear deficiency, achieve such greatness in one limited area? I have found that there are about as many theories attempting to answer this question as there have been investigators. Many of the theories stem from the study of a single case, so-called "undemocratic" research that often provides useful information but also is rather idiosyncratic and limited. Among the recent research, I have found no single finding or theory that could explain all savants. But several theories could explain aspects of the syndrome and are worth exploring.

Eidetic imagery. Some researchers link Savant Syndrome to this fairly rare phenomenon in which a person continues to "see" an object as an afterimage for as long as forty seconds after it has been taken away. The retained image is intensely vivid and absolutely accurate. The term also is used by some to describe what popularly is known as photographic memory (whereby the afterimage can be recalled later and viewed as if it were a photograph). While some studies have found a higher number of "eidekers" among savants than among non-savants, other studies have not documented this difference. At any rate, eidetic imagery is not uniformly present in all savants and thus could not serve as a universal explanation for the condition.

Heredity. Could the savant be the product of two coincidentally inherited genes—one for retardation and the other for special abilities? While some investigators have found higher incidences of special skills in the families of savants, others have not. Thus, like eidetic imagery, heredity cannot serve as the sole explanation.

Sensory deprivation. Other researchers have postulated that Savant Syndrome may be a consequence of social isolation or biologically impaired sensory input. While social isolation does apply to some savants—those in deprived institutional settings, for example—many others come from stimulating environments where they received a great deal of personal attention. There are similar problems with the theory that the syndrome results from some biological form of sensory deprivation such as blindness or deafness. While some sensorily deprived individuals do develop savant skills, most do not.

Impaired ability to think abstractly. Under this theory, organic brain damage reduces the savant's ability to think abstractly, and the savant compensates by developing and refining concrete abilities as well as a vivid memory. While this is an accurate characterization of many savants, it is only a description—not an explanation—of the syndrome.

Compensation for defects and reinforcement from praise. There is no doubt that the praise that savants receive for their unusual skills can compensate for feelings of inferiority and aid in their development of relationships. Yet these same dynamics are factors for many developmentally disabled people, and only a few achieve the performance level of the savant. There must be specific and unique factors that separate the savant from the rest of the mentally handicapped.

Right brain/left brain localization and other organic factors. While not an absolute rule, the left brain hemisphere generally is responsible for skills that require intellect, cognition and logic, such as reading and speaking. The right hemisphere deals with abilities that are more intuitive and nonverbal, such as painting, sculpting, and playing music. In general, skills most often seen in savants—are those associated with right hemisphere function, and those lacking tend to be left-hemisphere-related. Could Savant Syndrome result from damage to the left hemisphere of the brain?

One case lending impetus to this last theory involves a normal nine-year-old boy who suffered a gunshot wound very precisely confined to the left side of the brain, leaving him deaf, mute, and paralyzed on the right side. Following that injury, the boy developed a savant-like ability to troubleshoot and repair mechanical devices, presumably resulting from increased function in his undamaged right hemisphere.

Unfortunately, there has been very little research to confirm left brain damage in savants. It is interesting to note, however, that in two of the three reported cases where CAT scans (detailed x-rays of the brain) were performed on savants, there was clear evidence of such left brain damage. The other reported CAT scan—on a very high-functioning autistic savant with mathematical skills—showed an undamaged left brain.

No doubt some savants do have left brain damage as we generally think of it—trauma or injury before, during, or after birth. Yet, in the case of the identical twins George and Charles, both of whom had identical calculating skills, it seems most unlikely that both of them would have incurred such an injury in exactly the same area of the brain to give them their identical abilities. Their case argues for genetic or behavioral factors as well—or perhaps for some other process affecting the left brain.

Further insight into the damaged-left-brain theory is provided by the 1987 findings of Harvard neurologists Norman Geschwind and Albert Galaburda, who studied right brain/left brain development and cerebral dominance. The doctors note that, from conception onward, the left brain is larger than the right and that it completes its growth and development later than the right brain in utero, leaving it vulnerable for a longer period of time to a variety of prenatal influences and injury. One such influence is the male sex hormone testosterone, which in the male fetus reaches levels that have been shown to impair neural cell development in some instances. This testosterone effect could therefore produce the type of left brain "damage" postulated for the savant.

Such damage—coming before birth at a time when the brain is still developing—would result in right brain cells being recruited for what would ordinarily be left brain circuits. A "pathology of superiority" of the right brain would then develop, along with a preponderance of right-brain-type skills—the kind of skills seen in the savant.

According to Geschwind and Galaburda, testosterone-caused damage would account as well for the correspondingly high male-to-female ratios seen in savants and in other "left brain" disorders such as dyslexia, delayed speech, autism, stuttering, and hyperactivity. It correlates as well with the higher incidence of left-handedness in males.

Further implications can be drawn from the fact that a striking number of savants were born prematurely. The phenomenon of massive brain cell death in humans just before birth is well established and commonly accepted. There are many more brain cells in the fetus than can possibly make connections, and those unconnected neural cells are simply discarded late in the pregnancy.

Geschwind and Galaburda point out that when left brain injury occurs early in pregnancy—as postulated by the testosterone theory—there is still a large reservoir of spare right brain neurons available to accommodate a neuronal shift to the right hemisphere. Indeed, the right brain actually becomes enlarged compared to the left. Could the savant's premature birth prevent the normal brain-cell die-off and provide a large reservoir of right brain cells that, when recruited, produce the extraordinary right brain skills seen in the savant?

Another body of research that could be of importance in understanding the savant is the work of Mortimer Mishkin, M.D., and others at the National Institute of Mental Health. Mishkin outlined two types of memory, each with its own distinct pathways: cognitive or associative memory, in which facts or stimuli first are consciously recognized, then sorted, stored, and later recalled; and habit memory, more a system of conditioned reflexes, such as that used when driving a complex daily route to work while thinking about other things. It is the latter that more accurately characterizes savant memory—the "memory without consciousness" described over and over again in savant literature. Mishkin points to data suggesting two different neurological pathways, or circuits, for these two different kinds of memory. In the savant, it appears that habit memory pathways compensate for damaged cognitive memory circuits.

Clearly, the one quality or trait that all savants have in common, irrespective of their particular skills, is phenomenal memory. It is memory of a specific type: literal, vivid, reflex-like, unconscious, devoid of emotion, tremendously deep but impressively narrow. This is in dramatic contrast to memory in the rest of us, which tends to be much more conscious, highly associative, more abstract, less literal and precise, emotion-laden, and tremendously wide-ranging in subject matter but conspicuously limited in depth. Savants' unique memory function and circuitry distinguishes them from non-savants and points to the most fruitful area of further study.

Indeed, recent findings from new x-ray studies of the brain and autopsy data suggest that, in addition to the savant's left hemisphere damage, there is corresponding damage in lower brain areas, including those that control memory circuitry. This could explain the characteristic appearance in the savant of both right brain skills and an over developed reliance on habit memory.

Combining the various theories and new research, then, the talented savant emerges as an individual whose left-brain function has been disrupted as a result of some brain injury—perhaps sex-linked—occurring before, during, or after birth that leads to a compensatory increase in right brain function. The left brain damage is coupled with lower brain damage as well, causing a reliance on habit memory circuitry. These two factors somehow combine to produce the savant's characteristic cluster of abilities. Constant repetition and practice then refine these circuits, resulting in conspicuous talent within an exceedingly narrow range.

This scenario would account for the talented savants—those whose skills are remarkable simply in contrast to their obvious mental handicaps. However, in order to explain the prodigious savants, we must take into account some inherited factors as well. The prodigious savant's access to the vast rules of mathematics, art, or music could not be learned by practice alone. Some researchers have suggested that such extraordinary talents might be acquired from a shared field of knowledge similar to psychologist Carl Jung's "collective unconscious," or that these skills could reflect knowledge gained in so-called "past lives." These are explanations that no one can confirm or refute, but they are nevertheless explanations held by some.

Clearly, in both varieties of savant, intense concentration, practice, compensatory drives, and reinforcement play major roles in developing and polishing the skills made possible by this idiosyncratic brain function. But there is another factor as well: the deep care and concern that families or other caregivers have for the savants—not just for what they can do but for who they are; not just for what is missing but for all that remains. By radiating so much love, encouragement, and praise, they serve to reinforce and motivate in ways that are truly touching and inspirational.

Until recently, almost all of the technical advances in the study of the brain have allowed us to better and more precisely view brain *structure:* Are all the parts there? Now, for the first time, new technology, such as the positron emission tomography (PET) scan and similar devices, allows researchers to better study brain *function*, the actual way the brain works. Such new technology for studying the brain, coupled with new knowledge about the brain, has far-reaching implications for understanding savants—and thus ourselves.

For starters, the savant's "memory without consciousness"—Leslie's exact mimicry of an overheard German song or a random conversation, for example—can be studied in detail. Surely this distinct memory—so deep but so narrow, so vast but so emotionless—arises from circuitry far different from our ordinary memory, which is shallow and limited but far more flexible, associative, and creative.

By allowing us to better understand memory circuitry, savants may help us counteract the disruption of memory pathways by conditions such as Alzheimer's disease. Such brain repair might take any one of several forms: pharmacologic (with memory-enhancing drugs), neurologic (with brain cells recruited from unaffected areas and rerouted over new pathways), electrical (with brain-pacing devices such as those now used to treat certain types of epilepsy and to pace the electrical system of the heart), or neurosurgical (with brain grafts and neuronal transplants such as those now used in the treatment of Parkinson's disease).

Almost everything we have learned about health we have learned from the study of disease. Thus, from the research on Alzheimer's disease may come applications for expanding and enhancing normal memory. Each of us has tremendous numbers of memories—literally a lifetime's worth—stored in an organ to which we have relatively poor access. In our dreams, under hypnosis, or in sodium amytal interviews, some of this stored data cascades forth. And, as mentioned earlier, when neurosurgeons touch the cortex of a patient's brain with a tiny electrical probe, it also triggers thousands of memories of which the patient is unaware.

It seems "lost" memories have not disappeared; they have simply been misfiled, making them difficult to find. Normal memory enhancement, whether pharmocologic, electrical, or by some other method, promises to someday allow us to tap that tremendous reservoir of data we all possess but cannot now access.

The link between memory and creativity is another area in which studying savants may lead us to better understand ourselves. Their tremendous skills aside, savants almost exclusively echo and mimic—there is little or no creativity involved in what they do. Adding improvisation to existing music—as striking as that is—is still not the same as creating a new musical idea. Alonzo Clemons, a sculpting savant, can recreate fantastically what he sees but cannot do free-form sculpting. This is not to detract from such remarkable skills. It is simply to say that they differ from the creative process, and that difference warrants further study.

Savants, as a group, also demonstrate an unusual emotional flatness. Again, this trade-off is a mixed blessing. While they may miss some of the peaks of normal human emotion, they seem to be spared the valleys. While they may not shout at a ball game or weep at a movie, they also seem to be free of performance jitters or bouts of deep despair or cynicism. They may never feel ecstasy, but neither will they feel despondency. With further study, this emotional detachment may provide clues to the normal interplay of memory and emotion.

Indeed, we can learn a great deal about human potential from the jarring contradiction—the magnificent coexistence of deficiency and superiority—that is Savant Syndrome. We can learn that handicap need not necessarily blur hope and that stereotyping and labeling serve only to obscure—in a pernicious manner—an individual's strengths. We can learn the difference between paucity of emotion and purity of emotion. From the families, teachers, and therapists of the savant, we can learn that in dealing with people who have problems—even severe ones—it is not enough to care *for* those people: We must care *about* them as well. We can learn that there is a difference between sharing the spirit and shaping the spirit. We can learn how to work with a differently shaped soul—to understand, to actualize, and to appreciate it—while still respecting Its uniqueness.

In short, a complete understanding of human experience requires that we include and account for Savant Syndrome. Until then, we will be able only to marvel at people such as Leslie Lemke, Alonzo Clemons, or the calendar calculator named George who can compute twenty-digit prime numbers but cannot add two plus two. "it's fantastic I can do that," he says.

For now, it truly is.

The Truth about TV

Phil Catalfo

Just about all of us let our young children spend at least a little time in front of a television set. Many of us have found TV to be a very useful baby-sitter; while our preschoolers are happily engaged watching an hour or so of educational programming or videos, we can get a moment's rest or a bit of work done. Yet many of us occasionally wonder about the effects of TV on our children's development. Does the small screen have a negative influence on their attention span or their ability and desire to learn? Can it affect their behavior and attitudes?

"Many of the parents I speak to nationwide are quite concerned about whether TV damages kids," says Milton Chen, Ph.D., the director of education for public television station KQED in San Francisco and the author of the recently published book *The Smart Parent's Guide to Kids' TV* (KQED Books). "I've heard parents say, 'My God, I'm afraid to sit my two-year-old down in front of the television set for fear his brain will rot or his health will be affected.'"

Surveys show that a growing number of Americans feel similarly concerned. A 1994 poll conducted by the Gallup Organization and the Family Channel found that well over 50 percent of adults believe that TV has become more violent, more sexually explicit, and more profane in the last year. Eighty-three percent say that TV violence directly contributes to violent behavior by children. And 71 percent say they now monitor or restrict their children's access to TV—up from 63 percent in 1993 and 60 percent in 1991.

The creators of television shows, of course, stand behind their products, so television today has both its angry critics and its vehement defenders. But what do we really know about the risks and possible benefits of TV viewing? After decades of research, there should be some clear answers to parents' most pressing questions. To find those answers, *Sesame Street Parents* talked to the top experts in the field and combed through hundreds of research reports. Here is what we discovered.

1. Is there something about watching television that makes it bad for children?

In spite of alarms that have been raised during the last two decades, viewing television in moderate amounts is not, in itself, dangerous or harmful according to every expert we consulted.

The idea that there is something harmful about kids watching TV first attracted widespread public attention in the 1970s and 1980s, when a number of books were published attacking TV as a medium. *The Plug-in Drug*, by the critic Marie Winn, even argued that TV has inherent "druglike" properties and that educational children's programming can be "addictive" and "zap" kids' minds. "These are provocative claims, but there's no evidence to support them," says Ellen Wartella, Ph.D., the dean of the College of Communication at the University of Texas at Austin and a well-known researcher on television and children's issues. "The authors failed to study the physiological effect of TV on children, and they didn't observe real children watching TV."

Researchers who *have* observed the effects of TV on real children's physical, emotional, and mental development have found that watching television is no different in its impact on those areas of development than many other leisure-time activities that children pursue. Television viewing doesn't train kids to be passive, because kids are usually *not* passive while watching television, according to studies by Daniel R. Anderson, Ph.D., a professor of psychology at the University of Massachusetts at Amherst. Dr. Anderson says his research shows that, on average, children glance at and away from a TV screen between 100 and 200 times an hour and that, given a choice, kids will usually draw, eat, tumble, or play with toys while viewing.

And even if children do sit passively, their brains are active. In a comprehensive 1993 research report entitled "Television and the Brain: A Review," Katharine Fite, Ph.D., a professor of psychology and the director of the Neuroscience and Behavior Program at the University of Massachusetts, summarized the major findings of experiments measuring electrical activity in the brains of children as they watched TV. She concluded that children's "brain function while viewing is quite similar" to their brain function while playing with dolls or looking at books—in fact, doing anything other than sleeping. Based on these and other findings, Dr. Fite says that TV viewing isn't an unconscious, or sleeplike, activity, as the popular critics contend. An extensive review of the published scientific literature, Dr. Fite says, provides no evidence to substantiate such beliefs.

"Television itself is not the problem," sums up Dr. Chen. "The problem is programming. Our children watch TV programs, not TV, and we need to help them learn which programs to watch."

2. If certain television programs can be a problem for preschoolers, what can kids safely watch?

The short answer is: Your child can safely view just about any age-appropriate educational program, and some carefully chosen cartoons and light adult shows, such as family-oriented sitcoms and specials. The more pertinent answer is: The less violence your child encounters on TV, the better.

Nonviolent programming content is important for two reasons, Dr. Chen explains. One is that preschoolers can easily mistake violent or disturbing televised events for occurrences in real life, just as they can confuse fears with reality. As a result, young children can be seriously frightened by exposure to heavy adult TV programming, such as police dramas or news.

The second reason is that children can and often do imitate what they view on TV. A child as young as 14 months old "can and will simulate televised behavior," says Andrew N. Meltzoff, Ph.D., the head of developmental psychology at the University of Washington in Seattle. Dr. Meltzoff's research shows that babies can watch a gesture or action on TV one day, and when they return to the lab the next day can duplicate what they have seen from memory, "showing just how powerful TV can be, even at this preverbal age," he says. Older children are equally capable of reproducing the punching, kicking, and karate chopping motions they see on shows like *Mighty Morphin Power Rangers, Teenage Mutant Ninja Turtles,* or *X-Men.*

"American television programming is among the most violent in the world," asserts Dr. Chen, and studies confirm that commercial TV programs provide violent role models on a massive scale. To take one example: In 1994 a nonprofit research organization called the Center for Media and Public Affairs viewed ten network and cable channels in its hometown of Washington, D.C., during an 18-hour programming day. The agency counted 2,605 acts of violence—more than 10 acts per channel during every hour of programming. Worse, the leading source of violence was commercial *children's* shows, both programs and product commercials. These contained, on average, 36.7 violent events per hour. Much of that violence was, of course cartoon-style bops and bashes. But that's still more than three times the number of violent acts that appeared on other TV programs.

3. What effect does watching televised violence have on children?

This is one of the most thoroughly researched issues of our day. Most pertinent studies show that viewing realistic scenes of violence may lead children not only to imitate but to initiate aggressive, even violent, behavior. Furthermore, viewing violence can cause what some researchers call desensitization, "an increasing willingness to tolerate escalating levels of violence in the world around you," notes John P. Murray, Ph.D., the director of the School of Family Studies and Human Services at Kansas State University in Manhattan and an author of the American Psychological Association's 1992 report *Big World, Small Screen* (University of Nebraska). Dr. Murray cites a study by Ronald Thomas and Margaret Drabman in which one group of eight-year-old children was shown realistic violent programming, and a second group was shown less-violent fare. All children were then asked to watch a third group of children on a TV monitor and to call a teacher when the children's behavior became too unruly. According to Dr. Murray, the youngsters who had watched the violent programming "tolerated higher levels of aggressive behavior—throwing things, calling names—and took much longer to intervene."

A third effect of sustained viewing of TV violence is what Dr. Murray and others call mean world syndrome. Those afflicted with this syndrome, he explains, "begin to believe that the world is as mean and dangerous as it appears on TV"—in other words, much more dangerous than it really is.

4. What about cartoon aggression?

Most parents would agree that cartoon violence is different from live-action violence, such as that seen in the news. But experts point out that cartoon aggression still has an impact. "At the very least, cartoons teach young children to laugh at violence," says Deborah Prothrow-Stith, M.D., the assistant dean at the Harvard University School of Public Health and the author of *Deadly Consequences* (HarperCollins). "At worst they show children that violent behavior may be a cartoon hero's first recourse when solving problems."

And, in fact, preliminary results of a study at the Center for Research on the Influences of Television on Children at the University of Kansas in Lawrence indicate that preschoolers who watch cartoons are also more likely to watch violent adult programming by the grade-school years than are preschoolers who watch educational programming.

5. Do TV shows with powerful images and a fast pace—even educational programs—negatively affect a child's ability to concentrate on other activities, such as reading?

Some critics, including Marie Winn and Jerome L. Singer, Ph.D. a Yale University clinical psychologist, say yes, they can. These critics argue that fast-paced TV programs promote distractibility and inattention in children and can engender shallow thought processes. Says Dr. Singer, "I'm concerned that the rapid changes of pace and disconnected images train children to expect highly exciting material all the time, and not to take the time to think about what they're experiencing."

But other experts question these conclusions. Dr. Anderson, who has published a study comparing the effects on children of fast-paced and slower-paced educational programs, reports that he has found no measurable difference between the two paces of programming on children's impulsivity or ability to persevere with a mental task. He ascribes Dr. Singer's research results to the *amount* of viewing the kids in his studies have done, not to the viewing of fast-paced programs. Dr. Chen adds that studies summarized by Keith Mielke, Ph.D., a senior research fellow at Children's Television Workshop, "show that if kids watch a moderate amount of television, particularly educational television, they can prove to be excellent students."

6. How much TV viewing is okay for children? What amount is too much?

Most experts claim there is an upper limit on children's healthy viewing, and most put that limit at one to two hours a day. In fact, many experts say that what they call heavy viewing—more than three hours a day—raises the likelihood of a range of negative outcomes that have been associated with kids watching TV.

Many authorities claim that this is so because heavy viewing generally means at least some viewing of violence; others point out that kids who watch a lot of TV are probably being shortchanged on other activities they need for their development, including reading, talk, and outdoor play. As a result, some researchers contend that a diet of entertainment that's too rich in TV hours mutes children's imagination, intellectual responsiveness, and ability to learn quickly.

Among the strongest proponents of that claim are Dr. Singer and his wife, Dorothy Singer, Ed.D., who are codirectors of Yale University's Family Television Research and Consultation Center. "In our studies," Dr. Jerome Singer says, "we've found that kids who watch more than three hours of television a day are much more restless and less able to focus on a task." In a 1984 series of longitudinal studies, Dr. Singer also identified a correlation between heavy viewing during the preschool years and below-average storytelling skills by the age of eight. Similarly, research by Dr. Murray, of Kansas State, on children's storytelling abilities found that children who watch more than four hours a day of television can give elaborate accounts of stories they've seen on TV but can't invent stories as original or full of detail as those made up by viewers of the same age who watch less.

The consensus: Heavy viewing is to be avoided, if only because children need to engage in a range of other activities, including reading and outdoor play. Says Dr. Chen: "I wouldn't recommend that children watch more than a couple of hours of TV a day, on average, and I'd encourage parents to vary the TV diet—on some days do not allow kids to watch any television and on others, when it's raining or cold outside, allow them to watch more."

7. Can educational television programs really help my preschooler learn?

"Television can be quite useful in child development," says Dr. Wartella. "It can be used to enhance education-related skills and also to introduce children to an incredible wealth of information, knowledge, and intelligence about the world." Dr. Murray adds that educational children's programming "has been demonstrated again and again to have a tremendous effect on enhancing a child's preparation for reading and for school."

Television programs can also teach and reinforce important social values, such as nonviolence, tolerance of others, and altruism, notes Gerald S. Lesser, Ph.D., a professor of education and psychology at Harvard University's Graduate School of Education and one of the founders of *Sesame Street*. For example, Dr. Lesser notes, research shows that young children who view *Mister Rogers' Neighborhood* demonstrate increased "Sharing, nurturing, and cooperative behaviors."

8. In addition to steering my children away from violent or frightening programs, is there something I can do to shield them from any ill effects of TV watching?

There's a great deal parents can do, research suggests. The first thing, of course, is to restrict *what* kids watch and *how much* they watch. Second, parents can help kids get positive benefits from TV by making a concerted effort to integrate what the child sees on screen with her own experience and with other people and activity in the room, according to Dr. Singer. In one study he found some increase in imaginative play when the children viewed TV with an adult (such as a parent) who called attention to specific program elements and encouraged them to occasionally imitate the learning activities that were shown. "There has to be an interactive element," he says. "If TV just does all the work for the child, then the child doesn't get the chance to practice make-believe play."

Indeed, according to research and to every expert we spoke to, parental supervision is the key to mitigating any negative effects and enhancing the benefits of television viewing. In families that emphasize nonaggressive behavior and in which the parents themselves aren't aggressive, children are much less likely to exhibit aggressiveness, even if they watch it on TV, says Aimee Dorr, Ph.D., a professor of education at the University of California at Los Angeles and the author of *Television and Children* (Sage).

Needless to say, parents are the ones who are truly raising their children. But when TV baby-sits too often, notes Dr. Chen, children's behavior has been shown to reflect some of the confusion of images and of good and bad values they see on television. When we actively raise kids, he adds—with attention, games, books, balanced meals, outdoor play, hugs, some TV, and lots and lots of talk—their world widens with possibility.

Adolescence: Whose Hell Is It?

Virginia Rutter

The image of teenagers as menacing and rebellious is a big fiction that's boomeranging on kids. We've mythologized adolescence to conceal a startling fact: It is indeed a difficult and turbulent time—for parents. The trouble is, kids look like adults much sooner than ever before. Kids wind up feeling abandoned—and angry at the loss of their safety net. If we haven't got adolescence exactly figured out yet, there's some consolation in the fact that it's a brand-new phenomenon in human history.

I recently spent the weekend with a friend's 13-year-old son. In contrast to the tiny tots most of my friends have, Matthew seemed much more like an adult. The time spent with him wasn't so much like baby-sitting; it was like having company. It was impressive to see how self-sufficient he was. Simple matters struck me: he didn't need someone to go to the bathroom with him at the movies; he could help himself to ice cream; he was actually interested in following the O.J. Simpson story, and we discussed it.

He was polite, thoughtful, and interesting. While the intensive caretaking necessary for smaller children has its own rewards (I suppose), Matthew's contrasting autonomy was pleasant to me. And so I imagined it would be for parents of adolescents. But then, I am not a parent. And most parents report not feeling pleasant about their adolescents.

The weekend reminded me of how easy it is to think of these youngsters as adults. Compared to an eight-year-old, an adolescent is a lot like an adult. Can't reason like an adult, but doesn't think like a child anymore, either. Some parents are tempted to cut 'em loose rather than adjust to the new status of their teenager. Others fail to observe their adolescent's new adultlike status, and continue monitoring them as closely as a child. But it's obvious that adolescents aren't miniature adults. They are individuals on their way to adulthood; their brains and bodies—to say nothing of their sexuality—stretching uneasily toward maturity.

Yet the sight of kids reaching for some form of adult status commonly evokes contempt rather than curiosity. Negative feelings about teenagers have a strong grip on American culture in general, and on surprising numbers of parents in particular. It's not uncommon for parents to anticipate their child's adolescence with fear and trepidation—even before they've gotten out of diapers. They expect a war at home.

"It becomes a self-fulfilling prophesy that adolescence is seen as this bizarre, otherworldly period of development, complete with a battleground set for World War III," says Tina Wagers, Psy.D., a psychologist who treats teens and their families at Kaiser Permanente Medical Center in Denver.

We were all once 13, but it seems we can no longer imagine what kind of parenting a 13-year-old needs. Perhaps it's gotten worse with all the outside opportunities for trouble kids have—gangs, guns, drugs. Families used to extend their turf into their children's schools, friends, and athletic activities. But kids now inhabit unknown territory, and it is scary for parents. "I think this fear and lack of understanding makes some parents more likely to back off and neglect teenagers," reports Wagers. "There is an expectation that you can't influence them anyhow."

This skeptical, sometimes hostile view of teens, however, was countered by my experience with Matthew. I found him hardly a "teenager from hell." Like most teens, Matthew prefers to be with his own friends more than with family or other grown-ups. He's not good with time, and music, basketball, and girls are more central to him than achievement, responsibility, and family. (Despite his tastes, he does very well in school.) At home there is more conflict than there has been in the past, though not less love and commitment to his mom, with whom he lives in eastern Washington.

The story of Matthew falls in line with new research on adolescents, and it's causing psychologists to totally revise conventional wisdom on the subject. According to psychologist Laurence Steinberg, Ph.D., of Temple University, the majority of adolescents are not contentious, unpleasant, heartless creatures. They do not hate their parents—although they do fight with them (but not as much as you might think). "In scrutinizing interviews with adolescents and their families, I reaffirmed that adolescence is a relatively peaceful time in the house." Kids report continued high levels of respect for their parents, whether single, divorced, or together, and regardless of economic background.

When fighting does occur, it's in families with younger teenagers, and it has to do at least in part with their burgeoning cognitive abilities. Newly able to grasp abstract ideas, they can become absorbed in pursuing hypocrisy or questioning authority. In time, they learn to deploy relativistic and critical thinking more selectively.

Not a Disease

If adolescents aren't the incorrigibles we think—then what to make of the endless stream of news reports of teen sexism, harassment, drug abuse, depression, delinquency, gangs, guns, and suicide?

Any way you measure it, teens today are in deep trouble. They face increasing rates of depression (now at 20 percent), suicide (12 percent have considered it, 5 percent attempted), substance abuse (20 percent of high school seniors), delinquency (1.5 million juvenile arrests—about 1 percent of teens—in 1992), early sexual activity (29 percent have had sexual relations by age 15), and even an increased rate of health problems (20 percent have conditions that will hamper their health as adults). And kids' problems appear to be getting worse.

How to reconcile the two parts of the story: adolescents aren't so bad, but a growing number are jeopardizing their future through destructive behavior? Though we look upon teenagers as time bombs set to self-destruct at puberty, in fact the problems teens face are not encoded in their genes. Their natural development, including a surge of hormonal activity during the first few years of adolescence, may make them a little more depressed or aggressive—but how we treat them has much more to do with teenagers' lives today. From the look of it, we aren't treating them very well.

A Crisis of Adults

If what goes on in adolescence happens largely in the kids, what goes wrong with adolescence happens primarily in the parents. "It wasn't until I turned to the parents' interviews that I really got a sense that something unusual was going on," reports Steinberg of his ongoing studies of over 200 adolescents and their families. As he details in his recent book,

Crossing Paths: How Your Child's Adolescence Triggers Your Own Crisis (Simon & Schuster), Steinberg finds that adolescence sets off a crisis for parents.

Parents do not have positive feelings during the time their kids go through adolescence, and it isn't simply because they expect their kids to be bad (although that's part of it). Scientists have studied the behavior and emotions of parents as well as their adolescent children, and found that when children reach puberty, parents experience tremendous changes in themselves. What's more, they shift their attitudes toward their children. It isn't just the kids who are distressed. Parents are too. Consider the following:

- Marital satisfaction, which typically declines over the course of marriage, reaches its all-time low when the oldest child reaches adolescence. Married parents of adolescents have an average of seven minutes alone with each other every day. For the marriages that don't pass the point of no return during their kids' teen years, there is actually an increase in satisfaction after the kids complete adolescence.
- Happily married parents have more positive interactions with their kids than unhappy parents. In single-parent families, parental happiness also influences their response to adolescence.
- In a surprising finding, the marital satisfaction of fathers is directly affected by how actively their adolescents are dating. Especially when sons are busy dating, fathers report a marked decline in interest in their wives. Dad's aren't lusting for the girls Johnny brings home, they just miss what now seem like their own good old days.
- In family discussions, parent's become increasingly negative toward their adolescents—there's more criticism, whining, frustration, anger, and defensiveness expressed verbally or in grimaces. While the kids are always more negative than their parents (it comes with increasing cognitive ability, in part), the parents are actually increasing the amount of negativity toward their children at a higher rate.
- Working mothers don't spend less time at home with their teenagers than non-working moms do, but they do risk higher levels of burnout, because they continue to cover the lioness' share of work at home. On the other hand, a mother's employment makes her less vulnerable to the ups and downs of parenting an adolescent. Maternal employment also benefits kids, especially teen daughters, who report higher levels of self-esteem.
- Despite their fulfillment, mothers' self-esteem is actually lower while they are with their adolescents than when they are not. After all, a mother's authority is constantly being challenged, and she is being shunted to the margins of her child's universe.
- Teenagers turn increasingly to their friends, a distancing maneuver that feels like an emotional divorce to parents. Since mothers are generally more emotionally engaged with their children than are fathers, the separation can feel most painful to them. In fact, mothers typically report looking forward to the departure of their kids after high school. After the kids leave, mothers' emotional state improves.
- Fathers emotional states follow a different course. Fathers have more difficulty launching their adolescents, mostly because they feel regret about the time they didn't spend with them. Fathers have more difficulty dealing with their kids growing into adolescence and adulthood; they can't get used to the idea that they no longer have a little playmate who is going to do what daddy wants to do.

Add it all up and you get a bona fide midlife crisis in some parents, according to Steinberg. All along we've thought that a midlife crisis happens to some adults around the age of 40. But it turns out that midlife crisis has nothing to do with the age of the adult—and everything to do with the age of the oldest child in a family. It is set off by the entry of a family's first-born into adolescence.

Once the oldest child hits adolescence, parents are catapulted into a process of life review. "Where have I been, where am I now, where am I going?" These questions gnaw at parents who observe their children at the brink of adulthood.

It hits hardest the parent who is the same sex as the adolescent. Mothers and daughters actually have more difficulty than fathers and sons. In either case, the children tend to serve as a mirror of their younger lost selves, and bear the brunt of parents' regrets as parents distance themselves.

Steinberg tracks the psychological unrest associated with midlife crisis in parents:

- The onset of puberty is unavoidable evidence that their child is growing up.
- Along with puberty comes a child's burgeoning sexuality. For parents, this can raise doubts about their own attractiveness, their current sex life, as well as regrets or nostalgia for their teenage sexual experiences.
- The kids' new independence can make parents feel powerless. For fathers in particular this can remind them of the powerlessness they feel in the office if their careers have hit a plateau.
- Teens also become less concerned with their parents' approval. Their peer group approval becomes more important. This hits mothers of daughters quite hard, especially single mothers, whose relationship to their daughters most resembles a friendship.
- Finally, de-idealization—kids' often blunt criticism of their parents—is a strong predictor of decline in parental mental health. Parents who used to be the ultimate expert to their kids are now reduced to debating partner for kids who have developed a new cognitive skill called relativism.

A clear picture begins to emerge: parents of a teenager feel depressed about their own life or their own marriage; feel the loss of their child; feel jealous, rejected, and confused about their child's new sexually mature looks, bad moods, withdrawal into privacy at home, and increasing involvement with friends. The kid is tied up in her (or his) own problems and wonders what planet mom and dad are on.

Emotional Divorce

The sad consequence is that parents who experience a midlife crisis begin avoiding their adolescent. Although a small proportion of parents are holding on to their teens too closely—usually they come from traditional families and have fundamentalist religious beliefs—more parents are backing off. The catch is that these teenagers want their parents' guidance. But more and more they just aren't getting it.

Some parents back away not out of their own inner confusion but because they think it's hip to do so. Either way, letting go causes confusion in the kids, not help in making their way into adulthood. Even if they are irritating or irritable, or just more withdrawn than they used to be, teens are seeking guidance.

"I have this image of a kid groping through adolescence, kind of by himself," confides therapist Wagers, who sees a lot of parents out of touch with their kids. "The parents swarm around him, but don't actually talk to him, only to other people about him."

The mantra of therapists who work with adolescents and their families is "balance." Parents have to hold on, but not too tightly. They need to stay involved, even when their kids are ignoring them. Roland Montemayor, Ph.D., professor of psychology at Ohio State, finds it is not so different from learning how to deal with a two-year-old. You must stay within earshot, and be available whenever they falter or get themselves into trouble.

With a two-year-old, trouble means experimenting with mud pies or bopping a playmate; with a 14-year-old, it means experimenting with your car keys or sex. The task is the same—keep track of them and let them know what the rules are. Parents unfortunately taken up with their own midlife concerns may not embrace the task. God knows, it isn't easy. But it is vital.

Among parents who have gone through a real divorce, the emotional divorce that occurs between adolescents and their parents can heighten difficulty. It may reawaken feelings of sadness. Parents who don't have many interests outside the family are also vulnerable. Their kids are telling them to "Get a life!"—and that is exactly what they need to do.

Dropout Parents

As an adolescent reaches age 13, the time she is spending with parents is typically half that before age 10. "Teens come home and go into their bedrooms. They start to feel more comfortable by themselves than with siblings or parents around. They talk on the phone with friends, and their biggest worry usually has to do with a romantic interest," explains Reed Larson, Ph.D., who studies families and adolescents at the University of Illinois, Champaign-Urbana. Larson, coauthor of the recent book, *Divergent Realities: The Emotional Lives of Mothers, Fathers, and Adolescents,* studied 55 families who recorded their feelings and activities for one week, whenever prompted at random intervals by a beeper. He surveyed another 483 adolescents with the beeper method.

The families' reports revealed that a mutual withdrawal occurs. "When kids withdraw, parents get the message. They even feel intimidated. As a result they don't put in the extra effort to maintain contact with their kids," observes Larson. The kids feel abandoned, even though they're the ones retreating to their bedroom. The parents, in effect, cut their kids loose, just when they dip their toes in the waters of autonomy.

Separation is natural among humans as well as in the animal kingdom, Larson notes. Yet humans also need special care during this life transition—and suffer from reduced contact with parents and other adults. They still need to be taught how to do things, how to think about things, but above all they need to know that there is a safety net, a sense that their parents are paying attention and are going to jump in when things go wrong. The kids don't need the direct supervision they received at age two or eight, but they benefit emotionally and intellectually from positive contact with their parents.

Despite the tensions in family life, studies continue to confirm that the family remains one of the most effective vehicles to promote values, school success, even confidence in peer relationships. When it works, family functions as what Larson calls a "comfort zone," a place or a relationship that serves as a home base out of which to operate. Kids feel more secure, calm, and confident than those without a comfort zone. Similarly, Steinberg finds, the one common link among the many successful adolescents in his studies is that they all have positive relationships with their parents. Without positive relationships, the kids are subject to depression and likely to do poorly in school.

Parental withdrawal is a prime characteristic of families where adolescents get into trouble. It often catapults families into therapy. Wagers tells the story of a single parent who wasn't simply withdrawn, her head was in the sand: "I was seeing a mother and her 12-year-old son, who had depression and behavior problems. The mother called me up one time to say she had found all this marijuana paraphernalia in her son's room, in his pocket. She said she wasn't sure what it means. When I said 'it means that he's smoking pot,' she was very reluctant to agree. She didn't want to talk to her son about why he was getting into trouble or smoking pot. She wanted me to fix him." (Eventually, in therapy, the mother learned how to give her son a curfew and other rules, and to enforce them. He's doing much better.)

Marital problems also enter into the distancing equation. Although the marital decline among teens' parents is part of the normal course of marriage, the adolescent can exacerbate the problem. "Here is a new person challenging you in ways that might make you irritable or insecure," explains Steinberg. "That can spill over into the marriage. The standard scenario involves the adolescent and the mother who have been home squabbling all afternoon. Well, the mom isn't exactly going to be in a terrific mood to greet her husband. It resembles the marital problems that occur when a couple first has a new baby." Trouble is, when the parents' marriage declines, so does the quality of the parenting—at a time when more parental energy is needed.

As if there are not enough psychological forces reducing contact between parents and adolescents today, social trends add to the problem, contends Roland Montemayor. Intensified work schedules, increased divorce and single parenthood, and poverty—often a result of divorce and single parenthood—decrease parent–child contact. A fourth of all teenagers live with one parent, usually their mother. Families have fewer ties to the community, so there are fewer other adults with whom teens have nurturing ties. The negative images of teenagers as violent delinquents may even intimidate parents.

Alone and Angry

Whatever the source, parental distancing doesn't make for happy kids. "The kids I work with at Ohio State are remarkably independent, yet they are resentful of it," says Montemayor. "There is a sense of not being connected somehow." Kids are angry about being left to themselves, being given independence without the kind of mentoring from their parents to learn how to use their independence.

Adult contact seems to be on teenagers' minds more than ever before. Sociologist Dale Blythe, Ph.D., is an adolescence researcher who directs Minneapolis' noted Search Institute, which specializes in studies of youth policy issues. He has surveyed teens in 30 communities across the country, and found that when you ask teens, they say that family is not the most important thing in their lives—peers and social activities are. Nevertheless a large proportion of them say that they want more time with adults—they want their attention and leadership. They want more respect from adults and more cues on how to make it in the adult world. What a shift from 25 years ago, when the watchword was "never trust anyone over 30"!

So it's up to parents to seek more contact with their kids—despite the conflict they'll encounter. "The role of parents is to socialize children, to help them become responsible adults, to teach them to do the right thing. Conflict is an inevitable part of it," says Montemayor. He notes that one of the biggest sources of conflict between parents and teens is time management. Teens have trouble committing to plans in advance. They want to keep their options wide open all the time. The only sure-fire way to reduce conflict is to withdraw from teenagers—an equally surefire way to harm them.

"In other countries parents don't shy away from conflict. In the United States we have this idea that things are going to be hunky-dory and that we are going to go bowling and have fun together. Most people in the world would find that a pretty fanciful idea. There is an inevitable tension between parents and adolescents, and there's nothing wrong with that."

Silenced Sex

Who can talk about teens without talking about sex? The topic of teenage sexuality, however, heightens parents' sense of powerlessness. Adults hesitate to acknowledge their own sexual experience in addressing the issue. They resolve the matter by pretending sex doesn't exist.

Sexuality was conspicuous by its absence in all the family interviews Steinberg, Montemayor, or Larson observed. Calling sex a hidden issue in adolescence verges on an oxymoron. Sprouting pubic hair and expanding busts aren't particularly subtle phenomena. But adolescent sexuality is only heightened by the silence.

A postpubescent child introduces a third sexually mature person into the household, where once sex was a strictly private domain restricted to the older generation. It's difficult for everyone to get used to.

No matter how you slice it, sex can be an awkward topic. For parents, there's not only the feeling of powerlessness, there's discomfort. Most parents of adolescents aren't experiencing much sexual activity—neither the mechanics of sex nor its poetry—in this stage of the marriage (though this eventually improves).

The fact that fathers' marital satisfaction decreases when their kids start to date suggests the power of kids' sexuality, no matter how silenced, to distort parental behavior. Sex and marital therapist David Schnarch, Ph.D., points out that families, and the mythology of the culture, worship teen sexuality, mistakenly believing that adolescence is the peak of human sexuality. Boys have more hard-ons than their dads, while girls have less cellulite than their moms.

These kids may have the biological equipment, says Schnarch, but they don't yet know how to make love. Sex isn't just about orgasms, it is about intimacy. "All of our sex education is designed to raise kids to be healthy, normal adults. But we are confused about what we believe is sexually normal. Textbooks say that boys reach their sexual peak in late adolescence; girls, five to 10 years later. The adolescent believes it, parents believe it, schools believe it. In the hierarchy dictated by this narrow biological model of sexuality, the person with the best sex is the adolescent. On the one hand we are telling kids, 'we would like you to delay sexual involvement.' But when we teach a biological model of sexuality, we imply to the kids 'we know you can't delay. We think these are the best years of your life.'"

Parents can help their children by letting them know that they understand sex and have valuable experience about decisions related to sex; that they know it isn't just a mechanical act; that they recognize that teens are going to figure things out on their own with or without guidance from their parents; and that they are willing to talk about it. But often, the experience or meaning of sex gets lost.

I asked a woman whose parents had handed her birth control pills at age 15 how she felt about it now, at age 30. "1 wish sex had been a little more taboo than it was. I got into a lot more sexual acting out before I was 20, and that didn't go very well for me. Even though my parents talked about the health consequences of sex, they did not mention other consequences. Like what it does to your self-esteem when you get involved in a series of one-night stands. So I guess I wish they had been more holistic in their approach to sex. Not just to tell me about the pill when I was 15, but to understand the different issues I was struggling with. In every other aspect of my life, they were my best resource. But it turns out sex is a lot more complicated than I thought it was when I was 15. At 30, sex is a lot better than it was when I was a teenager."

The distortions parents create about teen sexuality lead directly to events like the "Spur Posse," the gang of teenage football stars in Southern California who systematically harassed and raped girls, terrorizing the community in the late 80s. The boys' fathers actually appeared on talk shows—to brag about their sons' conquests. "The fathers were reinforcing the boys' behavior. It was as if it were a reflection on their own sexuality," observes Schnarch.

By closing their eyes to teen sexual behavior, parents don't just disengage from their kids. They leave them high and dry about understanding anything more than the cold mechanics of sex. Kids raised this way report feeling very alone when it gets down to making intimate decisions for the first time. They feel like they haven't been given any help in what turns out to be the bigger part of sex—the relationship part of it.

Returning to the authoritarian, insular family of Ward, June, Wally, and the Beaver is not the solution for teenagers any more than it is for their parents. But teenagers do need parents and other responsible adults actively involved in their lives, just as younger children do. Only when it comes to teenagers, the grown-ups have to tolerate a lot more ambiguity—about authority, safety, responsibility, and closeness—to sustain the connection. If they can learn to do that, a lot of young people will be able to avoid a whole lot of trouble.

The Invention of Adolescence

Are Romeo and Juliet the quintessential adolescents? On the yes side, they were rebelling against family traditions, in the throes of first love, prone to melodrama, and engaged in violent and risky behavior. But the truth is that there was no such thing as adolescence in Shakespeare's time (the 16th century). Young people the ages of Romeo and Juliet (around 13) were adults in the eyes of society—even though they were probably prepubescent.

Paradoxically, puberty came later in eras past while departure from parental supervision came earlier than it does today. Romeo and Juliet carried the weight of the world on their shoulders—although it was a far smaller world than today's teens inhabit.

Another way to look at it is that in centuries past, a sexually mature person was never treated as a "growing child." Today sexually mature folk spend perhaps six years—ages 12 to 18—living under the authority of their parents.

Since the mid-1800s, puberty—the advent of sexual maturation and the starting point of adolescence—has inched back one year for every 25 years elapsed. It now occurs on average six years earlier than it did in 1850—age 11 or 12 for girls; age 12 or 13 for boys. Today adolescents make up 17 percent of the U.S. population and about a third of them belong to racial or ethnic minorities.

It's still not clear exactly what triggers puberty, confides Jeanne Brooks-Gunn, Ph.D., of Columbia University Teachers College, and expert on adolescent development. "The onset of puberty has fallen probably due to better nutrition in the prenatal period as well as throughout childhood. Pubertal age—for girls, when their first period occurs—has been lower in the affluent than the nonaffluent classes throughout recorded history. Differences are still found in countries where starvation and malnutrition are common among the poor. In Western countries, no social-class differences are found." Although adolescence is a new phenomenon in the history of our species, thanks to a stable and abundant food supply, we've already hit its limits—it's not likely puberty onset will drop much below the age of 12.

If kids look like adults sooner than ever before, that doesn't mean they are. The brain begins to change when the body does, but it doesn't become a grown-up thinking organ as quickly as other systems of the body mature. The clash between physical maturity and mental immaturity not only throws parents a curve—they forget how to do their job, or even what it is—it catapults teens into some silly situations. They become intensely interested in romance, for example, only their idea of romance is absurdly simple, culminating in notes passed across the classroom: "Do you like me? Check yes or no."

Puberty isn't the only marker of adolescence. There's a slowly increasing capacity for abstract reasoning and relative thinking. Their new capacity for abstraction allows teens to think about big things—Death, Destruction, Nuclear War—subjects that depress them, especially since they lack the capacity to ameliorate them.

The idea that everything is relative suddenly makes every rule subject to debate. As time passes, teens attain the ability to make finer abstract distinctions. Which is to say, they become better at choosing their fights.

Teens also move toward autonomy. They want to be alone, they say, because they have a lot on their minds. Yet much of the autonomy hinges on the growing importance of social relationships. Evaluating the ups and downs of social situations indeed requires time alone. Family ties, however, remain more important than you might expect as teens increase identification with their peers.

Whatever else turns teens into the moody creatures they are, hormones have been given far too much credit, contends Brooks-Gunn. In fact, she points out, the flow of hormones that eventually shapes their bodies actually starts around age seven or eight. "Certain emotional states and problems increase between ages 11 and 14, at the time puberty takes place. These changes are probably due to the increased social and school demands, the multiple new events that youth confront, their own responses to puberty, and to a much lesser extent hormonal changes themselves."

The nutritional abundance that underlies a long adolescence also prompted the extension of education, which has created a problem entirely novel in the animal kingdom—physically mature creatures living with their parents, and for more years than sexually mature offspring ever have in the past. College-bound kids typically depend on their parents until at least age 21, a decade or more after hitting puberty.

Historically, children never lived at home during the teen years, points out Temple University's Laurence Steinberg. Either they were shipped out to apprenticeships or off to other relatives.

Among lower primates, physically mature beasts simply are not welcome in the family den; sexual competition makes cohabiting untenable. But for animals, physical maturity coincides with mental acuity, so their departure is not a rejection.

The formal study of adolescence began in the 1940s, just before James Dean changed our perception of it forever. There is a long-standing tradition of professional observers looking at adolescence as a pathology—and this one really did start with Freud. It continues still.

A 1988 study reported that although the under-18 population actually declined from 1980 to 1984, adolescent admissions to private psychiatric hospitals increased 450 percent! The study suggests a staggering cultural taste for applying mental health care to any problem life presents. It also hints at the negative feelings Americans have toward adolescence—we consider it a disease.

The study of adolescence has come with a context—a culture of, by, and for youth, arising in the postwar boom of the 1950s and epitomized by James Dean. Once the original badass depressive teenager from hell, Dean seems quaintly tame by today's standards. But the fear and loathing he set in motion among adults is a powerful legacy today's teens are still struggling to live down.

"A couple of teachers are my heroes. My history teacher is great because he listens to what everybody has to say and never judges."

—Chelsea, 14, Bakersfield, California

"Teenagers say that parents are not understanding and I don't think it is always that way."

—Gabriel, 16, Albuquerque, New Mexico

"Adults want kids to learn to take care of themselves. Kids need guides and advice. That is how you help people mature—not by leaving them alone."

—Michelle, 16, Clackamas, Oregon

"I don't think adults understand how complicated kids' minds are today, how much they think; they don't just accept something but wonder why it is."
—Adam, 14, Bethesda, Maryland

"Teenagers know what is happening around them in school but adults hide things. Parents should shield their kids from some things but not so much that kids are afraid to go out into the world."
—Sarah, 17, Hanover, NH

"I am insecure about my future. The main view toward people in my generation is that we are all slackers and it's kind of disturbing. We are actually trying to make something of ourselves."
—Jasmine, 16, Brooklyn, New York

"I think there is going to be a lot of destruction and violence. There are all these peace treaties, but I don't think they are going to work out."
—Julia, 12, Albuquerque, NM

"The future sounds alright. It is probably going to be more modern and really scientific. Things will be run by computers and computers will do more for people."
—Emily, 13, New York City

"My hero is Queen Latifah. She is herself and doesn't try to be somebody else. My mother is also my hero because she raises me as well as she can and she is a single parent."
—Maria, 15, Bronx, New York

"Jackie Joyner-Kersee, the Olympic track star, is my hero because she has accomplished so much and she is one of the main female athletes."
—Kristy, 13, Woodbridge, New Jersey

"Doing the right thing and being good at what you're doing is important to me. As teenagers we have a lot of things on our back, a lot of people are looking for us to do many great things. We also take in a lot of things and we know a lot of things. I care about the environment because it's a place that we all have to live in, not just us but our families and children. Even though I'm 15, 1 still have to keep those things in mind because it's serious. As for my own future, I've had a good upbringing and I see all open doors."
—Semu, 15, New York City

"I don't feel any pressure about sex. It's a frequent topic of conversation, but we talk about other things, too—when I'm going to get my history paper done, movies, music. I listen to classical music a lot. I think about my maturity a lot, because I've recently had losses in my immediate family and it feels like I am maturing so fast. But then sometimes I feel so young compared to everything out there. I think adults have always felt that teens were more reckless."
—Amanda, 16, New York City

"Adults need to understand that it is very difficult to be a teenager nowadays. It takes a lot of understanding with so many problems like guns, drugs, AIDS, and gangs."
—Melissa, 14, Dallas, Texas

"Teenagers, like adults, are all different. One has a job that is hard, another has more money and more education, and one just gets by. It is unfair to look at an teens the same way. You have maturity in you, but you just don't want to show it because it's no fun. We've got problems, but not really big ones like my uncle who came over from China when he was 16, or going to war when you're 18. If teenagers make it through this era, adults will just bash the next generation of teenagers."
—Mike, 14, Brooklyn, New York

"I think Al Gore is a super environmentalist. With no ozone layer, the world is just going to melt. It's hard not to worry. The environment is really messed up and with no environment there will be no economy, no education, nothing. I hate it when people throw six-pack rings in the lake. We need to think about the environment because we need to get on with the rest of our lives. I don't think adults generally look to kids for opinions."

—Sam, 13, New York

"Many times teenagers are thought of as a problem that no one really wants to deal with. People are sometimes intimidated and become hostile because teenagers are willing to challenge their authority. It is looked at as being disrespectful. Teenagers are, many times, not treated like an asset and as innovative thinkers who will be the leaders of tomorrow. Adults have the power to teach the younger generation about the world and allow them to feel they have a voice in it."

—Zula, 16, Brooklyn, NY

How Advertising Can Use Psychology's Rules of Learning

Steuart Henderson Britt

Most advertising men don't realize it, but their work requires them to use psychological principles of learning. Both advertising men and psychologists want to know more about people's minds.

Every time an advertisement or commercial appears, the objective is to have the reader or viewer *learn* something . . . and *remember* what he learned.

In other words, whether advertising men are aware of it or not, they constantly employ psychological principles. And when psychologists pin down additional facts about learning, they may be making contributions to advertising.

This article presents 20 principles of learning which have been established experimentally by psychologists, and which have practical applications for advertising men. While some of these principles may have been followed by more experienced advertising people, others may be new to them. And all the principles should prove useful to advertising practitioners.

1. Unpleasant things may sometimes be learned as readily as pleasant things, but the most ineffective stimuli are those which arouse little or no emotional response.

The application is that it is better to have rewarding conditions than unpleasant conditions, but either is preferable to learning under neutral conditions. The annoying radio or TV commercial works, but not as well as a message which gives the audience a promise of a rewarding experience.

The closer the actual rewarding experience is to the presentation of the message, the more likely it is to be remembered. Thus, the procedure of giving out samples at the point of purchase is a good one, providing the proper advertising message is used at the time.

2. The capacities of learners are important in determining what can be learned and how long it will take.

The implication of this principle is that *advertisers should know their audience.* Bright people can grasp a complex message that is over the heads of less bright ones. And they grasp the significance of a simple message in less time.

The ability to learn changes with age. For most people, ability to learn reaches a peak around 16 years of age, then begins to decline steadily. Consequently, an advertiser should know his market and be more patient if he is trying to reach an older audience, or one of lower intelligence.

Editor's Note: this article was written in 1955, when few women were employed as advertising managers. Please forgive what today would be considered chauvinistic language.

3. Things that are learned and understood tend to be better retained than things learned by rote.

Mere repetition of ads is of no great value unless the message is understood by the people who see and hear it. It must be remembered, however, that extensive drill is still very important in getting facts across. For example, LS/MFT *can* be put across, but only by an enormous expenditure of money. Experimental evidence indicates that understanding contributes more to remembering than merely frequent repetition.

4. Practice distributed over several periods is more economical in learning than the same amount of practice concentrated into a single period.

In planning a campaign, the prospects should usually be exposed to the advertising over a relatively long period. Brief, concentrated, and temporary high pressure campaigns should be avoided, except in exceptional circumstances, such as making a favorable impression on channels of distribution. Thus, a campaign would probably be more effective if spaced over a period of months rather than concentrated in one week.

5. When teaching people to master mechanical skills, it is better to show the performance in the same way that the learner would see it if he were doing the job himself.

For example, in a TV commercial in which a sequence of acts is being demonstrated which you want the viewers to repeat, it may be better to employ "subjective camera angle," that is, place the camera so it is shooting over the demonstrator's shoulder.

In this way the viewers can see the demonstration in the same way they would see it if they were doing it themselves. This is somewhat comparable to writing copy from the "you" attitude.

6. The order of presentation of materials to be learned is very important.

Points presented at the beginning and end of the message are remembered better than those in the middle. Thus, if 4 reasons "why" are given in a series in copy, the 2 most important points should be given first and last.

7. If material to be learned is different, or unique, it will be better remembered.

An outdoor poster may be better recalled if it stands alone than if it is one of a group. If a magazine contained *nothing but* 4-color advertisments, a black-and-white one might get greater attention value than another color one, just because of the uniqueness. Likewise, a TV or radio commercial employing unusual sounds tends to stand out. The "man in the Hathaway shirt" will be long remembered as the first model who wore an eye patch.

8. Showing errors in how to do something can lead to increases in learning.

The effectiveness of a demonstration on television might be increased by showing not only *"what to do"* but *"what not to do."* Thus, to show how not to use a product and also how to use a product may be very useful. In print advertising, Sanforized has done an outstanding job of showing the shrunken garments that are not Sanforized.

9. Learning situations which are rewarded only occasionally can be more efficient than those where constant reward is employed.

For example, it is more efficient to employ deals or premiums over fairly short periods rather than over extended periods. The reason is that short-time deals are looked upon as some sort of bonus, whereas extended deals come to be expected, and consumers feel cheated if they are cut out. There is likely to be more brand switching away from a product after an extended deal than after a temporary one.

10. It is easier to recognize something than it is to recall it.

The application is obvious. Make the name of your product . . . your package . . . and your sales message easy to recognize. A fine example is the detergent *All* for automatic washing machines. Its distinctive type face stands out in both advertising and packaging.

11. The rate of forgetting tends to be very rapid immediately after learning.

Accordingly, the *continuing repetition of the advertising message is desirable.* It usually takes a lot of advertising in the early weeks of a campaign to overcome rapid forgetting. In fact, it takes a lot of advertising all the time, since the advertising by competitors helps people to forget your product.

12. Messages attributed to persons held in high esteem influence change in opinion more than messages from persons not so well-known, but after several weeks both messages seem equally effective.

The implication for advertising is that it is not essential to employ high-priced, well-known talent in testimonials if you are trying to build a long-range favorable climate for your product. The use of less well-known people should also prove effective and less expensive.

13. Repetition of identical materials is often as effective in getting things remembered as repeating the same story but with variations.

Psychologists term this *identical* vs. *varied* repetition. Using training films, they have failed to find significant differences in learning, after employing a lot of different examples *versus* repeating the same few over again. The implication is that exactly the same advertisements can be run over and over again, with real sales effectiveness each time.

14. In a learning situation, a moderate fear appeal is more effective than a strong fear appeal.

This means that a fear appeal that is too strong is likely to lead to a rejection of the whole sales message.

To take a far-fetched example, it would be poor strategy for a cigarette manufacturer to claim that he now uses treated tobaccos that prevent cancer. The mere association of cancer with smoking may set up a fear that is so strong as to lead to a rejection of the whole sales message.

15. Knowledge of results leads to increases in learning.

If you are interested in teaching a given amount of material to people, knowledge of how well they are doing as they are learning leads to greater learning gains. Advertisers should use this principle, by telling the consumer what specific benefits he will get from the product or service advertised.

16. Learning is aided by active practice rather than passive reception.

This point is of great importance to advertisers. If you can get your audience members to "participate" in your sales message, they are much more likely to remember your brand.

Participation can be accomplished in a number of ways. Get consumers to repeat key phrases, fill in coupons, or even make puns about the brand name. Whatever you do, get the audience to take part in the sales message. Contests with "I like __________ because" tend to put people in a buying mood.

17. A message is more easily learned and accepted if it does not interfere with earlier habits.

Thus, a sales theme which draws upon prior experiences of the audience will help the learning of the sales message. Recent examples are the new uses of aluminum foil, which show how familiar jobs may be done *better* rather than how familiar jobs may be done *differently.*

18. The mere repetition of a situation does not necessarily lead to learning. Two things are necessary—"belongingness," and "satisfiers."

Belongingness means that the elements to be learned must seem to belong together, must show some form of relationship or sequence. As an example, it is easier to learn 2, 4, 6, 8, 10, which seem to belong together, than to learn 2, 1, 4, 7, 43, which do not.

Satisfiers are real or symbolic rewards, as distinguished from annoying consequences that may be present in the learning process. In many learning experiments, it has been demonstrated that merely to say the word "right" when the person is making the correct response is a satisfier and helps to speed up the learning process. To say the word "wrong" is an annoyer or "punishment" and is relatively less effective.

Because of the importance of belongingness and of satisfiers, a good deal of advertising could gain in effectiveness if more attention were paid to the organic unity of the total advertising message (belongingness), and also the element of reward or consumer benefits (satisfiers).

19. When two ideas are of equal strength but of unequal age, new repetition increases the strength of the earlier idea more than that of the newer idea.

By the same token, if there are two ideas of the same strength but of unequal age, the older idea will not be forgotten as rapidly as the newer idea.

The application to various brands of merchandise is obvious. For instance, if there are two different brands—one older and one newer—which have equal association with a product, and if both brands are given the same amount of advertising, the older brand will probably benefit more from the advertising than the newer brand. Similarly, the older brand will not be forgotten to as great an extent as the newer brand.

20. Learning something new can interfere with the remembering of something learned earlier.

Psychologists refer to this as retroactive inhibition. As a hypothetical case, if you study French for an hour and then study Italian for an hour, your ability to recall the French will probably be less than it would have been had you substituted an hour's interval of rest in place of the hour's study of Italian.

There are many applications of the principles of retroactive inhibition to advertising. Suppose that a person has been looking at a one-hour television show, sponsored by just one advertiser. He is much more likely to remember that sponsor and his advertising message than in the situation where there is multiple sponsorship. The later commercial or commercials tend to interfere with the remembrance of the earlier commercial. The more similar the later commercials are to the earlier ones, the greater is the interference. That is why it is poor practice to have similar products advertised on shows which are too close together.

We should not just blindly apply every one of these principles to the field of advertising. However, we can point out certain applications that these principles suggest to the advertising practitioner.

After all, individuals exposed to advertising and people used in learning experiments are much the same kind of people; and all are reacting to materials that someone wants them to learn.

Beating Depression

Erica E. Goode

with Nancy Linnon and Sarah Burke

It is as if the person Dr. Peter Kent used to be is now buried somewhere inside this man who cannot summon the energy to get out of bed, who lies for hours staring blankly, sighing, his thoughts traveling in bleak circles. Kent's colleagues at the hospital have been told by his secretary that the 41-year-old cardiologist is on "personal leave," nothing more. They have not been told about the psychiatric ward that resembles an exclusive college dormitory, about the faint institutional smell, Monet's vision of Giverny on the wall, the living room where patients play pool or sit smoking cigarettes. They do not know that Kent is, for the moment, spending his afternoons in group therapy and watching the "Oprah Winfrey Show."

Kent's secretary is protecting him from what people—his patients, other doctors, the public—might think. It is very hush-hush, his illness. Indeed, this magazine is protecting him, too. We have changed his name in order to write about him, creating a new identity for this altered, sluggish self, the ailing Dr. Kent who finds it painfully difficult to string words into a sentence, who yawns every few minutes and shifts his gaze away, up to the ceiling, over to the daffodils on the table. "It's like being in quicksand," he says. "There's a sense of doom, of sadness."

The need for secrecy is troubling. Kent has not embezzled money, cheated on his income tax or seduced 16-year-old girls. He is not a bad person; on the contrary, his gentleness and quiet concern must be reassuring to patients who are recovering from heart attacks or facing bypass surgery. He is guilty only of having fallen victim to an illness that, because it affects the mind and the personality, is still tinged with shame, as if to suffer from it were somehow an admission of poor character, or weak will.

Though it is more common than diabetes, serious depression—the kind that can lead to suicide or land one in a mental hospital—remains an issue that can unhorse presidential candidates or bind a family in embarrassed silence. There are signs, however, that this view is shifting, that science is at last making headway against fear. Those who have sampled depression's dark offerings are speaking out, describing both the depth and harrowing intensity of their ordeal. Some of their faces are familiar: An actress, a prominent attorney, a talk-show host, a businesswoman. Most recently, author William Styron, writing in *Vanity Fair,* has described his own plunge into despondency, "a veritable howling tempest in the brain," that nearly cost him his life. With each declaration the curtain is drawn back a little further, a kind of mental *glasnost* reminiscent of the thaw that followed Betty Ford's public discussion of her struggle with breast cancer.

There are wider reflections of the changing climate. Large corporations, once oblivious to the impact of psychological factors, are beginning to pay more attention to their employees' state of mind, realizing that mental well-being is essential for high productivity and lower medical costs. They have reason for concern: A recent study by the Rand Corporation found that depression can be as disabling as coronary-artery disease or arthritis, with depressed individuals spending more days in bed than those with chronic lung or gastrointestinal problems. And, perhaps sensing growing interest in the subject, the media, too, have become expansive when it comes to mental illness. Public television this winter launched a new series, "Moods & Music," spotlighting the link between creativity and mood disorders (see page 50). Says Dr. Robert Hirschfeld, chief of the Mood, Anxiety, and Personality Disorders Research Branch of the National Institute of Mental Health (NIMH): "People are now recognizing depression as an illness and not a character flaw."

1 in 12 Americans

In part, this new-fledged openness rests upon an expanding body of research that in the last three decades has given scientists a much greater understanding of mood disorders—illnesses that will afflict more than 20 million Americans at some point in their lifetime. The treatment of depression and manic depression is "psychiatry's No. 1 success story," says Dr. Frederick Goodwin, administrator of the U.S. Alcohol, Drug Abuse and Mental Health Administration and co-author of *Manic Depressive Illness,* to be published by Oxford University Press this spring.

A new generation of drugs allows a sophistication and flexibility in treatment that was not possible in the past. One such antidepressant, Anafranil, also used to treat obsessive-compulsive disorder, won final approval from the Food and Drug Administration last month. Other medications are in the pipeline. For the first time, studies are also beginning to reveal how and where psychoactive drugs exert their action on the brain. Further, scientists have taken the initial steps toward solving the difficult problem of which pharmacological treatments work most reliably for different manifestations of the illness. Experts know more, too, about the types of psychotherapy best suited to defeating the feelings of hopelessness and paralysis that infuse the depressive state.

By far the most powerful lever for changing public attitudes comes from the growing body of work that establishes depression as a disease that is biologically based, at least in its most disabling forms. Both severe depression and manic depression involve dramatic physiological changes, and the evidence points to a hereditary vulnerability that is then triggered by environmental stress. Using high-tech scanners, chemical probes and genetic mapping techniques—the newest tools of a rapidly developing science—researchers are starting to fill in the unknowns of an immensely complicated equation, one capable of leaving the brain, as Lord Byron imagined it in *Childe Harold,* "In its own eddy boiling and o'erwrought, A whirling gulf of phantasy and flame."

Mood disorders take many forms, and researchers historically have been hard pressed to draw iron-clad distinctions among types, or even to differentiate reliably between "normal" dips in mood and the psychic transformation that constitutes depressive illness. Confusing the issue further is the colloquial use of the word *depression* to describe a range of unpleasant, but inevitable, consequences of living. One is "depressed" after a bad day at the office, or the breakup of a love relationship.

Clinical depression is at once more intense and longer lasting than the brooding funks that seize everyone from time to time. Of patients hospitalized for depression, 40 to 60 percent suffer from the disease in its classical form, once referred to as "melancholia." Submerged in recrimination and self-doubt, these patients lose their appetite, suffer an array of bodily aches, show little interest in sex and awaken in the early-morning hours. They may pace the floor in agitation, or their speech and movement may be drastically slowed, almost as if they had suddenly developed a peculiar and sudden form of brain damage. Yet this facade of lethargy is deceptive. In fact, says Dr. Philip Gold, chief of the NIMH Clinical Neuroendocrinology Branch, severe depression may be a state of hypervigilance and intense arousal: "Such patients are so overwhelmed and overstimulated," says Gold, "that they just kind of sit still."

Winter's Discontent

Less common than melancholia is a pattern in which the symptoms are reversed. Patients eat more than usual and sleep for long hours, only reluctantly emerging into wakefulness. In recent years, more and more patients have also been reporting to clinics with still other forms of depression that researchers are only beginning to categorize. In seasonal affective disorder (SAD), despair sets in with the disappearance of the lingering daylight hours of summer and persists for as long as short days and the cold winter sun remain. As spring returns, however, patients with SAD feel their energy return. Their desolation lifts, and their lives return to normal. "Dysthymia," on the other hand, is a chronic, if milder, form of depression that can last for months or even years. Researchers estimate that nearly 9 million Americans are locked in dysthymia's dispiriting grip. "It's like a low-grade infection," says Virginia Commonwealth University clinical psychologist James McCullough. "Dysthymics never really feel good."

At the most extreme end of the spectrum, a depressed patient can cross the border into psychosis. "I heard a voice, a male voice; it was the voice of death," says a 31-year-old entertainer, hospitalized for severe depression after she told friends she was afraid she might hurt herself or someone else. "The voice said, 'Hey, kiddo, you know I'm waiting right on the horizon for you.' It was telling me how my body was going to die, trying to catch me off guard. 'Jump in front of that car,' it told me."

Mania shares this departure from reality. Possessed of limitless energy, thoughts racing, manic-depressive patients in the elated phase of the illness may stay up all night, insist they are in touch with creatures from outer space, become uncharacteristically promiscuous or run up thousands of dollars in credit-card bills. One woman, a West Coast business executive, packed her briefcase, put on her best tailored suit and flew to Washington, D.C. Her mission: To convince the Federal Bureau of Investigation that a dangerous conspiracy threatened national security. The FBI agents were perplexed. Should they heed the woman's conservative attire and articulate manner or their hunch that something about her tale was not quite right?

The demographics of depression have changed dramatically in the last half-century. Cornell University psychiatrist Gerald Klerman and Columbia University epidemiologist Myrna Weissman, reviewing studies tracking fluctuating patterns of illness in 10 countries, have found that in developed nations, including the U.S., rates of depression increased markedly for postwar baby-boomers—those born in the period between 1945 and 1955—with the incidence peaking between 1975 and 1980. This upward trend seems to have been only temporary, however. Klerman's newest data, still unpublished, suggest that as the baby-boom generation turns 40, "the turmoil is subsiding," the curve sloping downward again. Suicides also declined in the '80s for baby-boomers, Klerman says, and rates of depression for those born in succeeding decades show a similar downward trend.

A Host of Theories

What accounts for these shifts? Researchers can only speculate. Fiercer competition in the labor force during the 1960s and '70s, a greater gap between expectations and fulfillment than in previous generations, increased drug use and greater mobility all have been proposed as possible reasons for the increases in the 1970s. Some even suggest that a change in biological factors is at work, but conclusive evidence for any of these theories is not yet in hand. Nor can experts at present convincingly account for changes in the male-to-female ratio among depressed patients. Women with "unipolar" depression—that is, without manic swings—have traditionally outnumbered men 3 to 1. But Weissman has found indications that men are catching up, with women now diagnosed with the illness at rates only twice those of men.

I should have done things differently.

This is one of the thoughts that Peter Kent cannot stop thinking as he eats chicken teriyaki for lunch in the psychiatric ward's dining room, or walks down the long, gray-carpeted hallway. He has a mental image of himself talking on the telephone, listening to his fiancée tell him it is over. He can see himself calling a few weeks later, hearing the metallic whir of her answering machine, her voice saying (impossibly, astoundingly), "You have reached the residence of Mr. and Mrs. . . ."

There were other things—events that, though he did not know it at the time, were leading him toward this spinning descent. Problems in his medical practice. Arguments with a friend. Indeed, there is the matter of his illness seven years ago, an episode of mania that lasted for several weeks, causing him to believe that a stranger was, in fact, his father in disguise. Yet none of these things is, in itself, an explanation, a solution to the riddle of "Why here, why now?"

Tracing the origins of mood disorders, illnesses that affect not only behavior and physiology but our very sense of ourselves, is a formidable task. For mind and body are inextricably joined, and everything we imagine, dream, experience or fear is ultimately translated into the firing of nerve cells and the ebb and flow of chemicals in the brain. How do we sort out the events that began internally, in a strip of DNA or a malfunctioning neuron, from those that have their roots in external events: A broken love affair, the death of a friend, the loss of a job? It is with this conundrum that scientists who would understand mental illness struggle. The answers that emerge are always somewhat murky, always two-sided, always a compromise of nature and nurture—which, after all, work hand in hand.

Melancholy's Creative Side

"As an experience, madness is terrific I can assure you, and not to be sniffed at," British novelist Virginia Woolf once wrote in a letter to a composer friend. Woolf, author of *To The Lighthouse* and *Orlando,* among other works, careened from feverish periods of writing to weeks immersed in bottomless gloom, according to the memoirs of her husband Leonard Woolf.

Neither the novelist's mood swings nor the conviction that her work was enhanced by them is unusual in creative individuals. Indeed, mood disorders seem to have a predilection for artistic victims, and the list of painters, composers and writers who suffered from depression—or, even more commonly, manic depression—is a long one. "Creativity involves making associations between unrelated ideas," says Kay Jamison, associate professor of psychiatry at Johns Hopkins University School of Medicine and executive producer of the PBS series "Moods & Music." "In a slightly manic phase, you can link things that before were just isolated ideas."

George Frideric Handel, who scholars believe may have been manic depressive, composed his "Messiah," a work that takes almost 4 hours to perform, in a mere three weeks—presumably riding on the frenetic high of his illness. Gustav Mahler, in a letter to a friend, described with uncanny precision a type of "rapid cycling" manic depression in which moods shift precipitously, sometimes within weeks or even days. "The fires of a supreme zest for living and the most gnawing desire for death alternate in my heart, sometimes in the course of a single hour," Mahler wrote.

Poets Anne Sexton and Robert Lowell, Vincent van Gogh and photographer Diane Arbus all fought the demons of mental disintegration, and all managed to turn the battle to their creative advantage. Far too often, however, artists also pay with their lives, choosing suicide as a balm for their psychic wounds.

The link between creativity and mood disorders is validated by research. Harvard University researchers Dr. Ruth Richards and Dennis Kinney gave creativity tests to 33 Danish patients diagnosed with manic depression or a milder form of the illness. The same tests were given to heir relatives. The scientists found that both patients and relatives scored higher than normal subjects. Similarly, in a study of creative writers enrolled in the prestigious University of Iowa Writers' Workshop, psychiatrist Nancy Andreasen discovered that 80 percent of the writers had suffered at least one episode of depression or mania in their lifetime, compared with 30 percent in a control group of lawyers, hospital administrators and social workers. The writers also showed a significantly higher incidence of alcoholism than the other subjects. It is possible, suggests Andreasen, that the sensitivity, openness, adventuresome nature and independent character of creative individuals in some way makes them more vulnerable to mental illness, in particular mood disorders.

Tailoring Treatment for Depression's Many Forms

Drugs and psychotherapy are targeting specific symptoms

A hot bath or some friendly encouragement may be all it takes to banish a normal case of the blues. But the "black dog" of depression, as Winston Churchill once described it, does not respond to jollying, distraction, or well-meaning exhortation. A depressed person cannot merely "cheer up" or "snap out of it." Yet depressive illnesses are eminently treatable, and with expert assistance—including medication, psychotherapy and in some cases hospitalization—up to 80 percent of patients can get better.

Antidepressant drugs form a cornerstone of therapy for mood disorders because they work relatively quickly (most show their effects in two to three weeks) and often produce dramatic results in launching patients on their way back to health. Today, doctors have a wider range of drugs to choose from than in the past. More than 20 antidepressants are available by prescription, and new drugs, with fewer side effects and more-specific action, are being tested in the laboratory. Perhaps just as important, professionals are noticing a change in patients' attitudes toward mood-elevating drugs. Says Dr. Daniel X. Freedman, Judson Braun Professor of Psychiatry at the University of California at Los Angeles: "You see fewer patients who pit themselves against the medicine, as if their integrity or ability to exercise willpower were at issue."

Chemistry of mood. Antidepressants work by altering the levels of brain chemicals, and different drugs target different substances when they first enter the brain. Scientists are finding that these highly specific effects make some classes of drugs more helpful than others in treating various types of depression. The so-called tricyclic antidepressants, for example, appear more effective in combatting the disturbed sleep patterns, apathy and appetite loss of melancholic depression. Another group of drugs, the "monoamine oxidase inhibitors," seem to work well for patients suffering from "atypical depression," that is, eating and sleeping more than usual, rather than less.

Of particular interest to psychiatrists are two drugs that recently entered the market. Prozac and Anafranil both act principally to increase brain levels of serotonin, a neurotransmitter that scientists believe plays a role in some forms of depression. Anafranil just received approval by the Food and Drug Administration in January and is expected to be available in pharmacies this month. Prozac, approved in 1987, has fewer side effects than most antidepressants, is energizing rather than sedating and has proved much less toxic in overdoses—a boon since antidepressants are often used in suicide attempts. A third drug, Wellbutrin, has a unique chemical structure and also produces fewer side effects than most mood-elevating medications.

For some years, the gold standard in treatment for mania's frenetic highs has been lithium carbonate, a salt that was in use as a therapy for gout in the 1950s when an Australian researcher noticed its quieting effects. Lithium works well for about 70 percent of patients in the manic phase of "bipolar" disorder, and can act as an antidepressant as well. Now, however, two antiseizure drugs—carbamazepine and valproic acid—also provide relief for some manic patients when lithium doesn't, and they can be combined with lithium for greater effect. Says Dr. Victor Reus, professor of psychiatry at the University of California at San Francisco: "We are clearly much more sophisticated in the recognition and treatment of bipolar depression than we were even five years ago."

Yet as effective as they are, psychiatric drugs are far from perfect. All have side effects, most commonly annoyances such as dry mouth and constipation, but in rare cases there can be more serious consequences. Nor does medication work for everyone. Some people don't respond to drugs; others find side effects intolerable. Experts caution that once you find a drug that works, it's important to stay on it long enough. Dr. David Kupfer, of Western Psychiatric Institute in Pittsburgh, recommends taking an antidepressant for at least four months after the major symptoms of depression disappear. Studies show that this decreases the chance of falling ill again.

When drugs aren't right. Sometimes using any drug is too risky. Elderly patients often react unpredictably to medicine, for example, and sometimes the risk of suicide precludes waiting the weeks needed for a given drug to take effect. In these cases, psychiatrists may turn to electroconvulsive therapy (ECT), a technique still recovering from the dubious reputation it acquired in the 1960s. ECT has been refined in recent years, and generally works quickly. Like drugs, however, it can have side effects: Patients may suffer memory loss and confusion right after treatment, and there are reports of longer-term memory problems.

Other innovative treatment methods for specific forms of depression have sprung up in recent years. In light therapy, for example, patients sit for a few hours each day in front of very bright, full-spectrum lights, a tactic found effective for sufferers of seasonal affective disorder.

Though medication plays an important role in treating severe depression, few experts would argue that it is, by itself, sufficient. Indeed, some types of moderate or mild depression may respond to talking therapy alone. The consensus is, however, that in most serious cases drugs and psychotherapy complement each other and are best used jointly. A recent National Institute of Mental Health study demonstrated that two forms of short-term psychotherapy—cognitive therapy, which helps change negative patterns of thinking, and interpersonal therapy, which addresses problems in personal relationships—are effective even in treating severe depression. They work more slowly than a standard antidepressant, however. Other kinds of brief therapy, including those that draw their guiding principles from psychoanalysis, may also succeed, but they have not yet undergone as much rigorous study. Ultimately, Dr. T. Byram Karasu suggests in this month's *American Journal of Psychiatry*, research on talking therapies may reveal that each has specific strengths, allowing therapists to pick and choose, tailoring psychotherapy to an individual patient's needs.

Yet there are some certainties. Researchers now know, for example, that certain forms of mood disorder—specifically manic depression and severe, recurrent, unipolar depression—run in families. This fact is demonstrated by dozens of research projects, including a 1986 study that examined the family pedigrees of depressed adults adopted as children and found an increase, incidence of mood disorders in biological, as opposed to adoptive, relatives. As Columbia University's Weissman puts it: "Depression is a family affair."

Both depression and mania are also accompanied by changes in brain chemistry, though these changes are not fully understood. In the early days of research, scientists thought in terms of relatively simple models of chemical imbalance: Depression, for example, was thought to stem from an insufficiency of norepinephrine, one of many substances mediating the transmission of nerve impulses in the brain. Now, few experts talk about "too much" or "too little" of a single chemical. Instead, they believe mood disorders are the result of a complex interplay among a variety of chemicals, including neurotransmitters and hormones.

Genetic Legacy

How much of this is influenced by heredity? The consensus is that genetic factors are at work, and in the last few years, laboratories all over the world have set out to track down the gene, or multiple genes acting in concert, that predispose an individual to depression or manic depression. This search has proceeded in fits and starts. Discoveries are announced, only to be called into question when other scientists fail to duplicate the findings. Most recently, the highly publicized results of a 1987 study of manic depression in the Amish—results that seemed to locate the gene for the illness on the short arm of chromosome 11—fell through when a research team re-analyzed the Amish pedigree, adding new subjects.

The team, which included some of the original researchers, concluded in an article published in *Nature* last November that while the evidence for a genetic marker in the Amish is still strong, the chances are slim that it is on chromosome 11. Another study, this one of an Israeli family, linked the gene for manic depression to the X chromosome. But so far, attempts to replicate this association have also been unsuccessful. Nonetheless, few researchers doubt that genetic studies will eventually yield results.

Even when they do, however, heredity will not tell the whole story. Depression and manic depression appear to be triggered by stress. And in some milder forms of mood disorder, experience—rather than genetics—may play the starring role. Traumatic events clearly are capable of precipitating changes in mood and behavior. In particular, scientists consistently find that being the child of a depressed parent may double or even triple the risk of depression in later life. Parents who suffer from depressive illnesses, these studies indicate, are more likely to be withdrawn, critical, inconsistent and irritable in child-rearing. Their own pain, expressed in this way, may thus become a burden for their offspring. According to a new report published last month, some children in this difficult atmosphere develop intense, exaggerated feelings of guilt—states of mind that then pave the way for depression and other emotional problems.

Losses in Childhood

Perhaps most devastating is the loss of a parent in childhood, either through death or abandonment. The evidence suggests, according to British psychoanalyst John Bowlby, that those who have lost a parent, especially the mother, are more likely to develop serious psychiatric problems and, more specifically, to become psychotically depressed and suicidal. Work by University of London researchers George Brown and Tirril Harris demonstrates that women who lose their mothers before the age of 17 are significantly more prone to depression as adults. The crucial factor, Brown and Harris say, is how the father, or parental surrogate, provides for the child: "Inadequate care . . . roughly doubled the risk of depression in adulthood."

Any true understanding of mood disorders must take into account this intricate interplay between psychology and biology. NIMH psychiatrist Dr. Robert Post and others have done just that in the theory of "kindling," an attempt to explain the fact that episodes of mania and depression appear initially in response to some external stress, but later seem to acquire a momentum of their own. Repeated low-level stresses, Post suggests, might build up until they trigger a manic swing in mood, much as experimenters can "kindle" seizures in the brain by delivering low-level electrical shocks to cells deep in its interior. Or conversely, the brain may become progressively "sensitized" to the effect of environmental stress. Eventually, bouts of illness may occur with no help from outside events.

Such analogies are approximations, hypothetical road maps for an as yet uncharted territory. Yet those who suffer in depression's depths or negotiate mania's precarious heights may count themselves fortunate. Emerging from their illness is not dependent upon perfect scientific knowledge, and tools for treatment are already in hand.

What will happen when he goes home?

Peter Kent's psychiatrist at the hospital asks him this. The nurses who monitor his mood, who cajole and counsel him, who keep track of how much he eats and whether he wakes up at night, ask him this as well. His chances of full recovery are good, but not assured. Perhaps 30 percent of severely depressed patients "get better on antidepressants but do not get completely well," says Dr. Jan Fawcett, chairman of psychiatry at Rush Presbyterian–St. Luke's Medical Center in Chicago.

Leaving the hospital, Kent will rest for a while, filling his time with volunteer work before returning to his medical practice. In part, how the cardiologist fares will be determined by other people. His colleagues. His friends. Can they accept a doctor who has become a patient? He has his doubts: "They would look at it negatively," he says. "It's best if they don't find out." Yet it is possible, though far from certain, that Kent is mistaken and that he will find good will where he expects ostracism or disdain. It is possible that the time for secrecy is nearly over, that what Styron has called "Darkness Visible" is, at last, an illness like any other.

Resources and Information on Depression

Help is readily available for the millions who suffer

The Warning Signs of Depression:

- Persistent sad, anxious or empty mood
- Feeling hopeless or worthless
- Loss of interest or pleasure in activities, including sex
- Sleep disturbances (early-morning waking or oversleeping)
- Decreased appetite, losing weight or eating more than usual
- Recurrent thoughts of death or suicide
- Difficulty concentrating, remembering, making decisions
- Irritability, excessive crying
- Physical symptoms such as headaches, digestive disorders, nausea or chronic pain

The Warning Signs of Mania:

- Increased energy and decreased need for sleep
- Unrealistic or exaggerated beliefs in abilities
- Inappropriate elation
- Increased talking, moving and sexual activity
- Racing thoughts
- Impulsive behavior without regard to consequences

Where to Go for Help:

- See your family doctor to rule out other illnesses
- Medical-school psychiatry department
- Community mental-health center
- Local mental-health association

The National Alliance for the Mentally Ill (NAMI)
P.O. Box NAMI-Depression
Arlington, Va. 22216

DEPRESSION/Awareness, Recognition, Treatment (D/ART)
National Institute of Mental Health
Rockville, Md. 20857

National Depressive and Manic Depressive Association
53 West Jackson Blvd.
Box USN
Chicago, Ill. 60604

National Mental Health Association
Information Center
1021 Prince Street
Alexandria, Va. 22314

The National Foundation for Depressive Illness
P.O. Box 2257
New York, N.Y. 10116
Include $5 and a self-addressed, stamped envelope for literature

American Psychiatric Association
1400 K Street, N.W.
Suite 501—Dept. USN
Washington, D.C. 20005
Include a self-addressed, stamped envelope for literature

National Association for Research on Schizophrenia and Depression
60 Cutter Mill Road, Suite 200
Great Neck, N.Y. 11021

Books

Depression and Its Treatment: Help for the Nation's #1 Mental Problem, by John H. Greist, M.D., and James W. Jefferson, M.D. (American Psychiatric Press, Washington, D.C., 1984; $7.95).

Overcoming Depression, by Demitri F. Papolos, M.D.. and Janice Papolos (Harper & Row, New York, 1987; $9.95).

Control Your Depression, by Peter M. Lewinsohn et al. (Prentice Hall Press, New York, 1986; $9.95).

Feeling Good: The New Mood Therapy, by David D. Burns, M.D. (New American Library, New York, 1980; $4.95)

Do You Have a Depressive Illness? by Donald F. Klein, M.D., and Paul H. Wender, M.D. (New American Library, New York, 1988; $7.95).

Is Your Child Depressed? by Joel Herskowitz, M.D. (Pharos Books, New York, 1988; $14.95).

The Crime of Commitment: Do We Banish Them to Bedlam for Society's Convenience?

Thomas Szasz

Physicians and laymen alike generally believe persons are involuntarily confined in mental hospitals because they are mentally ill, but don't know they are sick and need medical treatment. This view, to put it charitably, is nonsense. In my opinion, mental illness is a myth. People we label "mentally ill" are not sick, and involuntary mental hospitalization is not treatment. It is punishment.

Involuntary confinement for "mental illness" is a deprivation of liberty that violates basic human rights, as well as the moral principles of the Declaration of Independence and the U.S. Constitution. In short, I consider commitment a crime against humanity.

Any psychiatrist who accepts as his client a person who does not wish to be his client, who defines him as "mentally ill," who then incarcerates his client in an institution, who bars his client's escape from the institution and from the role of mental patient, and who proceeds to "treat" him against his will—such a psychiatrist, I maintain, creates "mental illness" and "mental patients." He does so in exactly the same way as the white man created slavery by capturing the black man, bringing him to America in shackles, and then selling and using the black man as if he were an animal.

To understand the injustice of commitment it is necessary to distinguish between *disease* as a *biological condition* and the *sick role* as a *social status.* Though a simple one, this distinction is rarely made in articles on mental illness, and there is a good reason for this. For once this distinction is made, psychiatry ceases to be what it is officially proclaimed, namely a medical specialty, and becomes, instead, social engineering.

Strictly speaking, *illness* is a biological (physicochemical) abnormality of the body or its functioning. A person is sick if he has diabetes, a stroke, or cancer.

The *sick role,* on the other hand, refers to the social status of claiming illness or assuming the role of patient. Like husband, father or citizen, the *sick role* denotes a certain relationship to others in the society.

A person may be ill, but may prefer not to assume the sick role, as when we have a severe cold but go about our business. Conversely, a person may be healthy, but choose to assume the sick role, as when we feel perfectly well but offer illness as an excuse for avoiding an obligation to go to the office or a party. Soldiers often assume the sick role—called "malingering"—to avoid the dangers of combat.

Where does the distinction between illness and sick role leave the alleged mental patient? He is said to be "very sick" by his relatives and the psychiatrists retained by them, but the patient maintains he is perfectly well and rejects medical or psychiatric help. Society then uses the police power of the state to force such a person into the sick role: this is done by calling the person a "mental patient," by incarcerating him in a "mental hospital" and by "treating" him for his "mental illness" whether he likes it or not. The underlying issue, however, is whether or not an individual has the right to refuse to be cast into the role of mental patient.

To answer this question, it is necessary to consider the problem of what mental illness is. Mental illness is not a physicochemical abnormality of the body, that is, an organic illness. If it were, we would simply call it illness and have no need for the qualifying adjective "mental." Actually, what we call "functional" mental diseases are not diseases at all. Persons said to be suffering from such disorders are socially deviant or inept, or in conflict with individuals, groups or institutions.

Not only does mental illness differ fundamentally from physical illness, but mental hospitalization differs from medical hospitalization. Mental hospitalization is typically involuntary, whereas medical hospitalization is typically voluntary. In a free society, a person can't be committed and treated against his will for cancer or heart diseases, but he can be committed for depression or schizophrenia.

Should future research establish that certain so-called functional mental illnesses are actual physical disorders, they would then be treated like other organic disorders and the question of involuntary hospitalization for them would become irrelevant.

If schizophrenia, for example, turns out to have a biochemical cause and cure, schizophrenia would no longer be one of the diseases for which a person would be involuntarily committed. Pellagra once sent many persons to mental hospitals with symptoms resembling schizophrenia until a vitamin deficiency was found to cause pellagra.

A person is said to be mentally ill if he behaves in certain "abnormal" ways. Since what is abnormal to one person is normal to another, mental illness is a kind of loose-fitting, quasi-medical synonym for bad or undesirable behavior. To a Christian Scientist, going to a doctor is abnormal. To a hypochondriac, *not* going is. To a Roman Catholic, using artificial birth control is abnormal. To a non-Catholic eager to avoid pregnancy, *not* using it is abnormal. The fact that mental illness designates a deviation from an ethical rule of conduct, and that such rules vary widely, explains why upper-middle-class psychiatrists can so easily find evidence of "mental illness" in lower-class individuals; and why so many prominent persons in the past 50 years or so have been diagnosed by their enemies as suffering from some type of insanity. Barry Goldwater was called a "paranoid schizophrenic"; Whittaker Chambers, a "psychopathic personality"; Woodrow Wilson, a "neurotic," frequently "very close to psychosis" (by no less a psychiatrist than Sigmund Freud!). Jesus himself, according to two psychiatrists quoted by Dr. Albert Schweitzer in his doctoral thesis, was a "born degenerate" with a "fixed delusional system"; manifesting a "paranoid clinical picture [so typical] it is hardly conceivable people can even question the accuracy of the diagnosis."

My argument that commitment is a crime against humanity is opposed on the grounds that commitment is necessary for the protection of the healthy members of society. To be sure, commitment does protect the community from certain threats. But the question should not be *whether* the community is protected, but precisely *from what,* and *how.*

Commitment shields nonhospitalized members of society from having to accommodate to the annoying or idiosyncratic demands of persons who have *not* violated any criminal statutes. The commitment procedure has already been used against General Edwin Walker and Ezra Pound. Conceivably it could be used against a Stokely Carmichael or an Eldridge Cleaver.

But what about those persons who are actually violent? Society could, if it were willing, protect itself from violence and threats of violence through our system of criminal laws, which provides for the imprisonment of violators in correctional institutions.

What about so-called emotionally disturbed persons who have not violated any statute but are believed to be violence-prone? Everything possible should be done to give them help, but is it just to hospitalize or treat them involuntarily for being "potentially dangerous"?

To be judged potentially violent, a patient must be interviewed by a psychiatrist, which in effect violates the patient's right under the Fifth Amendment to refuse to incriminate himself. Few "mental patients" receive legal advice prior to being committed, but if they refused to be seen or interviewed by a physician, commitment would be impossible.

Psychiatrists cannot predict whether a person will be violent. Many "mental patients" who lose their liberty never have been and never will be violent.

Being "potentially dangerous" is not a crime. Most of us equate emotional disturbance with being violence-prone. Studies show, however, that "mental" patients are no more violence-prone than "normals."

To further clarify the political dimensions and implications of commitment practices, let us note some of the fundamental parallels between master and slave on the one hand and the institutional psychiatrist and involuntarily hospitalized mental patient on the other. In each instance the former member of the pair defines the social role of the latter, and casts the latter in that role by force. The committed patient must accept the view that he is "sick," that his captors are "well," that the patient's own view of himself is false and his captors' view of him is true, and that to effect any change in his social situation, the patient must relinquish his "sick" views and adopt the "healthy" views of those who have power over him. By accepting himself as "sick" and the institutional environment and the various manipulations imposed by the staff as "treatment," the patient is compelled to authenticate the psychiatrist's role as that of benevolent physician curing mental illness. The patient who maintains the forbidden image of reality—that the psychiatrist is a jailer—is considered paranoid. Since most patients (like oppressed people generally) eventually accept the ideas imposed on them by their superiors, hospital psychiatrists are constantly immersed in an environment in which their identity as "doctor" is affirmed. The moral superiority of white men over black was similarly authenticated and affirmed.

Suppose a person wishes to study slavery. He might start by studying slaves—and he would then find that slaves are, in general, brutish, poor and uneducated. The student of slavery might then conclude that slavery is the slave's natural or appropriate social state. Such, indeed, have been the methods and conclusions of innumerable men through the ages. For example, Aristotle held that slaves were naturally inferior and hence justly subdued.

Another student, biased by contempt for slavery, might proceed differently. He would maintain there can be no slave without master holding the slave in bondage. This student would accordingly consider slavery a type of human relationship, a social institution, supported by custom, law, religion and force. From this perspective, the study of masters is at least as relevant to the study of slavery as is the study of slaves. I hold that the study of institutional psychiatrists is as relevant to the study of involuntary hospitalization as is the study of mental patients.

Mental illness has been investigated for centuries, and continues to be investigated today, in much the same way slaves were studied in the antebellum South and before. Men took for granted the existence of slaves. Scientists duly noted and classified the biological and social characteristics of the slaves. In the same way, we take for granted the existence of mental patients. Indeed, many Americans believe the number of such patients is steadily increasing. And it is generally believed that the psychiatrist's task is to observe and classify the biological, psychological and social characteristics of mental patients.

The defenders of slavery claimed the Negro was happier as a slave than as a free man because of the "peculiarities of his character." As historian S. M. Elkins has said, "The failure of any free workers to present themselves for enslavement can serve as one test of how much the analysis of the happy slave may have added to Americans' understanding of themselves." The failure of most persons with so-called mental illness to present themselves for hospitalization is a test of how much current analysis of mental health problems may have added to our understanding of ourselves.

Today, of course, involuntary mental hospitalization is a universally accepted method of social control, much as slavery was in the past. Our unwillingness to look searchingly at this problem may be compared to the unwillingness of the South to look at slavery. "A democratic people," wrote Elkins, "no longer reasons with itself when it is all of the same mind." Today the Supreme Court of Iowa can say: "Such loss of liberty [as is entailed in commitment of the insane] is not such liberty as is within the meaning of the constitutional provision that 'no person shall be deprived of life, liberty or property without due process of law.'" I submit, however, that just as slavery is an evil, so is hospitalizing anyone without his consent, whether that person is depressed or paranoid, hysterical or schizophrenic.

Commitment practices flourished long before there were mental or psychiatric "treatments" for "mental diseases." Indeed madness, or mental illness, was not always a requirement for commitment. The Illinois commitment laws of 1851 specified that, "Married women . . . may be entered or detained in the hospital on the request of the husband of the woman . . . *without* the evidence of insanity required in other cases." Regulations for the Bicètre and Salpêtrierè, the two Parisian "mental hospitals" that became world famous, made it possible in 1680 to lock up children (of artisans and poor people) who "refused to work or who used their parents badly." Girls "debauched or in evident danger of becoming so," and prostitutes or "women who ran bawdy houses" were also considered fit subjects for incarceration.

Today, commitment laws usually specify that, for involuntary hospitalization, a person not only must be mentally ill, but must also be dangerous to himself or to others. But even if a mental patient has expert legal advice, what facts can *he* offer to prove that he is not dangerous, when a psychiatrist claims he is? Clearly, it is impossible to *prove* that a person is not dangerous.

Involuntary mental hospitalization remains today what it has been ever since its inception in the 17th Century: an extra-legal, quasi-medical form of social control for persons who annoy or disturb others and whose nonconformity cannot be controlled through the criminal law. To be sure, the rhetoric has changed. Formerly, a housewife's commitment could be justified by her husband's disaffection and his unsupported complaints. Today, commitment must be justified by calling the housewife "mentally ill." The locus of confinement has changed. The Bedlams of old have been replaced by state mental hospitals and community mental health centers. But the social reality remains the same: commitment is still punishment without trial, imprisonment without time limit, and stigmatization without hope of redress.

On Being Sane in Insane Places

David L. Rosenhan

If sanity and insanity exist, how shall we know them?

The question is neither capricious nor itself insane. However much we may be personally convinced that we can tell the normal from the abnormal, the evidence is simply not compelling. It is commonplace, for example, to read about murder trials wherein eminent psychiatrists for the defense are contradicted by equally eminent psychiatrists for the prosecution on the matter of the defendant's sanity. More generally, there are a great deal of conflicting data on the reliability, utility, and meaning of such terms as "sanity," "insanity," "mental illness," and "schizophrenia" (*1*). Finally, as early as 1934, Benedict suggested that normality and abnormality are not universal (2). What is viewed as normal in one culture may be seen as quite aberrant in another. Thus, notions of normality and abnormality may not be quite as accurate as people believe they are.

To raise questions regarding normality and abnormality is in no way to question the fact that some behaviors are deviant or odd. Murder is deviant. So, too, are hallucinations. Nor does raising such questions deny the existence of the personal anguish that is often associated with "mental illness." Anxiety and depression exist. Psychological suffering exists. But normality and abnormality, sanity and insanity, and the diagnoses that flow from them may be less substantive than many believe them to be.

At its heart, the question of whether the sane can be distinguished from the insane (and whether degrees of insanity can be distinguished from each other) is a simple matter: do the salient characteristics that lead to diagnoses reside in the patients themselves or in the environments and contexts in which observers find them? From Bleuler, through Kretchmer, through the formulators of the recently revised *Diagnostic and Statistical Manual* of the American Psychiatric Association, the belief has been strong that patients present symptoms, that those symptoms can be categorized, and, implicitly, that the sane are distinguishable from the insane. More recently, however, this belief has been questioned. Based in part on theoretical and anthropological considerations, but also on philosophical, legal, and therapeutic ones, the view has grown that psychological categorization of mental illness is useless at best and downright harmful, misleading, and pejorative at worst. Psychiatric diagnoses, in this view, are in the minds of the observers and are not valid summaries of characteristics displayed by the observed (*3–5*).

Gains can be made in deciding which of these is more nearly accurate by getting normal people (that is, people who do not have, and have never suffered, symptoms of serious psychiatric disorders) admitted to psychiatric hospitals and then determining whether they were discovered to be sane and, if so, how. If the sanity of such pseudopatients were always detected, there would be prima facie evidence that a sane individual can be distinguished from the insane context in which he is found. Normality (and presumably abnormality) is distinct enough that it can be recognized wherever it occurs, for it is carried within the person. If, on the other hand, the sanity of the pseudopatients were never discovered, serious difficulties would arise for those who support traditional modes of psychiatric diagnosis. Given that the hospital staff was not incompetent, that the pseudopatient had been behaving as sanely as he had been outside of the hospital, and that it had never been previously suggested that he belonged in a psychiatric hospital, such an unlikely outcome would support the view that psychiatric diagnosis betrays little about the patient but much about the environment in which an observer finds him.

This article describes such an experiment. Eight sane people gained secret admission to 12 different hospitals (*6*). Their diagnostic experiences constitute the data of the first part of this article; the remainder is devoted to a description of their experiences in psychiatric institutions. Too few psychiatrists and psychologists, even those who have worked in such hospitals, know what the experience is like. They rarely talk about it with former patients, perhaps because they distrust information coming from the previously insane. Those who have worked in psychiatric hospitals are likely to have adapted so thoroughly to the settings that they are insensitive to the impact of that experience. And while there have been occasional reports of researchers who submitted themselves to psychiatric hospitalization (*7*), these researchers have commonly remained in the hospitals for short periods of time, often with the knowledge of the hospital staff. It is difficult to know the extent to which they were treated like patients or like research colleagues. Nevertheless, their reports about the inside of the psychiatric hospital have been valuable. This article extends those efforts.

Pseudopatients and Their Settings

The eight pseudopatients were a varied group. One was a psychology graduate student in his 20's. The remaining seven were older and "established." Among them were three psychologists, a pediatrician, a psychiatrist, a painter, and a housewife. Three pseudopatients were women, five were men. All of them employed pseudonyms, lest their alleged diagnoses embarrass them later. Those who were in mental health professions alleged another occupation in order to avoid the special attentions that might be accorded by staff, as a matter of courtesy or caution, to ailing colleagues (*8*). With the exception of myself (I was the first pseudopatient and my presence was known to the hospital administrator and chief psychologist and, so far as I can tell, to them alone), the presence of pseudopatients and the nature of the research program was not known to the hospital staffs (*9*).

The settings were similarly varied. In order to generalize the findings, admission into a variety of hospitals was sought. The 12 hospitals in the sample were located in five different states on the East and West coasts. Some were old and shabby, some were quite new. Some were research-oriented, others not. Some had good staff-patient ratios, others were quite understaffed. Only one was a strictly private hospital. All of the others were supported by state or federal funds or, in one instance, by university funds.

After calling the hospital for an appointment, the pseudopatient arrived at the admissions office complaining that he had been hearing voices. Asked what the voices said, he replied that they were often unclear, but as far as he could tell they said "empty," "hollow," and "thud." The voices were unfamiliar and were of the same sex as the pseudopatient. The choice of these symptoms was occasioned by their apparent similarity to existential symptoms. Such symptoms are alleged to arise from painful concerns about the perceived meaninglessness of one's life. It is as if the hallucinating person were saying, "My life is empty and hollow." The choice of these symptoms was also determined by the *absence* of a single report of existential psychoses in the literature.

Beyond alleging the symptoms and falsifying name, vocation, and employment, no further alterations of person, history, or circumstances were made. The significant events of the pseudopatient's life history were presented as they had actually occurred. Relationships with parents and siblings, with spouse and children, with people at work and in school, consistent with the aforementioned exceptions, were described as they were or had been. Frustrations and upsets were described along with joys and satisfactions. These facts are important to remember. If anything, they strongly biased the subsequent results in favor of detecting sanity, since none of their histories or current behaviors were seriously pathological in any way.

Immediately upon admission to the psychiatric ward, the pseudopatient ceased simulating *any* symptoms of abnormality. In some cases, there was a brief period of mild nervousness and anxiety, since none of the pseudopatients really believed that they would be admitted so easily. Indeed, their shared fear was that they would be immediately exposed as frauds and greatly embarrassed. Moreover, many of them had never visited a psychiatric ward; even those who had, nevertheless had some genuine fears about what might happen to them. Their nervousness, then, was quite appropriate to the novelty of the hospital setting, and it abated rapidly.

Apart from that short-lived nervousness, the pseudopatient behaved on the ward as he "normally" behaved. The pseudopatient spoke to patients and staff as he might ordinarily. Because there is uncommonly little to do on a psychiatric ward, he attempted to engage others in conversation. When asked by staff how he was feeling, he indicated that he was fine, that he no longer experienced symptoms. He responded to instructions from attendants, to calls for medication (which was not swallowed), and to dining-hall instructions. Beyond such activities as were available to him on the admissions ward, he spent his time writing down his observations about the ward, its patients, and the staff. Initially these notes were written "secretly," but as it soon became clear that no one much cared, they were subsequently written on standard tablets of paper in such public places as the dayroom. No secret was made of these activities.

The pseudopatient, very much as a true psychiatric patient, entered a hospital with no foreknowledge of when he would be discharged. Each was told that he would have to get out by his own devices, essentially by convincing the staff that he was sane. The psychological stresses associated with hospitalization were considerable, and all but one of the pseudopatients desired to be discharged almost immediately after being admitted. They were, therefore, motivated not only to behave sanely, but to be paragons of cooperation. That their behavior was in no way disruptive is confirmed by nursing reports, which have been obtained on most of the patients. These reports uniformly indicate that the patients were "friendly," "cooperative," and "exhibited no abnormal indications."

The Normal Are Not Detectably Sane

Despite their public "show" of sanity, the pseudopatients were never detected. Admitted, except in one case, with a diagnosis of schizophrenia (*10*), each was discharged with a diagnosis of schizophrenia "in remission." The label "in remission" should in no way be dismissed as a formality, for at no time during any hospitalization had any question been raised about any pseudopatient's simulation. Nor are there any indications in the hospital records that the pseudopatient's status was suspect. Rather, the evidence is strong that, once labeled schizophrenic, the pseudopatient was stuck with that label. If the pseudopatient was to be discharged, he must naturally be "in remission"; but he was not sane, nor, in the institution's view, had he ever been sane.

The uniform failure to recognize sanity cannot be attributed to the quality of the hospitals, for, although there were considerable variations among them, several are considered excellent. Nor can it be alleged that there was simply not enough time to observe the pseudopatients. Length of hospitalization ranged from 7 to 52 days, with an average of 19 days. The pseudopatients were not, in fact, carefully observed, but this failure clearly speaks more to traditions within psychiatric hospitals than to lack of opportunity.

Finally, it cannot be said that the failure to recognize the pseudopatients' sanity was due to the fact that they were not behaving sanely. While there was clearly some tension present in all of them, their daily visitors could detect no serious behavioral consequences—nor, indeed, could other patients. It was quite common for the patients to "detect" the pseudopatients' sanity. During the first three hospitalizations, when accurate counts were kept, 35 of a total of 118 patients on the admissions ward voiced their suspicions, some vigorously. "You're not crazy. You're a journalist, or a professor [referring to the continual note-taking]. You're checking up on the hospital." While most of the patients were reassured by the pseudopatient's insistence that he had been sick before he came in but was fine now, some continued to believe that the pseudopatient was sane throughout his hospitalization (*11*). The fact that the patients often recognized normality when staff did not raises important questions.

Failure to detect sanity during the course of hospitalization may be due to the fact that physicians operate with a strong bias toward what statisticians call the type 2 error (*5*). This is to say that physicians are more inclined to call a healthy person sick (a false positive, type 2) than a sick person healthy (a false negative, type 1). The reasons for this are not hard to find: it is clearly more dangerous to misdiagnose illness than health. Better to err on the side of caution, to suspect illness even among the healthy.

But what holds for medicine does not hold equally well for psychiatry. Medical illnesses, while unfortunate, are not commonly pejorative. Psychiatric diagnoses, on the contrary, carry with them personal, legal, and social stigmas (*12*). It was therefore important to see whether the tendency toward diagnosing the sane insane could be reversed. The following experiment was arranged at a research and teaching hospital whose staff had heard these findings but doubted that such an error could occur in their hospital. The staff was informed that at some time during the following 3 months, one or more pseudopatients would attempt to be admitted into the psychiatric hospital. Each staff member was asked to rate each patient who presented himself at admissions or on the ward according to the likelihood that the patient was a pseudopatient. A 10-point scale was used, with a 1 and 2 reflecting high confidence that the patient was a pseudopatient.

Judgments were obtained on 193 patients who were admitted for psychiatric treatment. All staff who had had sustained contact with or primary responsibility for the patient—attendants, nurses, psychiatrists, physicians, and psychologists—were asked to make judgments. Forty-one patients were alleged, with high confidence, to be pseudopatients by at least one member of the staff. Twenty-three were considered suspect by at least one psychiatrist. Nineteen were suspected by one psychiatrist *and* one other staff member. Actually, no genuine pseudopatient (at least from my group) presented himself during this period.

The experiment is instructive. It indicates that the tendency to designate sane people as insane can be reversed when the stakes (in this case, prestige and diagnostic acumen) are high. But what can be said of the 19 people who were suspected of being "sane" by one psychiatrist and another staff member? Were these people truly "sane," or was it rather the case that in the course of avoiding the type 2 error the staff tended to make more errors of the first sort—calling the crazy "sane"? There is no way of knowing. But one thing is certain: any diagnostic process that lends itself so readily to massive errors of this sort cannot be a very reliable one.

The Stickiness of Psychodiagnostic Labels

Beyond the tendency to call the healthy sick—a tendency that accounts better for diagnostic behavior on admission than it does for such behavior after a length period of exposure—the data speak to the massive role of labeling in psychiatric assessment. Having once been labeled schizophrenic, there is nothing the pseudopatient can do to overcome the tag. The tag profoundly color others' perceptions of him and his behavior.

From one viewpoint, these data are hardly surprising, for it has long been known that elements are given meaning by the context in which they occur. Gestalt psychology made this point vigorously, and Asch (*13*) demonstrated that there are "central" personality traits (such as "warm" versus "cold") which are so powerful that they markedly color the meaning of other information in forming an impression of a given personality (*14*). "Insane," "schizophrenic," "manic-depressive," and "crazy" are probably among the most powerful of such central traits. Once a person is designated abnormal, all of his other behaviors and characteristics are colored by that label. Indeed, that label is so powerful that many of the pseudopatients' normal behaviors were overlooked entirely or profoundly misinterpreted. Some examples may clarify this issue.

Earlier I indicated that there were no changes in the pseudopatient's personal history and current status beyond those of name, employment, and, where necessary, vocation. Otherwise, a veridical description of personal history and circumstances was offered. Those circumstances were not psychotic. How were they made consonant with the diagnosis of psychosis? Or were those diagnoses modified in such a way as to bring them into accord with the circumstances of the pseudopatient's life, as described by him?

As far as I can determine, diagnoses were in no way affected by the relative health of the circumstances of a pseudopatient's life. Rather, the reverse occurred: the perception of his circumstances was shaped entirely by the diagnosis. A clear example of such translation is found in the case of a pseudopatient who had had a close relationship with his mother but was rather remote from his father during his early childhood. During adolescence and beyond, however, his father became a close friend, while his relationship with his mother cooled. His present relationship with his wife was characteristically close and warm. Apart from occasional angry exchanges, friction was minimal. The children had rarely been spanked. Surely there is nothing especially pathological about such a history. Indeed, many readers may see a similar pattern in their own experiences, with no markedly deleterious consequences. Observe, however, how such a history was translated in the psychopathological context, this from the case summary prepared after the patient was discharged.

> This white 39-year-old male . . . manifests a long history of considerable ambivalence in close relationships, which begins in early childhood. A warm relationship with his mother cools during his adolescence. A distant relationship to his father is described as becoming very intense. Affective stability is absent. His attempts to control emotionality with his wife and children are punctuated by angry outbursts and, in the case of the children, spankings. And while he says that he has several good friends, one senses considerable ambivalence embedded in those relationships also. . . .

The facts of the case were unintentionally distorted by the staff to achieve consistency with a popular theory of the dynamics of a schizophrenic reaction (*15*). Nothing of an ambivalent nature had been described in relations with parents, spouse, or friends. To the extent that ambivalence could be inferred, it was probably not greater than is found in all human relationships. It is true the pseudopatient's relationships with his parents changed over time, but in the ordinary context that would hardly be remarkable—indeed, it might very well be expected. Clearly, the meaning ascribed to his verbalizations (that is, ambivalence, affective instability) was determined by the diagnosis: schizophrenia. An entirely different meaning would have been ascribed if it were known that the man was "normal."

All pseudopatients took extensive notes publicly. Under ordinary circumstances, such behavior would have raised questions in the minds of observers, as, in fact, it did among patients. Indeed, it seemed so certain that the notes would elicit suspicion that elaborate precautions were taken to remove them from the ward each day. But the precautions proved needless. The closest any staff member came to questioning these notes occurred when one pseudopatient asked his physician what kind of medication he was receiving and began to write down the response. "You needn't write it," he was told gently. "If you have trouble remembering, just ask me again."

If no questions were asked of the pseudopatients, how was their writing interpreted? Nursing records for three patients indicate that the writing was seen as an aspect of their pathological behavior. "Patient engages in writing behavior" was the daily nursing comment on one of the pseudopatients who was never questioned about his writing. Given that the patient is in the hospital, he must be psychologically disturbed. And given that he is disturbed, continuous writing must be a behavioral manifestation of that disturbance, perhaps a subset of the compulsive behaviors that are sometimes correlated with schizophrenia.

One tacit characteristic of psychiatric diagnosis is that it locates the sources of aberration within the individual and only rarely within the complex of stimuli that surrounds him. Consequently, behaviors that are stimulated by the environment are commonly misattributed to the patient's disorder. For example, one kindly nurse found a pseudopatient pacing the long hospital corridors. "Nervous, Mr. X?" she asked. "No, bored," he said.

The notes kept by pseudopatients are full of patient behaviors that were misinterpreted by well-intentioned staff. Often enough, a patient would go "berserk" because he had, wittingly or unwittingly, been mistreated by, say, an attendant. A nurse coming upon the scene would rarely inquire even cursorily into the environmental stimuli of the patient's behavior. Rather, she assumed that his upset derived from his pathology, not from his present interactions with other staff members. Occasionally, the staff might assume that the patient's family (especially when they had recently visited) or other patients had stimulated the outburst. But never were the staff found to assume that one of themselves or the structure of the hospital had anything to do with a patient's behavior. One psychiatrist pointed to a group of patients who were sitting outside the cafeteria entrance half an hour before lunchtime. To a group of young residents he indicated that such behavior was characteristic of the oral-acquisitive nature of the syndrome. It seemed not to occur to him that there were very few things to anticipate in a psychiatric hospital besides eating.

A psychiatric label has a life and an influence of its own. Once the impression has been formed that the patient is schizophrenic, the expectation is that he will continue to be schizophrenic. When a sufficient amount of time has passed, during which the patient has done nothing bizarre, he is considered to be in remission and available for discharge. But the label endures beyond discharge, with the unconfirmed expectation that he will behave as a schizophrenic again. Such labels, conferred by mental health professionals, are as influential on the patient as they are on his relatives and friends, and it should not surprise anyone that the diagnosis acts on all of them as a self-fulfilling prophecy. Eventually, the patient himself accepts the diagnosis, with all of its surplus meanings and expectations, and behave accordingly (*5*).

The inferences to be made from these matters are quite simple. Much as Zigler and Phillips have demonstrated that there is enormous overlap in the symptoms presented by patients who have been variously diagnosed (*16*), so there is enormous overlap in the behaviors of the sane and the insane. The sane are not "sane" all of the time. We lose our tempers "for no good reason." We are occasionally depressed or anxious, again for no good reason. And we may find it difficult to get along with one or another person—again for no reason that we can specify. Similarly, the insane are not always insane. Indeed, it was the impression of the pseudopatients while living with them that they were sane for long periods of time—that the bizarre behaviors upon which their diagnoses were allegedly predicated constituted only a small fraction of their total behavior. If it makes no sense to label ourselves permanently depressed on the basis of an occasional depression, then it takes better evidence than is presently available to label all patients insane or schizophrenic on the basis of bizarre behaviors or cognitions. It seems more useful, as Mischel (*17*) has pointed out, to limit our discussions to *behaviors*, the stimuli that provoke them, and their correlates.

It is not known why powerful impressions of personality traits, such as "crazy" or "insane," arise. Conceivably, when the origins of and stimuli that give rise to a behavior are remote or unknown, or when the behavior strikes us as immutable, trait labels regarding the *behaver* arise. When, on the other hand, the origins and stimuli are known and available, discourse is limited to the behavior itself. Thus, I may hallucinate because I am sleeping, or I may hallucinate because I have ingested a peculiar drug. These are termed sleep-induced hallucinations, or dreams, and drug-induced hallucinations, respectively. But when the stimuli to my hallucinations are unknown, that is called craziness, or schizophrenia—as if that inference were somehow as illuminating as the others.

The Experience of Psychiatric Hospitalization

The term "mental illness" is of recent origin. It was coined by people who were humane in their inclinations and who wanted very much to raise the station of (and the public's sympathies toward) the psychologically disturbed from that of witches and "crazies" to one that was akin to the physically ill. And they were at least partially successful, for the treatment of the mentally ill *has* improved considerably over the years. But while treatment has improved, it is doubtful that people really regard the mentally ill in the same way that they view the physically ill. A broken leg is something one recovers from, but mental illness allegedly endures forever (*18*). A broken leg does not threaten the observer, but a crazy schizophrenic? There is by now a host of evidence that attitudes toward the mentally ill are characterized by fear, hostility, aloofness, suspicion, and dread (*19*). The mentally ill are society's lepers.

That such attitudes infect the general population is perhaps not surprising, only upsetting. But that they affect the professionals—attendants, nurses, physicians, psychologists, and social workers—who treat and deal with the mentally ill is more disconcerting, both because such attitudes are self-evidently pernicious and because they are unwitting. Most mental health professionals would insist that they are sympathetic toward the mentally ill, that they are neither avoidant nor hostile. But it is more likely that an exquisite ambivalence characterizes their relations with psychiatric patients, such that their avowed impulses are only part of their entire attitude. Negative attitudes are there too and can easily be detected. Such attitudes should not surprise us. They are the natural offspring of the labels patients wear and the places in which they are found.

Consider the structure of the typical psychiatric hospital. Staff and patients are strictly segregated. Staff have their own living space, including their dining facilities, bathrooms, and assembly places. The glassed quarters that contain the professional staff, which the pseudopatients came to call "the cage," sit out on every dayroom. The staff emerge primarily for caretaking purposes—to give medication, to conduct a therapy or group meeting, to instruct or reprimand a patient. Otherwise, staff keep to themselves, almost as if the disorder that afflicts their charges is somehow catching.

So much is patient-staff segregation the rule that, for four public hospitals in which an attempt was made to measure the degree to which staff and patients mingle, it was necessary to use "time out of the staff cage" as the operational measure. While it was not the case that all time spent out of the cage was spent mingling with patients (attendants, for example, would occasionally emerge to watch television in the dayroom), it was the only way in which one could gather reliable data on time for measuring.

The average amount of time spent by attendants outside of the cage was 11.3 percent (range, 3 to 52 percent). This figure does not represent only time spent mingling with patients, but also includes time spent on such chores as folding laundry, supervising patients while they shave, directing ward clean-up, and sending patients to off-ward activities. It was the relatively rare attendant who spent time talking with patients or playing games with them. It proved impossible to obtain a "percent mingling time" for nurses, since the amount of time they spent out of the cage was too brief. Rather, we counted instances of emergence from the cage. On the average, daytime nurses emerged from the cage 11.5 times per shift, including instances when they left the ward entirely (range, 4 to 39 times). Late afternoon and night nurses were even less available, emerging on the average 9.4 times per shift (range, 4 to 41 times). Data on early morning nurses, who arrived usually after midnight and departed at 8 a.m., are not available because patients were asleep during most of this period.

Physicians, especially psychiatrists, were even less available. They were rarely seen on the wards. Quite commonly, they would be seen only when they arrived and departed, with the remaining time being spent in their offices or in the cage. On the average, physicians emerged on the ward 6.7 times per day (range, 1 to 17 times). It proved difficult to make an accurate estimate in this regard, since physicians often maintained hours that allowed them to come and go at different times.

The hierarchical organization of the psychiatric hospital has been commented on before (*20*), but the latent meaning of that kind of organization is worth noting again. Those with the most power have least to do with patients, and those with the least power are most involved with them. Recall, however, that the acquisition of role-appropriate behaviors occurs mainly through the observation of others, with the most powerful having the most influence. Consequently, it is understandable that attendants not only spend more time with patients than do any other members of the staff—that is required by their station in the hierarchy—but also, insofar as they learn from their superiors' behavior, spend as little time with patients as they can. Attendants are seen mainly in the cage, which is where the models, the action, and the power are.

I turn now to a different set of studies, these dealing with staff response to patient-initiated contact. It has long been known that the amount of time a person spends with you can be an index of your significance to him. If he initiates and maintains eye contact, there is reason to believe that he is considering your requests and needs. If he pauses to chat or actually stops and talks, there is added reason to infer that he is individuating you. In four hospitals, the pseudopatient approached the staff member with a request which took the following form: "Pardon me, Mr. [or Dr. or Mrs.] X, could you tell me when I will be eligible for grounds privileges?" (or ". . . when I will be presented at the staff meeting?" or ". . . when I am likely to be discharged?"). While the content of the question varied according to the appropriateness of the target and the pseudopatient's (apparent) current needs the form was always a courteous and relevant request for information. Care was taken never to approach a particular member of the staff more than once a day, lest the staff member become suspicious or irritated. In examining these data, remember that the behavior of the pseudopatients was neither bizarre nor disruptive. One could indeed engage in good conversation with them.

The data for these experiments are shown in Table 1, separately for physicians (column 1) and for nurses and attendants (column 2). Minor differences between these four institutions were overwhelmed by the degree to which staff avoided continuing contacts that patients had initiated. By far, their most common response consisted of either a brief response to the question, offered while they were "on the move" and with head averted, or no response at all.

TABLE 1. Self-initiated contact by pseudopatients with psychiatrists and nurses and attendants, compared to contact with other groups.

Contact	Psychiatric hospitals		University campus (nonmedical)	University medical center		
				Physicians		
	(1) Psychiatrists	(2) Nurses and attendants	(3) Faculty	(4) "Looking for a psychiatrist!"	(5) "Looking for an an internist!"	(6) No additional comment
Responses						
Moves on, head averted (%)	71	88	0	0	0	0
Makes eye contact (%)	23	10	0	11	0	0
Pauses and chats (%)	2	2	0	11	0	10
Stops and talks (%)	4	0.5	100	78	100	90
Mean number of questions answered (out of 6)	*	*	6	3.8	4.8	4.5
Respondents (No.)	13	47	14	18	15	10
Attempts (No.)	185	1283	14	18	15	10

* Not applicable.

The encounter frequently took the following bizarre form: (pseudopatient) "Pardon me, Dr. X. Could you tell me when I am eligible for grounds privileges?" (physician) "Good morning, Dave. How are you today?" (Moves off without waiting for a response.)

It is instructive to compare these data with data recently obtained at Stanford University. It has been alleged that large and eminent universities are characterized by faculty who are so busy that they have no time for students. For this comparison, a young lady approached individual faculty members who seemed to be walking purposefully to some meeting or teaching engagement and asked them the following six questions.

1) "Pardon me, could you direct me to Encina Hall?" (at the medical school: ". . . to the Clinical Research Center?).

2) "Do you know where Fish Annex is?" (there is no Fish Annex at Stanford).

3) "Do you teach here?"

4) "How does one apply for admission to the college?" (at the medical school: ". . . to the medical school?").

5) "Is it difficult to get in?"

6) "Is there financial aid?"

Without exception, as can be seen in Table 1 (column 3), all of the questions were answered. No matter how rushed they were, all respondents not only maintained eye contact, but stopped to talk. Indeed, many of the respondents went out of their way to direct or take the questioner to the office she was seeking, to try to locate "Fish Annex," or to discuss with her the possibilities of being admitted to the university.

Similar data, also shown in Table 1 (columns 4, 5, and 6), were obtained in the hospital. Here too, the young lady came prepared with six questions. After the first question, however, she remarked to 18 of her respondents (column 4), "I'm looking for a psychiatrist," and to 15 others (column 5), "I'm looking for an internist." Ten other respondents received no inserted comment (column 6). The general degree of cooperative responses is considerably higher for these university groups than it was for pseudopatients in psychiatric hospitals. Even so, differences are apparent within the medical school setting. Once having indicated that she was looking for a psychiatrist, the degree of cooperation elicited was less than when she sought an internist.

Powerlessness and Depersonalization

Eye contact and verbal contact reflect concern and individuation; their absence, avoidance and depersonalization. The data I have presented do not do justice to the rich daily encounters that grew up around matters of depersonalization and avoidance. I have records of patients who were beaten by staff for the sin of having initiated verbal contact. During my own experience, for example, one patient was beaten in the presence of other patients for having approached an attendant and told him, "I like you." Occasionally, punishment meted out to patients for misdemeanors seemed so excessive that it could not be justified by the most radical interpretations of psychiatric canon. Nevertheless, they appeared to go unquestioned. Tempers were often short. A patient who had not heard a call for medication would be roundly excoriated, and the morning attendants would often wake patients with, "come on, you m——f——s, out of bed!"

Neither anecdotal nor "hard" data can convey the overwhelming sense of powerlessness which invades the individual as he is continually exposed to the depersonalization of the psychiatric hospital. It hardly matters *which* psychiatric hospital—the excellent public ones and the very plush private hospital were better than the rural and shabby ones in this regard, but, again, the features that psychiatric hospitals had in common overwhelmed by far their apparent differences.

Powerlessness was evident everywhere. The patient is deprived of many of his legal rights by dint of his psychiatric commitment. (*21*). He is shorn of credibility by virtue of his psychiatric label. His freedom of movement is restricted. He cannot initiate contact with the staff, but may only respond to such overtures as they make. Personal privacy is minimal. Patient quarters and possessions can be entered and examined by any staff member, for whatever reason. His personal history and anguish is available to any staff member (often including the "grey lady" and "candy striper" volunteer) who chooses to read his folder, regardless of their therapeutic relationship to him. His personal hygiene and waste evacuation are often monitored. The water closets may have no doors.

At times, depersonalization reached such proportions that pseudopatients had the sense that they were invisible, or at least unworthy of account. Upon being admitted, I and other pseudopatients took the initial physical examinations in a semipublic room, where staff members went about their own business as if we were not there.

On the ward, attendants delivered verbal and occasionally serious physical abuse to patients in the presence of other observing patients, some of whom (the pseudopatients) were writing it all down. Abusive behavior, on the other hand, terminated quite abruptly when other staff members were known to be coming. Staff are credible witnesses. Patients are not.

A nurse unbuttoned her uniform to adjust her brassiere in the presence of an entire ward of viewing men. One did not have the sense that she was being seductive. Rather, she didn't notice us. A group of staff persons might point to a patient in the dayroom and discuss him animatedly, as if he were not there.

One illuminating instance of depersonalization and invisibility occurred with regard to medications. All told, the pseudopatients were administered nearly 2100 pills, including Elavil, Stelazine, Compazine, and Thorazine, to name but a few. (That such a variety of medications should have been administered to patients presenting identical symptoms is itself worthy of note.) Only two were swallowed. The rest were either pocketed or deposited in the toilet. The pseudopatients were not alone in this. Although I have no precise records on how many patients rejected their medications, the pseudopatients frequently found the medications of other patients in the toilet before they deposited their own. As long as they were cooperative, their behavior and the pseudopatients' own in this matter, as in other important matters, went unnoticed throughout.

Reactions to such depersonalization among pseudopatients were intense. Although they had come to the hospital as participant observers and were fully aware that they did not "belong," they nevertheless found themselves caught up in and fighting the process of depersonalization. Some examples: a graduate student in psychology asked his wife to bring his textbooks to the hospital so he could "catch up on his homework"—this despite the elaborate precautions taken to conceal his professional association. The same student, who had trained for quite some time to get into the hospital, and who had looked forward to the experience, "remembered" some drag races that he had wanted to see on the weekend and insisted that he be discharged by that time. Another pseudopatient attempted a romance with a nurse. Subsequently, he informed the staff that he was applying for admission to graduate school in psychology and was very likely to be admitted, since a graduate professor was one of his regular hospital visitors. The same person began to engage in psychotherapy with other patients—all of this as a way of becoming a person in an impersonal environment.

The Sources of Depersonalization

What are the origins of depersonalization? I have already mentioned two. First are attitudes held by all of us toward the mentally ill—including those who treat them—attitudes characterized by fear, distrust, and horrible expectations on the one hand, and benevolent intentions on the other. Our ambivalence leads, in this instance as in others, to avoidance.

Second, and not entirely separate, the hierarchical structure of the psychiatric hospital facilitates depersonalization. Those who are at the top have least to do with patients, and their behavior inspires the rest of the staff. Average daily contact with psychiatrists, psychologists, residents, and physicians combined ranged from 3.9 to 25.1 minutes, with an overall mean of 6.8 (six pseudopatients over a total of 129 days of hospitalization). Included in this average are time spent in the admissions interview, ward meetings in the presence of a senior staff member, group and individual psychotherapy contacts, case presentation conferences, and discharge meetings. Clearly, patients do not spend much time in interpersonal contact with doctoral staff. And doctoral staff serve as models for nurses and attendants.

There are probably other sources. Psychiatric installations are presently in serious financial straits. Staff shortages are pervasive, staff time at a premium. Something has to give, and that something is patient contact. Yet, while financial stresses are realities, too much can be made of them. I have the impression that the psychological forces that result in depersonalization are much stronger than the fiscal ones and that the addition of more staff would not correspondingly improve patient care in this regard. The incidence of staff meetings and the enormous amount of record-keeping on patients, for example, have not been as substantially reduced as has patient contact. Priorities exist, even during hard times. Patient contact is not a significant priority in the traditional psychiatric hospital, and fiscal pressures do not account for this. Avoidance and depersonalization may.

Heavy reliance upon psychotropic medication tacitly contributes to depersonalization by convincing staff that treatment is indeed being conducted and that further patient contact may not be necessary. Even here, however, caution needs to be exercised in understanding the role of psychotropic drugs. If patients were powerful rather than powerless, if they were viewed as interesting individuals rather than diagnostic entities, if they were socially significant rather than social lepers, if their anguish truly and wholly compelled our sympathies and concerns, would we not *seek* contact with them, despite the availability of medications? Perhaps for the pleasure of it all?

The Consequences of Labeling and Depersonalization

Whenever the ratio of what is known to what needs to be known approaches zero, we tend to invent "knowledge" and assume that we understand more than we actually do. We seem unable to acknowledge that we simply don't know. The needs for diagnosis and remediation of behavioral and emotional problems are enormous. But rather than acknowledge that we are just embarking on understanding, we continue to label patients "schizophrenic," "manic-depressive," and "insane," as if in those words we had captured the essence of understanding. The facts of the matter are that we have known for a long time that diagnoses are often not useful or reliable, but we have nevertheless continued to use them. We now know that we cannot distinguish insanity from sanity. It is depressing to consider how that information will be used.

Not merely depressing, but frightening. How many people, one wonders, are sane but not recognized as such in our psychiatric institutions? How many have been needlessly stripped of their privileges of citizenship, from the right to vote and drive to that of handling their own accounts? How many have feigned insanity in order to avoid the criminal consequences of their behavior, and, conversely, how many would rather stand trial than live interminably in a psychiatric hospital—but are wrongly thought to be mentally ill? How many have been stigmatized by well-intentioned, but nevertheless erroneous, diagnoses? On the last point, recall again that a "type 2 error" in psychiatric diagnosis does not have the same consequences it does in medical diagnosis. A diagnosis of cancer that has been found to be in error is cause for celebration. But psychiatric diagnoses are rarely found to be in error. The label sticks, a mark of inadequacy forever.

Finally, how many patients might be "sane" outside the psychiatric hospital but seem insane in it—not because craziness resides in them, as it were, but because they are responding to a bizarre setting, one that may be unique to institutions which harbor nether people? Goffman (4) calls the process of socialization to such institutions "mortification"—an apt metaphor that includes the processes of depersonalization that have been described here. And while it is impossible to know whether the pseudopatients' responses to these processes are characteristic of all inmates—they were, after all, not real patients—it is difficult to believe that these processes of socialization to a psychiatric hospital provide useful attitudes or habits of response for living in the "real world."

Summary and Conclusions

It is clear that we cannot distinguish the sane from the insane in psychiatric hospitals. The hospital itself imposes a special environment in which the meanings of behavior can easily be misunderstood. The consequences to patients hospitalized in such an environment—the powerlessness, depersonalization, segregation, mortification, and self-labeling—seem undoubtedly counter-therapeutic.

I do not, even now, understand this problem well enough to perceive solutions. But two matters seem to have some promise. The first concerns the proliferation of community mental health facilities, of crisis intervention centers, of the human potential movement, and of behavior therapies that, for all of their own problems, tend to avoid psychiatric labels, to focus on specific problems and behaviors, and to retain the individual in a relatively nonpejorative environment. Clearly, to the extent that we refrain from sending the distressed to insane places, our impressions of them are less likely to be distorted. (The risk of distorted perceptions, it seems to me, is always present, since we are much more sensitive to an individual's behaviors and verbalizations than we are to the subtle contextual stimuli that often promote them. At issue here is a matter of magnitude. And, as I have shown, the magnitude of distortion is exceedingly high in the extreme context that is a psychiatric hospital.)

The second matter that might prove promising speaks to the need to increase the sensitivity of mental health workers and researchers to the *Catch 22* position of psychiatric patients. Simply reading materials in this area will be of help to some such workers and researchers. For others, directly experiencing the impact of psychiatric hospitalization will be of enormous use. Clearly, further research into the social psychology of such total institutions will both facilitate treatment and deepen understanding.

I and the other pseudopatients in the psychiatric setting had distinctly negative reactions. We do not pretend to describe the subjective experiences of true patients. Theirs may be different from ours, particularly with the passage of time and the necessary process of adaptation to one's environment. But we can and do speak to the relatively more objective indices of treatment within the hospital. It could be a mistake, and a very unfortunate one, to consider that what happened to us derived from malice or stupidity on the part of the staff. Quite the contrary, our overwhelming impression of them was of people who really cared, who were committed and who were uncommonly intelligent. Where they failed, as they sometimes did painfully, it would be more accurate to attribute those failures to the environment in which they, too, found themselves than to personal callousness. Their perceptions and behavior were controlled by the situation, rather than being motivated by a malicious disposition. In a more benign environment, one that was less attached to global diagnosis, their behaviors and judgments might have been more benign and effective.

References and Notes

1. P. Ash, *J. Abnorm. Soc. Psychol.* 44, 272 (1949); A. T. Beck, *Amer. J. Psychiat.* 119, 210 (1962); A. T. Boisen, *Psychiatry* 2, 233 (1938); N. Kreitman. *J. Ment. Sci.* 107, 876 (1961); N. Kreitman, P. Sainsbury, J. Morrisey, J. Towers, J. Scrivener, *ibid.*, p. 887; H. O. Schmitt and C. P. Fonda, *J. Abnorm. Soc. Psycho.* 52, 262 (1956); W. Seeman, *J. Nerv. Ment. Dis.* 118, 541 (1953). For an analysis of these artifacts and summaries of the disputes, see J. Zubin, *Annu. Rev. Psychol.* 18, 373 (1967); L. Phillips and J. G. Draguns, *ibid.* 22, 447 (1971).
2. R. Benedict, *J. Gen. Psychol.* 10, 59 (1934).
3. See in this regard H. Becker, *Outsiders: Studies in the Sociology of Deviance* (Free Press, New York, 1963); B. M. Braginsky, D. D. Braginsky, K. Ring. *Methods of Madness: The Mental Hospital as a Last Resort* (Holt, Rinehart & Winston, New York, 1969); G. M. Crocetti and P. V. Lemkan, *Amer. Sociol. Rev.* 30, 577 (1965); E. Goffman, *Behavior in Public Places* (Free Press, New York, 1964); R. D. Laing. *The Divided Self: A Study of Sanity and Madness* (Quadrangle, Chicago, 1960); D. L. Phillips, *Amer. Sociol. Rev.* 28, 963 (1963); T. R. Sarbin, *Psychol. Today* 6, 18 (1972); E. Schur, *Amer. J. Sociol.* 75, 309 (1969); T. Szasz, *Law, Liberty and Psychiatry* (Macmillan, New York, 1963); *The Myth of Mental Illness: Foundations of a Theory of Mental Illness* (Hoeber-Harper, New York, 1963). For a critique of some of these views, see W. R. Gove, *Amer. Sociol. Rev.* 35, 873 (1970).
4. E. Goffman, *Asylums* (Doubleday, Garden City, N.Y., 1961).
5. T. J. Schaff, *Being Mentally Ill: A Sociological Theory* (Aldine, Chicago, 1966).
6. Data from a ninth pseudopatient are not incorporated in this report because, although his sanity went undetected, he falsified aspects of his personal history, including his marital status and parental relationships. His experimental behaviors therefore were not identical to those of the other pseudopatients.
7. A. Barry, *Bellevue Is a State of Mind* (Harcourt Brace Jovanovich, New York, 1971); I. Belknap, *Human Problems of a State Mental Hospital* (McGraw-Hill, New York, 1956); W. Caudill, F. C. Redlich, H. R. Gilmore, E. B. Brody, *Amer. J. Orthopsychiat.* 22, 314 (1952); A. R. Goldman, R. H. Bohr, T. A. Steinberg, *Prof. Psychol.* 1, 427 (1970); unauthored, *Roche Report* 1 (No. 13), 8 (1971).

8. Beyond the personal difficulties that the pseudopatient is likely to experience in the hospital, there are legal and social ones that, combined, require considerable attention before entry. For example, once admitted to a psychiatric institution, it is difficult, if not impossible, to be discharged on short notice, state law to the contrary notwithstanding. I was not sensitive to these difficulties at the outset of the project, nor to the personal and situational emergencies that can arise, but later a writ of habeas corpus was prepared for each of the entering pseudopatients and an attorney was kept "on call" during every hospitalization. I am grateful to John Kaplan and Robert Bartels for legal advice and assistance in these matters.
9. However distasteful such concealment is, it was a necessary first step to examining these questions. Without concealment, there would have been no way to know how valid these experiences were; nor was there any way of knowing whether whatever detections occurred were a tribute to the diagnostic acumen of the staff or to the hospital's rumor network. Obviously, since my concerns are general ones that cut across individual hospitals and staffs, I have respected their anonymity and have eliminated clues that might lead to their identification.
10. Interestingly, of the 12 admissions, 11 were diagnosed as schizophrenic and one, with the identical symptomatology, as manic-depressive psychosis. This diagnosis has a more favorable prognosis, and it was given by the only private hospital in our sample. On the relations between social class and psychiatric diagnosis, see A. deB. Hollingshead and F. C. Redlich, *Social Class and Mental Illness: A Community Study* (Wiley, New York, 1958).
11. It is possible, of course, that patients have quite broad latitudes in diagnosis and therefore are inclined to call many people sane, even those whose behavior is patently aberrant. However, although we have no hard data on this matter, it was our distinct impression that this was not the case. In many instances, patients not only singled us out for attention, but came to imitate our behaviors and styles.
12. J. Cumming and E. Cumming. *Community Ment. Health* 1, 135 (1965); A. Farina and K. Ring. *J. Abnorm. Psychol.* 70, 47 (1965); H. E. Freeman and O. G. Simmons. *The Mental Patient Comes Home* (Wiley, New York, 1963); W. J. Johannsen. *Ment. Hygiene* 53, 218 (1969); A. S. Linsky, *Soc. Psychiat.* 5, 166 (1970).
13. S. E. Asch. *J. Abnorm. Soc. Psychol.* 41, 258 (1946); *Social Psychology* (Prentice-Hall, New York, 1952).
14. See also I. N. Mensh and J. Wishner, *J. Personality* 16, 188 (1947); J. Wishner, *Psychol. Rev.* 67, 96 (1960); J. S. Bruner and R. Tagiuri, in *Handbook of Social Psychology*, G. Lindzey, Ed. (Addison-Wesley, Cambridge, Mass., 1954), vol. 2, pp. 634–654; J. S. Bruner, D. Shapiro, R. Tagiuri, in *Person Perception and Interpersonal Behavior.* R. Tagiuri and L. Petrullo, Eds. (Stanford Univ. Press, Stanford, Calif., 1958), pp. 277–288.
15. For an example of a similar self-fulfilling prophecy, in this instance dealing with the "central" trait of intelligence, see R. Rosenthal and L. Jacobson, *Pygmalion in the Classroom* (Holt, Rinehart & Winston, New York, 1968).
16. E. Zigler and L. Phillips, *J. Abnorm. Soc. Psychol.* 63, 69 (1961). See also R. K. Freudenberg and J. P. Robertson, *A.M.A. Arch. Neurol. Psychiatr.* 76, 14 (1956).
17. W. Mischel, *Personality and Assessment* (Wiley, New York, 1968).
18. The most recent and unfortunate instance of this tenet is that of Senator Thomas Eagleton.
19. T. R. Sarbin and J. C. Mancusol, *J. Clin. Consult. Psychol.* 35, 159 (1970); T. R. Sarbin, *ibid.* 31, 447 (1967); J. C. Nunally, Jr., *Popular Conceptions of Mental Health* (Holt, Rinehart & Winston, New York, 1961).
20. A. H. Stanton and M. S. Schwarz, *The Mental Hospital: A Study of Institutional Participation in Psychiatric Illness and Treatment* (Basic, New York, 1954).
21. D. B. Wexler and S. E. Scoville, *Ariz. Law Rev.* 13, 1 (1971).
22. I thank W. Mischel, E. Orne, and M. S. Rosenhan for comments on an earlier draft of this manuscript.

The author is professor of psychology and law at Stanford University, Stanford, California 94305. Portions of these data were presented to colloquiums of the psychology department at the University of California at Berkeley and at Santa Barbara; University of Arizona, Tucson; and Harvard University, Cambridge, Massachusetts.

The Three Faces of Love

Robert J. Trotter

Brains and sex are the only things in life that matter. Robert J. Sternberg picked up that bit of wisdom from a cynical high school classmate and appears to have taken it to heart. "I spent the first part of my career studying brains, and now along comes sex," he says, claiming to be only partly facetious.

Sternberg, IBM Professor of Psychology and Education at Yale University, has, in fact, made a name for himself as one of the foremost theoreticians and researchers in the field of human intelligence (see "Three Heads are Better than One," *Psychology Today,* August 1986), but in recent years he has turned a good deal of his attention the study of love. Why? Because it's an understudied topic that is extremely important to people's lives. "It's important to my own life," he says. "I want to understand what's happening."

Sternberg began his attempt to understand love with a study for which he and graduate student Susan Grajek recruited 35 men and 50 women between 18 and 70 years old who had been in at least one love relationship. Participants rated their most recent significant love affair using the well-tested scales of loving and liking developed by psychologist Zick Rubin and the interpersonal involvement scale developed by psychologist George Levinger. The participants also rated their love for their mothers, fathers, siblings closest in age and best friends of the same sex.

Sternberg and Grajek found that men generally love and like their lover the most and their sibling the least. Women tend to love their lover and best friend about the same, but they like the best friend more than they like the lover. Sternberg thinks he knows why. "Women are better at achieving intimacy and value it more than do men, so if women don't get the intimacy they crave in a relationship with a man, they try to find it with other women. They establish close friendships. They can say things to another woman they can't say to a man."

Sternberg and Grajek concluded that, while the exact emotions, motivations and cognitions involved in various kinds of loving relationships differ, "the various loves one experiences are not, strictly speaking, different." In other words, they thought they had proved that love, as different as it feels from situation to situation, is actually a common entity. They thought they had discovered the basis of love in interpersonal communication, sharing and support.

This research generated a lot of publicity in 1984, especially around St. Valentine's Day, and earned Sternberg the appellation "love professor." It also generated a lot of phone calls from reporters saying things like, "You mean to tell me the way you love your lover is the same as the way you love your 5-year-old? What about sex?" Sternberg had to rethink his position.

He analyzed various relationships to figure out what differentiates romantic love from companionate love, from liking, from infatuation and from various other types of love. He finally concluded that his original theory accounted for the emotional component of love but left out two other important aspects. According to Sternberg's new triangular theory, love has motivational and cognitive components as well. And different aspects of love can be explained in terms of these components (see "How Do I Love Thee?").

Sternberg calls the emotional aspect of his love triangle intimacy. It includes such things as closeness, sharing, communication and support. Intimacy increases rather steadily at first, then at a lower rate until it eventually levels off and goes beneath the surface. Sternberg explains this course of development in terms of psychologist Ellen Berscheid's theory of emotions in close relationships.

According to Berscheid, people in close relationships feel increased emotion when there is some kind of disruption. This is common early in a relationship primarily because of uncertainty. Since you don't know what the other person is going to do, you are constantly learning and experiencing new things. This uncertainty keeps you guessing but also generates new levels of emotion and intimacy. As the other person becomes more predictable, there are fewer disruptions and less expressed, or manifest, intimacy.

An apparent lack of intimacy could mean that the relationship and the intimacy are dying out. Or, says Sternberg, the intimacy may still be there in latent form. The relationship may even be thriving, with the couple growing together so smoothly that they are hardly aware of their interdependence. It may take some kind of disruption—time apart, a death in the family, even a divorce—for them to find out just how they feel about each other. "Is it any wonder," Sternberg asks, "that some couples realize only after a divorce that they were very close to and dependent on each other?"

The motivational side of the triangle is passion, which leads to physiological arousal and an intense desire to be united with the loved one. Unlike intimacy, passion develops quickly. "Initially you have this rapidly growing, hot, heavy passion," Sternberg says, "but after a while it no longer does for you what you want it to—you get used to it, you habituate."

Passion is like an addiction, Sternberg says. He explains it according to psychologist Richard Solomon's opponent process theory of motivation, which says that desire for a person or substance involves two opposing forces. The first is a positive motivational force that attracts you to the person. It is quick to develop and quick to level off. The negative motivational force, the one that works against the attraction, is slow to develop and slow to fade. The result is an initial rapid growth in passion, followed by habituation when the more slowly developing negative force kicks in. "It's like with coffee, cigarettes or alcohol," Sternberg says. "Addiction can be rapid, but once habituation sets in, even an increased amount of exposure to the person or substance no longer stimulates the motivational arousal that was once possible.

"And then when the person dumps you, it's even worse. You don't go back to the way you were before you met the person," Sternberg explains. "You end up much worse off. You get depressed, irritable, you lose your appetite. You get these withdrawal symptoms, just as if you had quit drinking coffee or smoking, and it takes a while to get over it." The slow-starting, slow-fading negative force is still there after the person or the substance is gone.

The cognitive side of Sternberg's love triangle is commitment, both a short-term decision to love another person and a long-term commitment to maintain that love. Its developmental course is more straightforward and easier to explain than that of intimacy or passion. Essentially, commitment starts at zero when you first meet the other person and grows as you get to know each other. If the relationship is destined to be long-term, Sternberg says, the level of commitment will usually increase gradually at first and then speed up. As the relationship continues, the amount of commitment will generally level off. If the relationship begins to flag, the level of commitment will decline, and if the relationship fails, the level of commitment falls back to zero. According to Sternberg, the love of a parent for a child is often distinguished by a high and unconditional level of commitment.

Levels of intimacy, passion and commitment change over time, and so do relationships. You can visualize this, says Sternberg, by considering how the love triangle changes in size and shape as the three components of love increase and decrease. The triangle's area represents the amount of love and its shape the style. Large amounts of intimacy, passion and commitment, for example, yield a large triangle. And in general, Sternberg says, the larger the triangle, the more love.

Changing the length of the individual sides yields four differently shaped triangles, or styles of love. A triangle with three equal sides represents what Sternberg calls a "balanced" love in which all three components are equally matched. A scalene triangle (three unequal sides) in which the longest leg is passion represents a relationship in which physical attraction plays a larger role than either emotional intimacy or cognitive commitment. A scalene triangle with commitment as its longest leg depicts a relationship in which the intimacy and passion have waned or were never there in the first place. An isosceles triangle (two equal sides) with intimacy as its longest leg shows a relationship in which emotional involvement is more important than either passion or commitment. It's more like a high-grade friendship than a romance.

Sternberg admits that this triangle is a simplification of a complex and subtle phenomenon. There can be a variety of emotions, motivations and types of commitment in a loving relationship, and each would have to be examined to completely diagnose a relationship. Beyond that, he says, every relationship involves several triangles: In addition to their own triangles, both people have an ideal triangle (the way you would like to feel about the person you love) and a perceived triangle (the way you think the other person feels about you).

Sternberg and graduate student Michael Barnes studied the effects these triangles have on a relationship by administering the liking and loving scales to 24 couples. Participants were asked to rate their relationship in terms of how they feel about the other person, how they think the other person feels about them, how they would feel about an ideal person and how they would want an ideal person to feel about them. They found that satisfaction is closely related to the similarity between these real, ideal and perceived triangles. In general, the closer they are in shape and size, the more satisfying the relationship.

The best single predictor of happiness in a relationship is not how you feel about the other person but the difference between how you would ideally like the other person to feel about you and how you think he or she actually feels about you. "In other words," Sternberg says, "relationships tend to go bad when there is a mismatch between what you want from the other person and what you think you are getting.

"Were you ever the overinvolved person in a relationship? That can be very dissatisfying. What usually happens is that the more involved person tries to think up schemes to get the other person up to his or her level of involvement. But the other person usually sees what's going on and backs off. That just makes the overinvolved person try harder and the other person back off more until it tears the relationship apart. The good advice in such a situation is for the overinvolved person to scale down, but that advice is hard to follow."

An underlying question in Sternberg's love research is: Why do so many relationships fail? Almost half the marriages in the United States end in divorce, and many couples who don't get divorced aren't all that happy. "Are people really so dumb that they pick wrong most of the time? Probably not," he suggests. "What they're doing is picking on the basis of what matters to them in the short run. But what matters in the long run may be different. The factors that count change, people change, relationships change."

Sternberg can't predict how people or situations will change, but he and his assistant Sandra Wright recently completed a study that suggests what will and won't be important in the long run. They put this question, what's important in a relationship, to 80 men and women from 17 to 69 years old, and divided them into three groups according to the length of their most recent relationship. The short-term group had been involved for up to two years, the mid-term group between two and five years, the others for more than five years.

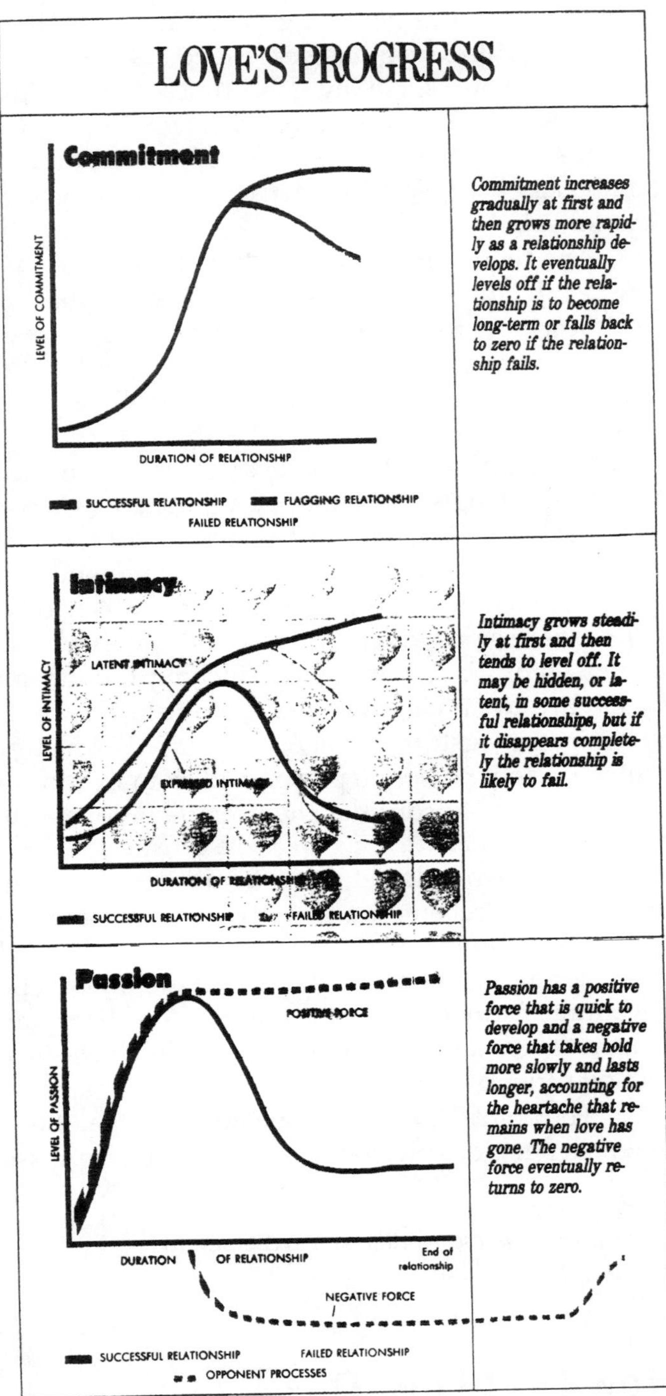

Among the things that increase in importance as a relationship grows are willingness to change in response to each other and willingness to tolerate each other's imperfections. "These are things you can't judge at the beginning of a relationship," Sternberg says. "In the beginning," he explains, "some of the other person's flaws might not seem important. They may even seem kind of cute, but over the long term they may begin to grate on you. You both have to be willing to make some changes to make the relationship work and you both have to be willing to tolerate some flaws."

Another thing that becomes increasingly important is the sharing of values, especially religious values. "When you first meet," says Sternberg, "you have this love-overcomes-all-obstacles attitude, but when the kids come along you have to make some hard decisions about the religion issue. All of a sudden something that wasn't so important is important."

Among the things that tend to decrease in importance is how interesting you find your partner. "In the beginning," Sternberg says, "it's almost as if the other person has to keep you interested or the relationship will go nowhere. Later on, it's not quite as critical because there are other things in your life that matter."

In addition to asking what is important at different times, Sternberg and Wright asked how much of these various things people had at different times in their relationships. The answers were not encouraging. The ability to make love, for example, often goes just at the time when it is becoming more important. In fact, Sternberg says, almost everything except matching religious beliefs decreased over time. The ability to communicate, physical attractiveness, having good times, sharing interests, the ability to listen, respect for each other, romantic love—they all went down. "That may be depressing," says Sternberg, "but it's important to know at the beginning of a relationship what to expect over time, to have realistic expectations for what you can get and what is going to be important in a relationship."

And Sternberg feels that his triangular theory of love can help people in other ways. "Just analyzing your relationship in terms of the three components can be useful," he says. "Are you more romantic and your partner more companionate? It's helpful to know where you and your partner are well-matched and where you are not and then start thinking about what you can do to make yourselves more alike in what you want out of the relationship."

If you decide to take steps to improve a relationship, Sternberg offers a final triangle, the action triangle. "Often there's quite a gap between thought or feeling and action," he explains. "Your actions don't always reflect the way you feel, so it could help to know just what actions are associated with each component of love."

Intimacy, he suggests, might be expressed by communicating inner feelings; sharing one's possessions, time and self; and offering emotional support. Passion, obviously, is expressed by kissing, hugging, touching and making love. Commitment can be expressed by fidelity, by staying with the relationship through the hard times that occur in any relationship or by getting engaged or married. Which actions are most important and helpful will vary from person to person and from relationship to relationship. But Sternberg feels it is important to consider the triangle of love as it is expressed through action because action has so many effects on a relationship.

Citing psychologist Daryl Bem's theory of self-perception, Sternberg describes how actions can affect emotions, motivations and cognitions. "The way we act shapes the way we feel and think, possibly as much as the way we think and feel shapes the way we act." Also, he says, certain actions can lead to other actions; expressions of love, for example, encourage further expressions of love. Furthermore, your actions affect the way the other person thinks and feels about you and behaves toward you, leading to a mutually reinforcing series of actions.

"The point," Sternberg concludes, "is that it is necessary to take into account the ways in which people express their love. Without expression, even the greatest of loves can die."

Robert J. Trotter is a senior editor at Psychology Today.

How Do I Love Thee?

Intimacy, passion and commitment are the warm, hot and cold vertices of Sternberg's love triangle. Alone and in combination they give rise to eight possible kinds of love relationships. The first is nonlove—the absence of all three components. This describes the large majority of our personal relationships, which are simply casual interactions.

The second kind of love is liking. "If you just have intimacy," Sternberg explains, "that's liking. You can talk to the person, tell about your life. And if that's all there is to it, that's what we mean by liking." It is more than nonlove. It refers to the feelings experienced in true friendships. Liking includes such things as closeness and warmth but not the intense feelings of passion or commitment.

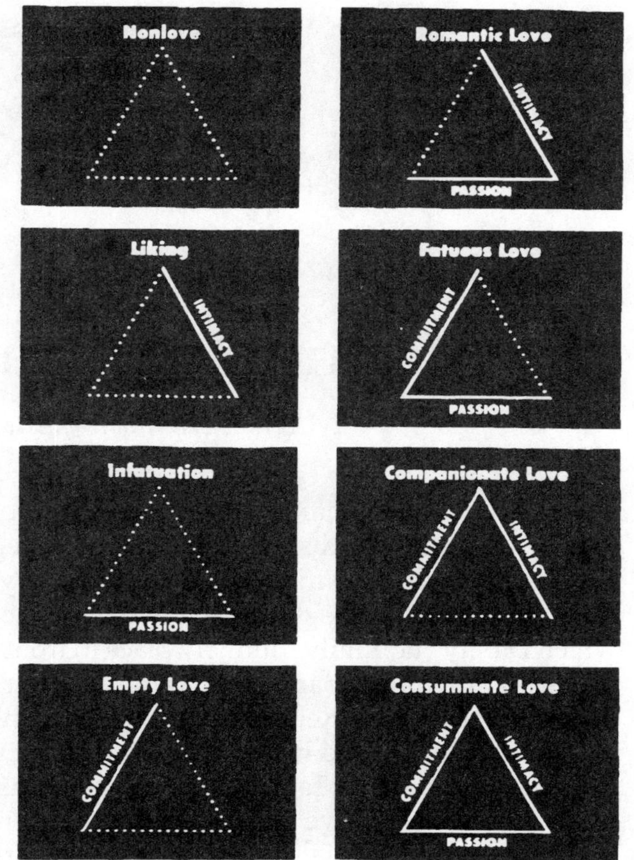

If you just have passion, it's called infatuated love—the "love at first sight" that can arise almost instantaneously and dissipate just as quickly. It involves a high degree of physiological arousal but no intimacy or commitment. It's the 10th-grader who falls madly in love with the beautiful girl in his biology class but never gets up the courage to talk to her or get to know her, Sternberg says, describing his past.

Empty love is commitment without intimacy or passion, the kind of love sometimes seen in a 30-year-old marriage that has become stagnant. The couple used to be intimate, but they don't talk to each other any more. They used to be passionate, but that's died out. All that remains is the commitment to stay with the other person. In societies in which marriages are arranged, Sternberg points out, empty love may precede the other kinds of love.

Romantic love, the Romeo and Juliet type of love, is a combination of intimacy and passion. More than infatuation, it's liking with the added excitement of physical attraction and arousal but without commitment. A summer affair can be very romantic, Sternberg explains, but you know it will end when she goes back to Hawaii and you go back to Florida, or wherever.

Passion plus commitment is what Sternberg calls fatuous love. It's Hollywood love: Boy meets girl, a week later they're engaged, a month later they're married. They are committed on the basis of their passion, but because intimacy takes time to develop, they don't have the emotional core necessary to sustain the commitment. This kind of love, Sternberg warns, usually doesn't work out.

Companionate love is intimacy with commitment but no passion. It's a long-term friendship, the kind of committed love and intimacy frequently seen in marriages in which the physical attraction has died down.

When all three elements of Sternberg's love triangle come together in a relationship, you get what he calls consummate love, or complete love. It's the kind of love toward which many people strive, especially in romantic relationships. Achieving consummate love, says Sternberg, is like trying to lose weight, difficult but not impossible. The really hard thing is keeping the weight off after you have lost it, or keeping the consummate love alive after you have achieved it. Consummate love is possible only in very special relationships.

Making the Grade as Parents

Michael Meyerhoff and Burton L. White

Danny and Emily Richardson and their 1-year-old daughter Rebecca live in a large, neatly kept home in the suburbs. The Richardsons, college graduates, have decided to give Rebecca the best possible start in life. She has a nursery that is stocked with all the latest educational toys. During the day, she spends much of her time in her well-equipped playpen, which Danny and Emily routinely place in front of the television set so she can be exposed to *Sesame Street.* Both parents set aside 30 minutes every day for "learning sessions," during which they teach Rebecca to recognize numbers, the alphabet and objects in pictures, and they have enrolled her in a professionally run playgroup two mornings a week.

David and Laura Taylor, high school graduates with two older children and a 1-year-old named Andrew, live in a crowded apartment that is clean but usually quite cluttered. They can't afford special toys or equipment, and their busy schedule does not allow them to set aside special blocks of time for Andrew. He spends much of his time roaming around the house playing with pots, pans, empty boxes and whatever else he can find. Sometimes he follows his parents around as they perform household chores, interrupting them every now and then to ask for help or to share his excitement over something he has discovered. David and Laura always respond warmly and enthusiastically, but they rarely can give Andrew more than a couple of minutes of their undivided attention.

On the surface, it would appear that the Richardsons have the advantage in the child-rearing game. But our 20 years of child-development research indicate that Andrew is more likely than Rebecca to develop into a well-adjusted, competent preschool child. Some of our findings often defy popular notions and even "common sense," but they are supported by our recently completed "New Parents as Teachers" project in Missouri.

The new parents project was based on the idea that a great deal of important learning takes place during the first three years of life, that home is the first schoolhouse and parents are the first teachers. If parents are adequately prepared for and supported in their role as teachers, they will have a better chance of doing that job well.

The roots of the project go back to the early 1960s when an increasing number of parents and educators began to realize that many children were already "educationally disadvantaged" by the time they entered kindergarten. Our research with the Harvard Preschool Project, which began in 1965, identified a large sample of preschool children who, by anyone's definition and in everyone's opinion, were "most likely to succeed." They came from a wide range of socioeconomic and cultural backgrounds but shared a variety of intellectual, linguistic and social skills that clearly set them apart from their average and below-average peers. It soon became clear to us that they were exhibiting this impressive pattern of abilities by the time they were 3 years old.

We then went to the families of these children and found out which ones were expecting another child. When the new infants were between 1 and 3 years old, we began visiting their homes every other week and recording everything we could about their experiences and the child-rearing practices of their parents.

Later, we took what we had learned, combined it with the research of other developmental psychologists and translated it into information and support programs for new parents. Although much research remained to be done, we were convinced that effective programs could be developed to provide new parents with a great deal of reliable, useful information that was not then routinely available to them.

With this in mind, we established in 1978 the Center for Parent Education in Newton, Massachusetts. The primary goals were to increase public awareness of these issues and to provide resource, consulting and training services to professionals concerned with the education of children during the first three years of life. We were especially interested in those who wanted to work with parents in their role as a child's first and most important teachers.

In 1981, the Missouri State Department of Education, with funding from the Danforth Foundation, hired us to design a model parent-education program and help set it up in four school districts across the state: one urban, one suburban, one small town and one rural. Together, the families they served represented the total population of Missouri, covering a wide range of social and economic backgrounds. One full-time and two part-time parent educators were hired to serve between 60 and 100 families in each district. We provided them with specialized training, helped equip resource centers and supplied ongoing guidance and supervision for the entire effort. By January of 1982, everything was ready, and services to families began. They continued for three years at a cost of approximately $800 per family per year.

The services included group get-togethers, at which 10 to 20 parents would meet with a parent educator at the resource center, and individual home visits by a parent educator. Services began during the final three months of pregnancy and continued until the child's third birthday, with increasing emphasis on private visits after the child was 5 or 6 months old. The average amount of contact with families was once a month for an hour to an hour and a half.

Comprehensive screening procedures were used to monitor each child's intellectual, linguistic and social progress, and an extensive referral system ensured that parents could obtain prompt assistance if there were any signs of educational difficulty. Parents who had monetary, medical or other noneducational problems were referred to appropriate agencies.

Parents also used the resource centers to examine books, magazines, toys and other materials related to early development and parenting and to get guidance from the staff in selecting the most useful items.

During group and private sessions, parents were given basic information about what kinds of parenting practices are likely to either help or hinder their children's progress (see "A Primer for Parents"). They watched videotapes that demonstrated typical behavior of infants and toddlers and were given pamphlets and other materials that outlined the interests and abilities of children at each stage of development, suggested appropriate activities and told them what new developments to expect.

The information and advice provided were remarkably simple. Since we were interested in promoting well-balanced, all-around development, we did not advocate high-pressure procedures designed to produce child prodigies. Unlike the many "infant stimulation" or "superbaby" programs that have sprung up in recent years, the Missouri program focused on a comfortable, constructive style of parenting designed to make the early educational process enjoyable as well as effective rather than intensive and highly structured. In our opinion, such high-pressure programs tend to dampen the children's intrinsic interest in learning and take much of the fun out of the typical daily interactions between parents and children.

All too often, for example, parents overemphasize the importance of their child's spoken vocabulary. Our research shows that although many well-developing children do not say much until they are almost 2 years old, their capacity to understand simple words and instructions begins well before their first birthday, usually when they are between 6 and 8 months old. Unfortunately, since most people tend not to talk to things that don't talk back—such as chairs, fire hydrants, and little babies—many parents miss out on many months worth of opportunities for teaching language.

In homes where children were developing impressive linguistic abilities, we noticed that the parents talked to them frequently almost from birth. Moreover, once the children showed an awareness of language, the parents did not push them into vocabulary exercises using flashcards, labeling books or other such devices. Instead, they simply waited for the many times every day their children approached them for comfort, assistance or to share their excitement over some discovery. When this happened, the parents would use simple language to talk about and expand upon whatever topic the child introduced.

Intellectual development is an area in which "doing what comes naturally" also can be counterproductive at times. For instance, when children reach the second half of the first year, they start crawling and climbing, making accidental falls, poisonings and other serious mishaps likely. Many well-meaning parents react by restricting their children to a small but safe area, such as a playpen. They then provide an abundance of "educational" toys to keep the children occupied and occasionally let them loose for supervised "learning" sessions.

We noticed, however, that in homes where children were developing impressive intellectual abilities, parents often took a much different tack. Rather than restricting their children, they simply redesigned their homes, making most of the living area safe for (and from) newly mobile babies. This gave the children access to a very large, interesting learning environment in which they could experiment with, explore and investigate a whole world of exciting and enriching objects virtually at will.

The parents of these exceptional children were also ready and willing to provide new learning opportunities, not through expensive toys or specific games, but by letting the children help bake cookies, accompany them on a trip to the supermarket and so on. In other words, instead of setting aside specific and structured "teaching" time, they set up interesting environments, allowed the children to indulge their natural curiosity and then followed the children's leads.

Social skills are also beginning to develop during the first three years, but many parents, especially first-timers, make the mistake of assuming that children come civilized, or at least acquire common courtesies on their own. Even when presented with increasing evidence to the contrary, a lot of parents have trouble cracking down on unacceptable behavior, fearing they might lose the child's love. The "terrible twos" and the unpleasant temper tantrums of the third year of life are an all too common result.

But they are not inevitable. Our earlier studies had shown that in homes where children were both bright and a pleasure to live with, the parents were not afraid to set realistic but firm boundaries on behavior before their children's first birthday. During the first months of life, these parents lavished love and attention on their children and responded almost unconditionally to every demand. However, starting at about 8 months, and especially during the normal period of "negativism" between 15 and 24 months of age, when many children's demands were simply tests of what they could get away with, these parents reacted by letting the children know in no uncertain terms that other people had rights, too.

We had also learned that persistency in setting such limits was most important. Sooner or later, all parents would admonish their children for certain undesirable activities. But the effective parents always made sure to follow through. If the admonishments were ignored, then or later, they acted swiftly, using disciplinary strategies appropriate to their children's level of understanding. For instance, with an 18-month-old, rather than saying something like, "If you don't stop pulling on the drapes, we won't take you to Nana's house next Christmas," they quickly removed the child from the scene and physically prevented a return.

These few examples represent the sorts of things we stressed and the style of child rearing we encouraged the parents to adopt. Since participation in the Missouri program was voluntary, we could not require them to follow our advice, but we've always found that first-time parents are eager for guidance that will help them cope.

As the children of the participating families approached their third birthdays, we had an independent organization, Research and Training Associates of Overland Park, Kansas, evaluate the effectiveness of the program. A group of 75 randomly selected children from our project was compared with a carefully matched sample of children who had not been in the project. The evaluators found that the social development of the project children was outstanding, but since it is difficult to measure social skills in such young children, there was no reliable way to make comparisons.

Sophisticated measures of linguistic and intellectual development, however, left little doubt that the program had enhanced the educational prospects of the children involved in the project. The Kaufman Assessment Battery for Children and the Zimmerman Preschool Language Scale were used to measure intellectual and linguistic development, and the Missouri project children scored significantly higher in both areas.

A Primer for Parents

The following recommendations are based on the lessons we learned from the parents of linguistically, intellectually and socially competent preschool children.

Things to Do

Provide your children with a maximum opportunity for exploration and investigation by making your home as safe and accessible as possible.

Remove fragile and dangerous items from low shelves and cabinets, and replace them with old magazines, pots and pans, plastic measuring cups and other suitable playthings.

Be available to act as your children's personal consultant during the majority of their waking hours. You don't have to hover, just be nearby to provide attention and support as needed.

Respond to your children promptly and favorably as often as you can, providing appropriate enthusiasm and encouragement.

Set limits—do not give in to unreasonable requests or permit unacceptable behavior to continue.

Talk to your children often. Make an effort to understand what they are trying to do and concentrate on what they see as important.

Use words they understand but also add new words and related ideas. For example, if your child gives you a red ball, say, "This ball is red, just like my shirt. Your shirt is blue and it matches your pants."

Provide new learning opportunities. Having children accompany you to the supermarket or allowing them to help you bake cookies will be more enriching than sitting them down and conducting a flashcard session.

Give your children a chance to direct some of your shared activities from time to time.

Try to help your children be as spontaneous emotionally as your own behavior patterns will allow.

Encourage your children's pretend activities, especially those in which they act out adult roles.

Things to Avoid

Don't confine your children regularly for long periods.

Don't allow them to concentrate their energies on you so much that independent exploration and investigation are excluded.

Don't ignore attention-getting devices to the point where children have to throw a tantrum to gain your interest.

Don't worry that your children won't love you if you say "no" on occasion.

Don't try to win all the arguments, particularly during the second half of the second year when most children are passing through a normal period of negativism.

Don't try to prevent your children from cluttering the house—it's a sure sign of a healthy and curious baby.

Don't be overprotective.

Don't bore your child if you can avoid it.

Don't worry about when children learn to count or say the alphabet. Don't worry if they are slow to talk, as long as they seem to understand more and more language as time goes by.

Don't try to force toilet training. It will be easier by the time they are 2.

Don't spoil your children, giving them the notion that the world was made just for them.

Not all families in the four school districts were included in the evaluation. In some cases children had severe problems, such as cleft palate or Down's syndrome. In others, the parents had overwhelming problems that overshadowed educational issues, such as alcoholism or abject poverty. We included these families in the project, but we made it clear that our program could not deal with their extraordinary circumstances. To that extent, we cannot say that this type of program will be successful for every family with young children.

On the other hand, the results of the evaluation seem applicable to the approximately 85 percent of the population without such special problems. We had success with families in which both parents had doctoral degrees and with families in which both parents had failed to finish high school. In some families, the annual income was more than $40,000, and in others it was below the poverty line. There were black families and white families. Some parents were in their late 30s, others were still teenagers and a number of them were single parents.

We feel that we have clearly demonstrated some basic principles that could revolutionize the traditional approach to education in this country and around the world. First, you are likely to make the greatest difference in the academic prospects of young children if you reach them during the first three years, when the foundations for later development are laid.

Furthermore, the most inexpensive and efficient method is to work through the people who have the greatest influence on children's lives during this period—their parents. Finally, most parents, regardless of social status, educational level or cultural background, are eager to receive and can benefit from the information and support they need to be effective in their role as their children's first and most important teachers.

Educational psychologists Michael K. Meyerhoff, Ed.D., and Burton L. White, Ph.D., publish a newsletter every other month for professionals through the Center for Parent Education in Newton, Massachusetts, and they regularly conduct professional workshops on "Educating the Infant and Toddler" throughout the United States and Canada.

How to Manage Your Kids

Frank Pittman, M.D.

"Children are life renewing itself, Captain Butler. And when life does that, danger seems very unimportant."

Melanie Wilkes in *Gone with the Wind*

"Babies, war, and taxes! There's never a convenient time for any of them."

Scarlett O'Hara in *Gone with the Wind*

Last week Justin Wesley Wagers, the first of what I hope will be many grandchildren, was born. My wife Betsy and I went out to Boulder to bond with him. I spent a week holding him and licking him and understanding that people have children to get grandchildren. In due time we turned Justin over to the alternate shift of grandparents, and came back to earth. We had been transposed. We glowed in the dark. We had been declared gods and turned into constellations. We were now immortal—maybe, a little.

When people have children, there is this hope for some little piece of immortality. Parents and grandparents don't actually become immortal, but if they are paying attention, they do become part of everything that has gone on before or that will go on after them. That is wonderful, but it is even more wonderful if they fully realize that their children and grandchildren (even those as perfect as my beloved grandson Justin) are no different, no more special, than everyone else's children and grandchildren, and that every other parent and grandparent is going through the same thing with them.

The Magic of Child Raising

Of course, *having* children has limited benefits at best, and can even be an expression of greediness and narcissism, an imposition upon one's neighbors and upon the planet itself. The magical experience, rather, is *raising* children. People who want the pride, the potential glory, and the self-expansion of parenthood without the humbling, enlightening turmoil of hands-on parenting are not just missing the magic but are cheating. Unless they are supplying much-needed children for people who cannot create their own, people who create babies they expect others to raise are like F. Scott Fitzgerald's spoiled-rotten rich kids in *The Great Gatsby:* "They were careless people, Tom and Daisy—they smashed up things and creatures and then retreated back into their money or their vast carelessness . . . and let other people clean up the mess they had made."

Naive scientists trying to make sense out of human sexuality would have us believe that childbearing is a biological imperative that stops at the delivery-room door. They tell us that the human animal has an overriding instinctive investment in the survival of its sperm and egg cells, and is drawn to behaviors that will spawn the largest numbers of fertilized eggs. But the human animal could not have survived, no matter how many of our ignorant, immobile, dependent offspring were deposited on the ground, if there were not parents around to raise them.

Human babies require parents not just for their physical survival but for their humanity. Feral children, raised in the woods by wolves or on the streets by peers, are not likely to be fully human—in large part because they lack the experience of parents investing love in an organism who is not yet able to give anything back.

The human species survived against all probability in a hostile environment because there were people who valued us enough to join forces and take care of us. Not just to feed and shelter us, but to teach us the increasingly complex things we soft, slow, unarmed beings need to survive and to serve our biological function of creating others—taking care of them, teaching them what they need to know, and loving them enough to make them yearn to love others and pass it on.

Child raising has always been the most important activity of the human animal, male or female. But since the Industrial Revolution, the outrageous idea has taken hold that child raising is women's work—that men have something vastly more important to do than the care, feeding, education, and emotional training of the next generation. (I can't imagine what would be more important—war? business? government? sports on TV? reassuring themselves of their masculinity by seducing other women?)

The man who cannot be servant to a child, who expects his children or those of other people to exist for his own glory or comfort, is the center of his own universe and is unlikely to be capable of loving anything outside himself. He may be stuck in the wrong generation.

Football, military school, prison, and war have been touted as the experience that can turn a boy into a man. Nonsense! The experience that makes a man is not insemination, but hands-on fathering. I have no desire to shake the hand that has never changed a diaper.

We Need More Parents

If you need a baby, we already have all you could ever need. (They may not come in your choice of colors, but that is your problem.) The rest of us certainly don't need you to have babies unless you are willing to dedicate your life to raising them, and to letting others share in the process. If you are too selfish, childish, ill-tempered, or out of control to share your life with a grown-up partner or a community of other adults, please don't inflict yourself on a helpless child.

You don't have to be perfect to be a parent, but you do have to be pleasant and accommodating enough to others so that they don't isolate you and your child. After all, child-raising is not just about sheltering, feeding, watering, and educating children, but about making kids part of the world around them. If you embark upon this most excellent adventure, be aware that all a child needs from you is you—completely.

Hodding Carter gave me my favorite quote about parents and children. He said "There are only two lasting bequests we can hope to give our children. One of these is roots; the other, wings." I would add to that. Roots and wings are exactly the two lasting bequests that children give parents, connecting you with your familial, biological, and personal origins, and enabling you to live many lives other than your own.

Never forget: the end product of child raising is not the child, who still must go forth in the world to raise him- or herself, but the parent. For the parent, raising children is magic.

What Parents Cannot Expect

With all the emotional exercise and the character building that goes into parenting, there are still things children cannot do for their parents, things parents cannot expect from their children.

1. You can't expect to get the benefits of parenthood from sperm donation or other forms of surrogate parenthood. Supporting your own children is no more gratifying or character enhancing than paying taxes to support other people's children. You'll just get angry because the people you support don't perform better or produce more. Even if you get your picture taken with the child on ceremonial occasions, or come home at night to a house filled with the child's artifacts, or hear the child's blood-curdling music coming from a locked bedroom, or see the child perform at athletic or artistic displays, the experience will have little impact on you if you are not totally involved in the experience of the child's life, and the corresponding revelations of your own life, your relationship to the world, and the human condition you both share.

2. You can't expect to run out on your family, or destroy it, or ignore it, without terrible repercussions on your children. I don't know who came up with the notion of "quality time," the idea that parenting could be done efficiently. Parenting is what happens when people of different generations hang out together and compare their experience of the world. It affects one just about as much as it affects the other. If what you are doing with your child is not changing your life, then don't expect it to change the child's.

I also don't know who came up with the idea that parents "shouldn't stay together for the children's sake." That's absurd, though I certainly agree that staying together while turning family life into a war zone and blaming it on the kids is not good for anybody's mental health, even the neighbors'. Children do not require perfect love or brilliant innovative parenting techniques, or a life that is made free of germs or disappointments or traumas, but they do require the security of knowing that their parents will put up with one another's mild to moderate obnoxiousness and repulsiveness for the sake of the family.

And it is not sufficient for parents to stay married for the children's sake; they must stay *happily* married for the children's sake. A happy marriage is a decision that comes when people decide that this is their real life, their real world, their real marriage—and that stomping their foot and holding their breath because it is not the life, world, and marriage of their dreams is not going to get them a better deal, so they might as well grin and bear it. No marriage is easy to stay in. Yet as couples measure the pros and cons of such drastic action as divorce, they must tally in the costs to their children. Parents may learn the hard way that running out on parenting for a while, to recapture some piece of their own lost youth, breaks a parent–child bond that may never be reforged.

There are limits, of course. It is hard to be married to someone who is not married to you, and it is foolhardy to be married to someone who is driving drunk, beating you up, or exposing you to deadly viruses. People sometimes must choose between suicide, homicide, and divorce—and that's a no-brainer. And if you are married to someone who expects you to be a single parent, you may have fantasies of cutting loose and finding someone who is the parent your child deserves. But that's risky.

The crippling trauma of a divorce and the child's resulting lifelong insecurity about life and relationships may be worse than the vague or even fairly certain hope that the next step-parent will be the magical one that will make everything rosy for you and your child. Every child needs a secure family, not a perfect one.

3. You can't expect to raise perfect children even if you are perfect parents. We like to think, and our therapists and the writers of our favorite self-help books like to reassure us, that everything that isn't ideal in our life is surely our parents' fault. You may be right in thinking that you are to blame for your kid's hang-up, that your child's teachers are going

to think your child's failures are because you are not sufficiently involved (even though your child's therapist is probably telling you the kid is a screwup because you are too involved). Your parents and in-laws overflow with wisdom that may or may not be applicable, and the neighbors have another set of ideas about how you are making a mess of things. Everybody will blame you except the child. But if you are too willing to blame yourself, the child will take the cue from you and blame you for his or her failures, and that's a lot worse.

Don't worry. Your children will probably turn out to be pretty much the way you are unless you try too hard to change them. If you raise your child violently, your child will learn to be violent. If you scream and yell, your child will learn to scream and yell. Certainly no child can change the thing you are always screaming about and still retain any self-respect. If you are anxious about your child's failures, you can make the child so nervous the failures will be inevitable.

Just stop trying to fix your normal children, show the joy you take in them, talk to them about their experience of the world and tell them about yours, make them face the world even if it scares you both, and they will become just like you. You have no way of making them turn out better than you; they have to do that on their own. And if you are really perfect in some way, they will have to find their own way to distinguish themselves.

You can't have a perfect child because you are in some contest with the other parents, or because you are afraid the inspection committee will come along and tell you what you have suspected all along: that you are a terrible parent and a terrible person. Anyway, children learn from their mistakes, not from their parents' anxiety that they will make mistakes. You can require that they face life, and even that they develop competence in the basic skills, but excellence can only come from their own hunger for it, and that can come only when their initial efforts are praised.

In some ways, damaged children are actually more gratifying to raise, especially if the disability shows. If the kid is blind or deaf or missing a body part or two, the world does what the world should do for all kids: assesses the child's performance on the basis of his or her own merits and the child's own development, rather than as part of some contest with other kids.

In other words, it is not a contest, so stop trying so hard to win at it, and just enjoy the wonder of it all.

4. You can't expect children to repay your investment in them. Some parents believe that if they put enough time and money into it, the child is supposed to reward them with a comparable amount of parental pride. I see men who know something about sports, the military, business, or all three, but nothing at all about being a human being. They attempt to turn their children into lucrative sports stars by investing their hard-earned time and energy into full-time basic training and coaching. At either the stroke of puberty or the last straw in personal humiliation, whichever comes first, the child must of course rebel, and the father, who really had only the best of intentions, doesn't understand what has happened. Children, however dutiful, can only dedicate their lives to their own dreams, not the fulfillment of their parents'. If parents' fantasies overwhelm their kids, if the children lose their sense of self by buckling under and merging with their parents' ego, they can't go on.

Kids must feel safe in an activity before they become competent at it and, finally, pull back and differentiate. Only then can they excel while remaining their own person, capable of pride in their skills and self-respect with their parents.

5. You can't expect the children to show appreciation for your efforts. If a child takes the parent quite for granted, without having to avoid giving or taking offense, without having to keep score on who owes whom what, that should be appreciation enough. It

shows that the child feels the parent's steady love and knows that the parent has gotten as much as has been given from the parenting process.

The child may adore and cherish the parent and may still take the parent for granted, and forget to send a card on Mother's Day.

6. You can't expect your children to give you the sort of exclusive loyalty, the almost monogamous dedication, that you might reasonably expect from marriage. A parent might naively assume that since "I was always there for the kids while he worked or played golf or screwed around," or that since "I supported them while she lay around watching TV and drinking," then the kids owe allegiance to me. It may feel like a terrible betrayal in a divorce or a marriage at war when the kids take the "good" parent for granted and throw themselves after the "bad" parent who escapes parenthood for another go at childhood, but it is necessary for the child who doesn't know a parent to find out personally what's missing, what's wrong.

There are those parents who destroy their children by getting between them and the other parent, getting between them and their grandparents, getting between them and the child's friends or mates, getting between them and their in-laws, and even getting between them and their own children.

When a parent tries to get his or her life from the grown child, it will destroy either the child or the relationship, and it indicates that when the parent was raising the child, the parent did not "get it." He or she didn't realize who was benefiting from the process, and therefore didn't become his or her own person. Recycling an adult through childhood, so the parents can feel loved without having to risk a relationship with another adult, is cumbersome.

If parents want unquestioning loyalty from a creature who will never desert them, perhaps they should get a dog. Dogs merely wag their tails and lick the hands of whoever feeds them, even if they get beaten as well. Dogs demand nothing more from life than food. Some parents would raise children like that, but even the best-trained humans are not so reliable in that role, and have been known to run away from the best-appointed homes.

Puppies can be paper-trained at a very early age, and while still quite young can be taken outside to pee on the lawn. Dogs are already learning entertaining tricks while human children can't do much more than pull things over on top of themselves. Dogs are a lot cheaper at every stage of development and you don't have to worry about them growing up, leaving you, and telling a therapist what a miserable parent you were.

7. You can't expect your children to serve as cheap labor for you. Some potential parents are seeking a practical use for children. Families used to breed children for labor, to work in the mines or the mills, and the children were rewarded with a little pay and a lot of honor. Growing up in the country, I had farm work to do and animals to feed and tend, and I loved it because it made me feel useful. In some parts of the world, families have seeing-eye children for the blind adults. Children are natural, eager apprentices, excited to learn whatever the parents know how to do, delighted to follow the parents around learning their skills. There should be no thought of having someone around the house who doesn't share in work needing to be done. Children, if they are to become adults, should be functional and proud of it.

Somehow it doesn't work out that way nowadays. For one, child labor is now illegal, as every child knows. And anyone who has tried to teach a child to do his or her chores can immediately see the folly in that effort. It takes far more effort to get a child to clean his room or take out the garbage than it does to do it yourself. I see rich kids who will cut a deal with their parents and earn what in other families might be a week's wages for washing the car. It is as if work and even punishment—is beneath the dignity of His Majesty The Child.

Of course, children may eagerly join parents in doing whatever work around the house they do themselves. Kids are so eager to work *with* parents, and so loathe to work *for* them. Moreover, a child who would declare global nuclear war rather than pick up his underwear may eagerly slave away for minimum wage at McDonald's. Working for someone other than parents can seem like a victory rather than a defeat.

8. You can't expect children to save a relationship. Some women foolishly have babies to save a bad marriage, to get some guy to marry them, or even just to get him to drop by from time to time and be nice to her. It is not a good idea. Having a baby with a guy who is afraid of commitment and family life, afraid of husbandhood and fatherhood, will not reliably bring him closer to you. And if he doesn't like you very much to start with, he's not likely to like you better when you wake him up in the middle of the night to throw a hungry, wet, feces-smeared, squishy noisemaker at him.

The most inescapable fact of human biology is that females can create life from their bodies and males cannot. Patriarchy was invented to give men some feeling of involvement in the creation of life. But beneath the patriarchal posturings of male ownership that cover the sterile shame of male uterus-envy, there is full awareness on the part of men that they can never experience anything comparable to the mother–child relationship. As a result, men are likely to distance themselves from the early stages of that symbiosis. Perhaps overwhelmed and fearful, a man may consider the mother-and-child unit to be complete but dependent and turn his attention to conquering the world and turning himself into a hero for them.

Of course, once the child is weaned and able to venture out into the world, the father is quite capable of joining in or taking over. But men who didn't get much fathering in recent generations may not know what a father is for, and women, who usually got even less fathering than men did, are likely to be even more misinformed about what men are capable of doing. If the father feels left out or if the mother leaves him out, it bodes badly for the relationship. He generally takes on the parenting role initially because of his commitment to the mother and if that relationship is not a loving one, he may have trouble bonding with his son or daughter—unless, of course, he has bonded well with his own father. In the long run, how a man does as father and husband is mostly dependent upon what his own dad did as father and husband.

9. You can't expect the benefits of child raising to come immediately. Like farming, child raising enforces patience. There is no way to speed it up, and any effort to do so will just screw it up. Child raising forces busy people to slow down and live their lives in real time, moving no faster than the earth does, blocked from taking any shortcuts. Once you are operating on earth time with your child, you begin to see and hear and smell and feel things you had forgotten all about. You may not get as much done, but you will get far more from everything you do. Don't worry, you won't miss a thing.

10. But finally, you must expect to make one crucial concession to child raising. As you raise your children you will have to forgive your parents, either for loving you too much or for not loving you enough. While that is the most important step in getting control of your own life, for those who endeavor to go through life as their own pampered child or as an indignant victim, it is a terrible loss. The act of becoming a parent involves the willingness to expose yourself to having your child feel toward you the way you feel toward your parents.

21 Tricks for Taming Children

1. Hold babies close to your skin for many hours every day. No matter how delicious your baby smells, resist the temptation to take a bite.
2. Play mostly Mozart or Haydn so the baby will grow up intelligent, secure, and prepared to join an orderly, graceful world.
3. Talk to your baby. Long before the baby is old enough to understand a word of it, tell the baby everything about you, all the wonderful things you're too modest to tell others, and all of the secrets you wouldn't want even your analyst to know. You will value the baby even more if he or she knows you better than anyone else.
4. Spend a lot of time on the floor with the baby seeing the world from the baby's perspective.
5. Be careful in naming the baby. The name should connect the baby with his or her heritage rather than his or her generation. Don't name your baby after movie stars, cartoon characters, or all the other babies born that year.
6. Share your baby with other parents, grandparents, aunts, and uncles. Never try to do it alone; you will exhaust one another with your needs. As the old African proverb says, "It takes a whole village to raise a child."
7. Take your baby with you wherever you can, but make sure you leave the baby some of the time. You both need to know that you can get along without one another.
8. Never punish a baby. Whatever the baby does is exactly what he or she is supposed to do, so just stand in awed wonder and adore the magical unfolding of the child.
9. Punish children rarely and minimally. Instead, talk to them about the complexities of knowing the right thing to do in a confusing world.
10. You can't teach a child too much. The child will eagerly and joyously learn everything you eagerly and joyously teach them. Learn together.
11. Shoot out the TV. If you read, the child will read. If you exercise, the child will exercise. If you watch TV, the child will become the lazy slacker you seem to be.
12. Always express your optimism about the child's basic goodness. Children will become whatever you tell them they are. You must never insult or ridicule a child.
13. Go with little children wherever they go and do whatever they do about half the time. Then take them with you to do whatever you are doing the other half of the time.
14. Don't drink or do drugs while you are with your children. You need all your faculties about you. If you must abuse your brain, do so at work, where your job is less important.
15. Provide structure, like meals and family outings, and expect the child to fit into it. Don't over-schedule a child's activities away from home. The child must, above all, be a member of the family.
16. Give the child something valuable to do, not as discipline or punishment or evidence of parental control, but because the family needs it done.
17. Insist children go to school even if they aren't feeling well that day, but let children take off a day from time to time when they feel particularly well.
18. Be polite to children. You are teaching them how to behave properly, so treat conflicts as exercises in manners rather than revelations of basic inner rottenness.
19. Try not to be too rich or too poor. Either extreme changes children's sense of reality, and the worth they put on their own efforts.
20. Express constant pride in your kids, not just for their successes, but for the workings of their mind, body, and emotions. Adore them just for letting you be part of it.
21. If your children don't seem to appreciate you, don't try to make them feel guilty about it, just disappear from time to time, leaving a vague note. Couples need to escape regularly. Children's greatest security comes from parents' relationship. Titillate them with your love.

21 Tricks for Taming Adolescents

1. Celebrate their puberty. If they take their sexuality underground because it embarrasses you, they will quickly follow it and may not emerge for a few years.
2. Don't let your teenage kids shock you. Insist upon hearing it all, and honestly compare your own adolescence. Adolescents aren't alienated; their parents are.
3. Stay connected with your adolescent kids. Get them out in the woods or up on a mountain, anyplace where you are not in control and you are dependent on one another.
4. Keep adolescents moving. They are only a problem when they stop. Sports and work save lives.
5. The rules must be clear. Negotiate them, write them out, have the child sign them, magnet them to the refrigerator, and follow them yourself.
6. Don't escalate the punishment as a way of getting an adolescent under control. Your efforts will only throw them out of control. Just keep them with you until they have heard your calm feelings about what they are doing and you have heard theirs.
7. If kids refuse to do what you tell them, refuse to provide goods and services for them. Don't fight with them, just starve them out.
8. Don't try to protect kids from natural consequences. That is how they learn about reality. Your punishment only teaches them unpleasant things about you.
9. Don't threaten anything you aren't willing to do. Underreact and make the kids wait for your reaction.
10. Don't turn matters of style into matters of substance. Let them get themselves up in weird ways without making it a moral issue.
11. Don't respect your children's privacy. Don't let them hide in their rooms and keep their lives secret from you.
12. If there are two or more parents you mustn't do anything unilaterally, you mustn't undercut one another, and you mustn't fight it out in front of the adolescent. You don't have to be right, but you do have to be together.
13. If you are a single mother of a teenage son, accept your authority and don't let your son think he is the boss. Don't bring in a new stepfather just now unless he is extraordinarily humble and powerless. If you feel the need for a male partner in parenting, pull in the real father, or perhaps an uncle or grandfather, but you stay in charge.
14. Try to listen to their music. You can't be expected to live with it: it loosens the wallpaper, undermines the foundation, and defrosts the refrigerator. But the lyrics help you to better understand how scary it is to be an adolescent.
15. Never let your kids embarrass you, or let the reactions of shocked friends, gawking strangers, or indignant teachers be more important than the feelings of your beloved child who just made a humiliating mess.
16. Cultivate a bad recent memory. Refuse to recall what they did wrong the day before. Start each day as if it were a new relationship. Adolescents change so very rapidly and self-consciously, it probably is.
17. Whatever age your kids, try to hold them every day.
18. Don't go nuts over what your adolescent is doing until you have talked it over with the family therapist. You may need one unless you have used the previous 38 tricks, are a particularly cooperative couple, or are backed up by a good team of aunts and uncles.
19. As a last resort, call the cops. Kids must understand that the world supports your efforts to raise them, unless you are violent or angrily insulting to a teenager; only a maniacal parent would be as foolhardy as that.
20. If older teenagers don't respect the comforts of family life, let them leave. If they get along O.K. without you, then they were right: they didn't need you after all. But if you're not too unpleasant, soon they'll see that they want you, and that's better for you both.
21. Remember that adolescence is a time of normal psychosis, the most painful time in anyone's life. You've been there, so you can see it from the adolescent's perspective but they can't see it from yours. Keep thinking about how wonderful it will be when it's over and your kids are free to become just like you. They will come to love you just as much as you love your parents because they'll learn this, as they'll learn everything, not from what you tell them is right, but from your example.

Ten Commandments for Parenting

1. Thou shalt not consider "your" child to be any different in kind or quality or rights or privileges than any other child on earth.
2. Thou shalt not teach children to be violent by being violent with them.
3. Thou shalt not teach children to be unpleasant and abusive by being unpleasant and abusive with them.
4. Thou shalt not shame a child for not excelling and leaving you feeling ashamed around the parents of more successful kids. Your need for "your" child to excel is your problem. You may shame a child only for not trying.
5. Thou shalt not make a child feel guilty for not loving you enough. Make a child feel guilty only for hurting other people.
6. Thou shalt not teach a child to fear. Instead you will let the child teach you to stop fearing the things you fear now.
7. Thou shalt not teach a child any of the traditional nonsense about gender, about what he or she is permitted to feel, what he or she is permitted to do.
8. Thou shalt not let your gender determine your functioning as a parent. Specifically, do not let yourself get trapped into doing a great deal more or less of the parenting then your partner. Such a triangle will eventually destroy all three relationships. Children need fathers as much as they need mothers; fathers need children even more.
9. Thou shalt not pull back from loving your adolescent just because they must pull back from you and your efforts to control, protect, or fix them. It is just when they hate you that they most need your steady, reliable love.
10. Thou shalt not destroy your child's childhood so you can relive yours. Don't worry, if you can stick it out you will ultimately be much rewarded. You may even be rewarded with a grandchild and get to start the process all over again.

Credits

The Maze, the painting on the back cover by William Kurelek, is used by permission of the Guttman-McClay Collections and William Kurelek. The schematic diagrams in the learning unit are reproduced with permission of the Ronald Press Company, from their text, *Principles of General Psychology.*

The author wishes to thank all of those former Psychology 101 students, teaching assistants, and teaching aides who assisted in the organization and evolution of this manual.

A special note of appreciation is due: Cindy Swan Clifton, David Dunn, Rodo Sofranac, Joseph Gregory Carroll, David Gluck, Preston Maynard, Andra Putenis, Holly Stein, Mary Robinson, Christine MacVicar, Karen Lee, Carol Howe, Myra Shapiro, Becky Smith, Gary Thompson, Kathrine Christ, David Levitan, Bernie Lohr, Jonathan Mork, Catherine deNeergaard, Kim Sue Hazelrigg, Lisa Basch, Kay Nero, Heidi Robinson, Kathleen Knipp, Mike Birnbaum, Karen Snelbecker, Caroline Calkins, Cindy Durbin, Matthew Reynolds, Brian Schilling, Phil Goldberg, Megan Wherry, Barbara Hogan, Jason Zamkoff, David Wolfe, Jon Wolfe, Lily Benjamin, Alexis Kahn, Vinnie Santo, David Axelrod, Jessica Karp, Brian Prager, Rebecca Hansen, Rebecca Selling, Kathleen Reynolds, Kara Malloy, Janelle Weinstock, Justin Maas, Laura Evans, Kristin Bisset, Laura Harding, Jenna Durbin, Caitlyn Durbin, Hanaah Applebaum and Carolyn Hirschmann.